Rhetorics of Order / Ordering Rhetorics in English Neoclassical Literature

Rhetorics of Order / Ordering Rhetorics in English Neoclassical Literature

Edited by
J. Douglas Canfield
and
J. Paul Hunter

DELAWARE

Newark: University of Delaware Press
London and Toronto: Associated University Presses

PR
445
R46
1989

Associated University Presses
440 Forsgate Drive
Cranbury, NJ 08512

Associated University Presses
25 Sicilian Avenue
London WC1A 2QH, England

Associated University Presses
P.O. Box 488, Port Credit
Mississauga, Ontario
Canada L5G 4M2

The paper used in this publication meets the requirements of the American National Standard for Permanence of Paper for Printed Library Materials Z39.48-1984.

Library of Congress Cataloging-in-Publication Data

Rhetorics of order/ordering rhetorics in English neoclassical literature / edited by J. Douglas Canfield and J. Paul Hunter.
   p.   cm.
  ISBN 0-87413-374-2
  1. English literature—18th century—History and criticism.
  2. Neoclassicism (Literature)   3. Classicism—Great Britain.
  4. Order in literature.   5. Rhetoric—1500–1800.   6. English literature—Early modern, 1500–1700—History and criticism.
  I. Canfield, J. Douglas (John Douglas), 1941–   . II. Hunter, J. Paul, 1934–   .
PR445.R46   1989
820.9′142—dc20   88-40578
                                                        CIP

PRINTED IN THE UNITED STATES OF AMERICA

To Aubrey Williams
from students and friends

Contents

Preface
JOHN IRWIN FISCHER
and CLIFFORD EARL RAMSEY

Aubrey Williams has contributed generously to the understanding of English neoclassical literature. And his contribution to students, colleagues, and friends has provided us all with a model of the dedicated scholar.

The gifts Aubrey brings in his published work are the easiest of his benefits to describe. His first book, *The Dunciad: A Study of Its Meaning*, was a seminal text in the revaluation of Pope and of satire. The book displays those attributes that have marked all his work: supple interpretive skill, extraordinary knowledge of intellectual history, and a rare gift for using that knowledge to tease out and validate meaning. Most importantly, the book displays Aubrey's intellectual morality, his characteristic, uniquely nuanced, passionate earnestness. This earnestness is not solemn, or ponderous; it is penetrating. It gives Aubrey's work a savor of the ground it grows in. That savor is detectable again in his contributions, especially the introductions for *Windsor Forest* and *An Essay on Criticism*, to the first volume of the Twickenham Edition of Pope's poetry. It is present, too, more gently, almost endearingly, in his Riverside Edition of Pope, a text that has introduced generations of students to eighteenth-century English literature. Finally, its savor is markedly present in his book on Congreve. Like all his other books and essays, *An Approach to Congreve* is insightful, learned, provocative. But it is also, more than any of his earlier works, conscious of its own stance: disinterested methodologically, yet passionately engaged by Congreve's efforts to imagine a possible comedic harmony within which women and men might fruitfully realize themselves.

The same passion for literature and the same commitment to learning have characterized Aubrey's teaching, so much so that it was at first as intimidating as it was inspiring to be his student. He was hard on us. Yet he thought better of us than we thought of ourselves. And he got better work from us than we thought we could do. He taught us to turn our fears about ourselves into enabling humility before the texts that we studied. His values and his example persist in those dozens of students scattered all over the world who attempt to profess the eighteenth century with some of his passion and some of his precision and some of his rigor and some of his humility. They often write and teach, we suspect, with the image of Aubrey nearby, rebuking, cajoling, prodding, provoking, inspiring, insisting, encouraging, demanding, always demanding.

Aubrey's colleagues and friends, too, value him and recognize, as his students recognize, that, with whatever degree or kind of piety one wishes to affirm it, for Aubrey Williams the academic life is a vocation. But a human vocation. In him the scholar and the human being are one. What is so often sundered in so many of us—intellect and emotion, mind and feeling, the physical and the spiritual—are integrated in him. Indeed, it is this integrity, in its several senses, that makes Aubrey Williams distinctive as well as distinguished. And it is this integrity we hope to honor with this volume.

Acknowledgments

The editors wish to acknowledge the gracious assistance of Elizabeth Reynolds and Jay Halio of the University of Delaware Press. We also owe a special debt of gratitude for advice along the way to Patricia Meyer Spacks. And we wish to thank our contributors for their patience.

Introduction

Intellectual historians have traditionally characterized the Enlightenment as a time when the rage for order dominated institutions and texts as well as thought. Out of the late-Renaissance crisis of authority had come belief that the world could be known in unprecedented ways. From new empirical science to new epistemology to "neoclassical" art, a new order promised an end to chaos and eternal night. In literature in particular, conscious of its vatic heritage and the power of a Logos it tried to share with revealed religion, the desire to find, or assert, or make order was a powerful motive to creativity. Looking back upon it from the perspective of the twentieth century, historians of English literature have been especially struck by the pervasiveness of the rage for order between the Restoration of Charles II in 1660 to the publication of *Lyrical Ballads* in 1798. The age they defined—sometimes called neoclassical, sometimes Augustan, sometimes an Age of Reason, sometimes something less printable or memorable—became prized for its calm and confident forms and structures, which imitated "the eighteenth-century mind." Literature was seen to reflect an ordered universe in highly ordered forms, often variations on classical genres that both embody and inculcate social order.

In recent years, however, that world picture has begun to change—partly because the nature of literary study has been modified to include many texts formerly relegated to the background or "subliterature," partly because historians have come to offer a far broader sense of those years as varied, bumptious, and unstable, and partly because philosophers, linguists, anthropologists, and cultural theoreticians have begun to offer a richer variety of disciplinary models. As the age itself has come to seem less homogeneous and secure, its cultural artifacts and literary forms have taken on new colorations, new interests, and new meanings. Historical work in the past few years, on all aspects of eighteenth-century life or art, has become very different, and although Anglo-American work has been slower to pick up on some of the new directions of thought, many of its disciplines have begun to produce major rethinkings of basic issues. On issues of order and ordering, literary critics and theorists have come nearly to see a rage for chaos, focusing on themes and forms reflecting madness, misrule, and disorder. Yet order, nearly everyone would agree, remains an important trope for the Enlightenment, and the relationship of the trope to what now seems a wilder and more complex age remains to be sorted out. What did the age's desire for order come to when it came to particulars? How did the possibilities of rhetoric and the need for a governing sense of things lead to lively engagements with the most recalcitrant issues of time and art? How did the ordering rhetorics of the past fare when they collided with rhetorics of new or emerging senses of order? The answers to these and related questions are by no means obvious, but such issues are on the minds of a wide variety of theorists, critics, and scholars of many backgrounds and persuasions who are concerned to discover the implications of the mimetic and representational aspirations of the age but also its persistent, if often frustrated, desire for an order that could be made to seem stable.

The essays collected here attempt to analyze some—although by no means all—of the several rhetorics of order. Our bookend essays, to which we shall return shortly, look at early and late resistances to those rhetorics. In between, several of the essays address works of art with troubled relations to the two most powerful of formal ordering rhetorics, those of traditional genres and teleological narratives. Other essays address rhetorics that compose imbalances or imbalances that discompose rhetorics. Yet another addresses rhetorics not so much of persuasion but of presentation, especially of an ordered self. All reveal an age preoccupied with and profoundly anxious over the forms of order employed to impose metaphysical, political, ethical, and epistemological stability in an era destabilized by tremulous revolutions of many kinds.

Rose A. Zimbardo examines two works that suggest slippage from one genre to another. *Don Sebastian* is a heroic tragedy that includes material which breaks out of the form into what she, following Mikhail Bakhtin, calls novelistic discourse—realistic detail that is gratuitous, extraneous, uncontainable; *Oroonoko* marks the transition from prose romance to tragic novel by embedding the ideal in the real, the discourse of authority in that of experience. These two works, then, feature competing discourses that fail to come to any easy resolution and that mark a moment of transition from an aristocratic to a bourgeois episteme.

Jackson I. Cope seeks to discover why Elkanah Settle would take a suggestion from Barton Booth to combine the seemingly incompatible rhetorics of two plays by Beaumont and Fletcher into *The City Ramble*. Cope's analysis of the historical concatenation of calls for theatrical reform and reactionary political nostalgia yields a surprising vision of self-reflexive generic mixing constituting a "suprasocial" mixing of love *and* money, country *and* city, theater *and* reform—aristocratic and bourgeois—at the same moment of historical transition.

James Thompson situates Pope's *Elegy to the Memory of an Unfortunate Lady* between two poles: the Renaissance elegy with its appeal to communal consolation and the romantic elegy with its appeal to private concerns. Using Lacan, Thompson sees Pope's poem as enigmatic and disturbing because it fails to participate in either ordering rhetoric but can only mark the lady's fundamental lack/absence and deny the efficacy of substitutes, including the poem itself. Thompson implies that for Pope the aristocratic rhetoric of mutuality is no longer viable, whereas the bourgeois rhetoric of individualism is not yet fully available.

Patricia Meyer Spacks explores the difference between attempts by threatened heroines in *Clarissa* and *The Italian* to order their own stories. Clarissa finally literalizes the Christian story of "humiliation, sacrifice, and transcendence" and employs it as an assertion of power and self—although the only self available to this beleaguered female is a negation through death that may make her a saint but leaves her sexless. Ellena's sentimentalized Catholicism provides no such narrative plot, and all her other attempts to project herself into a plot fail as she remains dominated not by male characters but by male constructs. Spacks provocatively suggests that this failure calls into question "the hegemony of order itself."

While not addressing a problem of mixed genres, Michael J. Conlon considers a mixed form of government in a critical moment of imbalance as portrayed in *Absalom and Achitophel*. Conlon argues that Dryden provides a rhetoric of *Kairos* or the "right time" for an intervention of the king's power, backed by Providence, to set the balance in equilibrium, a closure that cannot be permanent because the very tropes themselves suggest "the growing sense of contingency in Dryden's world." Conlon contests, moreover, recent criticism of the poem's ending as mere rhetoric, invoking Quentin Skinner's notion that such normative rhetoric can actually be constitutive and modify events.

In his analysis of one of the central ordering rhetorics of the neoclassical period, the shared language of wit, John Sitter examines first John Locke's slippery distinction between wit and judgment, then Joseph Addison's and Matthew Prior's responses to it. Sitter writes, "The problem dividing Locke from Addison and Prior can be seen as a question with particular pertinence to our own era and criticism: does it make more sense to think of 'things as they are' as represented (perhaps badly) by language or as constituted by lan-

guage?" While not trying to make Addison and Prior proto-poststruc-
turalists, Sitter nevertheless insists that we need to speak not of one
neoclassical logocentrism but of several, lest the term, like Locke's
wit, become merely "protective of its rhetorically contructed opposite."

Maynard Mack's tercentennial appreciation of Pope praises him for
his enduring qualities, especially his innovations and particularly his
new rhetorics of presentation. While focusing at one point on Pope's
presentations of women as "real" selves, as part of an emerging
rhetoric of resistance to moribund but nevertheless still-oppressive
patriarchal rhetorics, and while focusing at another point on the
pleasures of Pope's rhetorical effects, from simple, subtle, specific
tropes to a global rhetoric of specificity back down to the particulars of
prosody, Mack repeatedly returns to his central topic, Pope's strategies of self-presentation. The ordering of a self out of the particulars
of existence becomes a rhetoric of order that Mack relates to other
ordering rhetorics from poems to gardens to governments to the
creation itself.

Our own essays explore works that challenge the hegemony of
order in radically disordering ways. "Poetical Injustice" examines the
signal absence of one of drama's dominant rhetorics of order—poetical
justice as mimetic reflection of providential justice—in some deeply
disturbing plays. If there is no poetical justice, then perhaps there is
no ultimate justice, either, no validation of the bonds that hold society
together, that guarantee the peaceful transmission of power and property through the principle of genealogical, patrilineal succession.
Instead there is only the naked Will to Power of the Machiavel or the
libertine, and God himself is their ultimate avatar.

"Clocks, Calendars, and Names" examines the disordering impluse
of *Tristram Shandy* and the way it repeatedly interrupts or aborts
Shandean attempts to order—from chronology, authority, and identity to plot, patriarchy, and paternity. All of Tristram's rituals and
sacraments go awry, etiology betrayed by circumstance. Tristram's
anxiety about these ordering rhetorics (especially paternity, an anxiety shared with hero and heroine of many an eighteenth-century
novel) represents a larger historical anxiety of the age. Just as the
novel as a loose and baggy structure reflects a destabilized moment in
the transition from aristocratic to bourgeois patriarchy, Sterne prob-
lematizes the relationship between the worlds of fact and fiction.
Elizabeth Shandy, with little voice in the novel itself and almost
denied her own motherhood in the prevailing family myth, is the
shadowy presence who threatens all that tradition can muster, figur-
ing the novel's subversive rhetoric of disorder.

Other authors and works—Rochester, *Hudibras*, Swift, *The Dunciad*, Lady Mary, *Rasselas*, Gibbon, *Camilla*, and countless others—might readily have been included here. The point of the collection, however, is not to exhaust but to suggest: it invites readers to consider the age's preoccupation with order—aesthetic, philosophical, religious, political, social—and the ways in which its various literary rhetorics are problematized or problematize themselves by mixing or slipping or sliding. Sometimes these rhetorics all too glibly reaffirm themselves. Sometimes they cling in desperate contingency, trying to shore up the fragments in moments of crisis. Sometimes they fail tragically, frighteningly. And sometimes they fail with a smile. In all this, why—mirabile dictu—they resemble us critics, trying to find our own rhetorics to order them. In an important instance of our own attempt to order, for example, we retain the term "neoclassical," however problematical, precisely for its suggestion not of a theory or practice of imitation but the age's—and our—desire for order.

Rhetorics of Order / Ordering Rhetorics
in English Neoclassical Literature

Part 1
Drama

Poetical Injustice in Some Neglected
Masterpieces of Restoration Drama
J. DOUGLAS CANFIELD

Thanks especially to Aubrey Williams, we have come to understand the sense of an ending in Restoration drama. Most plays end in a poetical justice that mirrors Providence.[1] Or to put it my way, most heroic romances, tragicomedies, tragedies, and what I call "social" comedies end by reaffirming the feudal chivalric code with its under-writing religious rhetoric (see Canfield 1979, 1984, 1985). However, a rare tragicomedy (James Howard's *All Mistaken*) and several "subversive" comedies (the most famous of which is William Wycherley's *Country Wife*) have split endings, one half of which reaffirms the chivalric code while the other half leaves unpunished and free a single or a team of tricksters (for the Howard play, see Canfield 1984, 452; for the Wycherley, see Canfield 1989, chap. 4). Perhaps the most disturbing of these subversive comedies are Thomas Otway's *Friendship in Fashion*, Thomas Southerne's *Sir Anthony Love*, and Sir John Vanbrugh's *Relapse*.[2] Even more disturbing are satirical plays where not only the tricksters, however vicious, are unpunished, and the virtuous unrewarded, but the atmosphere of celebration is absent and we are left with a bleak world without justice. In this paper I shall examine three extremely disturbing examples of such satirical endings in some relatively unknown but excellent plays—Sir Robert Howard's *Duke of Lerma* (first performance 1668), Nathaniel Lee's *Princess of Cleve* (ca. 1682), and John Dryden's *Amphitryon* (1690)—plays that end so cynically as to suggest the death of the code poetical justice was employed to underwrite.

In his earlier play *The Vestal Virgin* (1664) Howard (anticipating John Fowles in *The French Lieutenant's Woman*) writes alternative endings, one tragic with no metaphysical consolation, the other comic with attribution of the dynamic of the denouement to "Justice," "just Fortune," and "Heaven" (5.1, 295–97).[3] Such an alternative suggests, as in Fowles, that the "happy" ending is the product of wish-fulfill-ment, that poetical justice as the rhetoric of order is merely the rhetoric of desire. In the later, much better *Great Favourite; or, The*

Duke of Lerma, Howard sets up in his audience full expectation of traditional poetic justice. The Duke of Lerma is a Renaissance Over-reacher, a Grand Machiavel characterized by enormous ambition, unscrupulousness, and magniloquence. As he proceeds in his quest for unlimited power to exalt his base followers, persecute the loyal nobility, prostitute his own daughter Maria in order to control the young King Philip, and murder the Queen Mother, he is portrayed as blasphemously irreverent, defiant, and positively satanic in his desire to supplant God himself. When the old king, who has thwarted Lerma's ambition and ordered him banished, finally dies, Lerma mocks traditional descriptions of such events as having cosmic, cata-clysmic consequences:

> I heard methoughts a Groan as horrible
> As if great Nature's Frame had crackt in two,
> And yet that Blow kill'd not a Fly, *Caldroon* [his own Mosca];
> Something is gone old Folks will talk on.
>
> (1.1, 320)

When a courtier announces the king is dead Lerma responds aside "Thanks be to Heaven" (ibid.). Appropriating the language of the code of word as bond, Lerma demands loyalty, faith, and trust from his equally vicious followers (1.1, 318; 2.2, 341; 3.3, 353) and accuses his truly loyal brother, the Duke of Medina, who is attempting to defend the young king from Lerma's schemes, of violating the bonds of "Nature" and abandoning brother, "Friends and Alliance" out of a specious "pious Love to Honour" (5.1, 372). Medina sees him as "a subtle Sophister," and in soliloquy Lerma articulates his antitrust ethic:

> He's gone; he durst not stay to hear me;
> He did begin to melt, good-natur'd Gentleman.
> I love to try Men's Tempers, to laugh at 'em;
> For I shou'd hardly trust a promis'd Kindness.
> I will not beg, that can command my Peace:
> He that secures himself well in the End,
> Must destroy Foes, and never trust a Friend.
>
> (5.1, 373)

Delivering Maria to King Philip supposedly out of "Loyalty" (2.2, 333), Lerma in ironically religious language justifies his and the Confessor's virtual pimping:

> you may tell her
> The Mistress of a King, is half a Saint,
> For she'll be worshipt. . . .
> You have a fine, large Text, to preach upon:
> And I will second you, and add new Motives,
> Hugging her Sin, and bless her for offending.
>
> (1.3, 323)

Falling down before his daughter and worshipping her as a "Divinity" who can save him from banishment by seducing the young king, Lerma blasphemously declares, "I ask no other Help but thine, / To make *Spain* know I am their Deity" (2.1, 329). When Maria mysteriously disappears and Lerma's designs begin to fail, he defiantly indicts heaven:

> Where is its Mercy then? for it ne'er had
> Another Way to bless, but by *Maria*.
> Could my profane and passionate Revenge
> Reach but the Hearts and Lips of the Religious,
> No Incense evermore shou'd upward fly,
> Of Prayer or Praise; I'd stop all Piety
> Till They restor'd *Maria* to me.
>
> (5.1, 370)

From the beginning, Lerma claims to control events, as he says to the Confessor, "If we but prosper now; not we on Fate, / But she on us, shall for Direction wait" (1.3, 324). Even as things begin to fall apart, Lerma proclaims, "Fortune and I did long ago agree, / I to make Work for her, and she for me" (4.2, 365). Seemingly more resigned to failure, he appropriates traditional Stoic discourse:

> Virtue can singly stand on its own Trust. . . .
> He only is above Envy and Fate,
> Whose Mind in sinking Fortunes keeps its Height.
>
> (3.3, 354; 4.2, 368)

Lerma's creature, Caldroon, however, employs a typical image for impending doom: "The Storm has overtook our greatest Speed. / Nor can the Duke himself find out a Shelter" (3.3, 351). Indeed, it would appear that Howard has set Lerma up for the traditional poetical, providential justice. While Lerma defiantly mocks romantic "Love" and naive "Confidence," the virtuous characters pledge their "Loyalties" to young King Philip and advise him to garner "the People's

Oaths," as Medina exults, "It is the Boast of *Spain*, and our best Glories, / That we have ever truly serv'd our Kings" (1.1–2, 321–22). As Lerma gains power, the virtuous appeal to Heaven. Horrified at the pimping Confessor, Maria cries, "Is this Divinity? Defend me, Heaven!" (2.1, 325). In contrast to Lerma's perverted Stoicism, Maria practices proper Christian Stoicism: "Virtue, thou shalt protect me before Heaven, / Though not from this bad World" (2.1, 330). Yet she responds to Lerma's blasphemy with both filial and religious piety: "Heaven defend my Father" (2.1, 327). And she resists the attempt to prostitute her, converts King Philip to ideal love, and proves her constancy and fidelity to the skeptical patriarchal judge, Medina. Meanwhile, the loyal Duke of Alva praises Medina's attempts to thwart Lerma and prays, "Heaven prosper and direct you" (2.2, 338). Finally the loyalists begin to purge the court of Lerma's favorites. In a spectacle designed to move Lerma to repent his atrocities, Caldroon is led to execution by friars carrying a crucifix and tapers (5.1). The Confessor poisons himself. And Medina draws his sword of "Justice" (5.1, 371), obviates Maria's plea for mercy, and confidently believes the approaching Lerma, despite his laughing defiance, "a tir'd o'er-hunted Deer" who "Treads fatal Paths offer'd by Chance, / And not design'd by him" (5.2, 375). The oxymoron, "fatal Paths" of "Chance," epitomizes all the contradictory references to Fate and Fortune throughout the play and reveals them to be sloppy metaphysics, for the force that governs events is finally portrayed neither as pure accident nor as pure necessity but as the "design" of a providential justice that employs Medina as its instrument. Or so it would seem.

The great shock at the end of the play is the complete frustration of expectation. Lerma enters in a *"Cardinal's Habit"* (5.2, 376s.d.), purchased from the Pope in Rome in the nick of time. As early as the end of the third act he has predicted, "in despight of my curst Enemies, / I'll find a Conquest in a safe Retreat, / And though they rise, I'll sink to be as great" (3.3, 354). As his followers earlier hide his treasure remaining from his secret papal purchase, he triumphs blasphemously, perverting the religious language that is supposed to underwrite feudal society:

> Here, set that Treasure in, for they are Reliques,
> And will preserve their faithful Worshipper;
> Why, here are Mysteries Canonical,
> That must not be search'd into by Disputes;
> 'Twas a good Purchase too, considering
> The deep Necessity; or if compar'd
> To the vast Sums I gave my Instruments

To turn them Fiends, and make my self a Devil;
For I am sainted at a cheaper Rate,
Thanks to his Holiness: My Pack of Counsellors,
I have out-gone you all.

(5.1, 369)

Indeed, one of the apparently triumphant counselors concludes, "He has o'er-reach'd us all" (5.2, 376).

Thus this Renaissance Overreacher does not end, as usual, by defeating himself, by going one step too far, by improvidently playing into the hands of Providence. And he taunts his would-be justicers by pretending to have received from the conferral on him of his cardinal's "Office" a gift of tongues, a call to preaching, as he upbraids them for being so "uncharitable" as to abominate his escape from their justice and as he counsels them to have "Patience" (5.2, 376–77). Even though King Philip and Maria will apparently finally be married as her religious vows yield to public (genealogical) necessity, and even though the play thus has something of the conventional resolution, the audience cannot shake the effects of Lerma's last great cynical attack, worth quoting in its entirety:

I will not longer trouble you, my Lords,
But leave you now to prey upon your selves.
He that devours the rest, in Time may be
A Monster, more o'ergrown than e'er I was.
When you are low and poor, you are all Friends,
And in one fair Pretence together join,
While every one conceals his own Design.
It is your Country's Cause, until full grown
In long sought Power, then it proves your own.
When you seem good, your Crimes are not the less;
Men have all new Creations by Success.
Ambition, like a wanton Woman's Haste,
Invites new Slaves, grown weary of the last.
Mankind each others Stories do repeat,
And Man to Man is a succeeding Cheat.
So to this Fate I leave you, and shall joy,
To see those Crimes you blame, your selves destroy.
May you all sink in Fates for me you meant,
And be too dull, your Ruins to prevent;
That when you're lost in this ambitious Toil,
I in my safe Retreat may sit and smile.

(5.2, 377)

Not only does Lerma frustrate expectations of justice, he indicts the virtuous as hypocrites. Like Hobbes (and Nietzsche after him), Lerma interprets the language of virtue, the rhetoric of ethical order, as a mask for desire, for the inevitable Will to Power that animates men. Medina is so captivated by Lerma's "Greatness" of "Spirit" in this speech that he "cou'd almost forgive him" (5.2, 377). Howard leaves us with a Nietzschean rather than Aristotelian magnanimity, a frightening great-spiritedness that threatens to translate virtue back into its root sense of manly power. Lerma's final mockery is directed as much at us as at his antagonists: "This holy Robe tells me, it is my Duty, / And I forgive: but sure I may laugh at you" (5.2, 376). An audience that expects poetical as a sign of providential justice, the rhetoric of metaphysical order, has been forced to take a nasty look into the nominalist abyss.

*   *   *

Nat Lee's Duke Nemours is another type of overreacher; he is an extreme example of the Restoration Rake, the libertine Don Juan whose unlimited pursuit of sexual variety threatens to destabilize patriarchal society by attacking the grid upon which its power is based, genealogy. The typical rake of Restoration social comedy (Etherege's Dorimant, Behn's Willmore) has his promiscuous sex urge socialized into marriage. The rake of subversive comedy remains a rover at large, but the plays end in celebration and marriage. But perhaps following Shadwell's lead in *The Libertine* (first performed 1675) or the numerous other seventeenth-century versions of the Don Juan story, only the most famous of which are those by Tirso de Molina (*El Burlador de Sevilla y Convidado de Piedra* [first performed 1623]) and Molière (*Dom Juan; ou, le festin de pierre* [first performed 1665]), Lee portrays a rake so extreme in his defiance of conventional morality and its validating metaphysic as to be utterly shocking.[4]

The play is structured like a split-plot tragicomedy, but Lee took the unusual measure of refusing to designate its genre (see the title page of the first edition and the dedication, Lee 1955, 2:147, 153), perhaps because he sensed its radical difference from other plays. As in a Dryden tragicomedy especially, the comic plot mirrors the concerns of the heroic or high plot. St. Andre and Poltrot are buffoons who mimic the lascivious behavior of their betters, searching for sexual game, pretending to lie with duchesses and other women of quality, much to the consternation—and sexual frustration—of their wives, Elianor and Celia. And Poltrot yearns to cuckold his friend. That is, he would play Nemours, but ironically he ends up a comic version of the Prince of Cleve, except that, unfortunately, he has actually experienced his bed rocked, his wife mounted, and himself apparently shot in the groin by one of the wits. Thus Poltrot receives a typical folk poetical justice. But the difference in Lee's play is that the wives of these comic butts also ape the vices of their betters. In the high plot, the Lady Tournon outrageously justifies being a bawd for Nemours and the other wits by appropriating the conventional language of morality ("Honesty" means "Pimping," for example, at 1.1.45–46; "true" means virile at 2.2.153), portraying all grave and apparently moral women as "Devils in a corner" who employ proper language with seductive double entendre (3.1.18), and praising clever women who succeed in the patriarchal system not by the high road of chastity but the low road of "Discretion" (4.2.7). Tournon calls attention to her having appropriated the main tool of male oppression— language—by joking, ". . . certainly I shou'd have made a rare Speaker in a Parliament of Women, or a notable Head to a Female Jury, when his Lordship gravely puts the question, whither it be Satis or Non Satis or Nunquam Satis, and we bring it in Ignoramus" (4.2.15–18). The fools' wives similarly employ language to free themselves from their husbands' tyranny, first in overt dialogue, then in masquerade by engaging in a witty repartee that they clearly win, as they waltz off with the wits. When the butts adopt Jonsonian disguises, humors, and cant to get even with their wives by abusing them misogynistically, the women turn the tables and defeat them verbally once more. Finally, they cuckold them with two of the wits, and even though discovered, they maneuver their husbands into reconciliation. Although the couples conclude the play swearing henceforth to be true to one another, Lee suggests through style alone that the women have learned too much. When Celia sues to Poltrot to be forgiven, in a parody of the Princess suing to the Prince of Cleve, she breaks into heroic couplets and Settlean quatrains. When that posturing fails, she resorts to prose and hilarious physical threats: "I'll have your Throat cut. . . . He that miss'd your Guts in the dark, shall take better aim at your Gullet by day-light" (5.1.73–77). It might be argued that the men have received no more than what they deserve, and that the women want nothing more than constancy and regular sexual service. But the fact that Poltrot complains throughout the play of Celia's romps with Lord Harebrain earlier in their relationship implies that she, like her male libertine counterpart, will never be satisfied and that the comic conclusion of apparent return to constancy is merely, satirically cosmetic.

Celia has a counterpart other than Tournon in the high plot— Marguerite. She begins the play as a Mrs. Loveit, railing violently at the perjured, inconstant Nemours. Like Loveit, she vows revenge, but that revenge takes the shape of a bed-trick, with Marguerite courting Nemours in a masquerade, punctuating their dialogue with asides condemning him for his devilish falsehood. She plans not to redeem him for herself, however, but simply to rekindle his desire for her, "enjoy him / With the last Pang of a revengeful Pleasure," exact from him vilification of herself and promises of constancy, then reveal herself and "leave him to the Horror of his Soul" (3.1.96–107). Like Celia, then, she would inflict on her unfaithful a poetical justice, one that here takes on religious overtones. Yet like Celia in another way, after she has worked her scam and, after exciting—and mocking— repeated vows of constancy from Nemours, unmasked in triumphant scorn, she proclaims that she'll beat Nemours at his own game of promiscuity:

> Yes, I will try the Joys of Life like you,
> But not with Men of Quality, you Devils of Honour;
> No, I will satisfie
> My Pride, Disdain, Rage and Revenge more safely,
> By all the Powers of Heav'n and Earth I will;
> I'll change my loving lying Tinsel Lord,
> For an obedient wholsome drudging Fool.
>
> (4.1.193–99)

Sounding like the voluble gadabout in Rochester's "Letter from Artemisia to Chloe," Marguerite announces a program of freeing herself from male oppression by choosing a fool for a husband, whom she can dominate in order to purchase her own sexual freedom.

Women who commit adultery and get away with it are relatively rare in Restoration drama, especially if they remain witty and desirable like Otway's Mrs. Goodvile or like Marguerite and Celia in this play. But Marguerite's triumph and program are short-lived, for at the end of the play she is resubordinated to patriarchy as Nemours claims her for his wife. Then perhaps the Princess of Cleve represents real freedom and independence from men, the kind of (silently) triumphant feminist heroine like the one Nancy Miller finds in Madame de La Fayette's original (1981, 43). At a crucial moment in the play, the Princess learns that her husband, the Prince, is to be accompanied by Nemours upon an important mission. Actually, the Prince is just testing her to discover the identity of the lover she has already confessed. As she speaks, she fatefully discloses her concern for the threat Nemours represents to her, to them, and to society. She pleads, "Perhaps 'tis not too late yet to supplant him" (3.2.21). She means *replace* Nemours in the entourage, but she calls attention to his role as supplanter, as what Jacques Derrida calls "That Dangerous Supplement" (1976, pt. 2, chap. 2), that constant threat to the perfection or completion of any human institution, from marriage to language itself. Nemours has already supplanted Cleve in her heart, but the Princess makes a heroic resistance, confesses her attraction to her husband, and remains constant to him. Nevertheless, the dangerous supplement continues to work. The Prince grows jealous; trust yields to distrust and finally to deadly rivalry between these best friends, Nemours and Cleve; the Prince receives at least a psychic wound if not an actual physical one, fades swiftly, and eventually dies. As he is languishing, he sees the Princess and Nemours together, concludes the affair has been consummated, and comes to exhort his wife to repentance before he dies. She maintains her innocence, and he declares their final reconciliation, but he refuses ever to see her again, and we must interpret why. He says,

> I do believe thee;
> Thou hast such Power, such Charms in those dear Lips,
> As might perswade me that I am not dying.
>
> (4.3.149–51)

Yet of course he knows he's dying, so he is referring to the power of language to make faith, trust, permanence, Presence seem possible despite the reality of the supplement. He says he believes, yet "Were I to live I shou'd not see thee more" (4.3.157), because to see her again would admit the possibility of further supplementation, further supplanting.

Even the Princess's heroic effort to overcome supplanting fails. After Cleve's death, when there is no legal reason why she and Nemours cannot fulfill their love in marriage, that is, why his final supplanting of Cleve should not take place, the Princess refuses because she has learned the danger of the supplement, how satiety leads ineluctably to the need for variety, a truth that is the wisdom of both high and low plots. Nemours's rhetoric of constancy, of his word as bond, she sees as "the Blandishments of Perjur'd Love" (5.3.201), and she poignantly asks, "What Power on Earth can give / Security that Bond shall prove Eternal?" (5.3.164–65). Thus she triumphantly declares, "I will, I must, I shall, nay, now I can, / Defie to Death the lovely Traytor Man" (5.3.202–3). She appears to have transcended earth with its patriarchal dominance and dangerous supplement and turned toward heaven with its permanence and Presence, as she calls on "Heav'n" throughout the scene for its forgiveness and support. She herself longs to die, for she has developed nothing but contempt for the false world. And yet. And yet. In an extraordinary departure from the line of her reasoning, she admits to Nemours,

> 'Tis true, my Lord, I offer much to duty,
> Which but subsists in thought, therefore have patience,
> Expect what time, with such a love as mine,
> May work in your behalf.
>
> (5.3.230–33)

In a weak moment she acknowledges that the language of transcendence is but abstraction, that time and supplementation are the underlying realities. She leaves imploring Nemours, "Believe that you shall never see me more" (5.3.247), but he recognizes that this is not really a declaration. Upon his knowledge of "the Souls of / Women" he self-assuredly proclaims to the Vidam, "Believe that you shall never see me more—she Lyes, I'll Wager my State, I Bed her eighteen months three weeks hence, at half an hour past two in the Morning" (5.3.254–59).

Such unmitigated cocksureness is the trademark of this extreme libertine. From the beginning he has defied time and death, morality and the gods themselves. Like the Duke of Lerma, he mocks man's moralizing memento mori over the death of the ultimate libertine, Count Rosidore (read Lord Rochester), whom he eulogizes as "the Spirit of Wit" who personified and exulted in the Dangerous Supplement itself: "He never spoke a Witty thing twice, tho to different Persons; his Imperfections were catching, and his Genius was so Luxuriant, that he was forc'd to tame it with a Hesitation in his Speech to keep it in view" (1.2.101–6). Nemours appreciatively paraphrases Rosidore's poetry celebrating carpe diem in defiance of death (3.1.125–33).

In typical libertine fashion, Nemours is a thoroughgoing nominalist. He chides Tournon for appealing to "Conscience" and continues:

> Vertue! An ill-bred crosness in the will;
> Honour a Notion, Piety a Cheat,
> Prove but successful Bawds and you are great.
>
> (1.2.58–69)

To Bellamore he makes a mockery of the important aristocratic virtue of obligation, for he had once saved the life of the prince he is about to cuckold: "I sav'd his Life, Sweet-heart, when he was assaulted by a mistake in the dark, and shall he grudge me a little Fooling with his Wife, for so serious an Obligation?" (2.3.7–9). To the Vidam he declares he would leap his mistress "in thy Face" (2.3.26). And like the Duke of Lerma, he chides all others as hypocrites: "Why 'tis the way of ye all, only you sneak with it under your Cloaks like Taylors and Barbers; and I, as a Gentleman shou'd do, walk with it in my hand" (2.3.34–36); "Now do I know the Precise will call me damn'd Rogue for wronging my Friend, especially such a soft sweet natur'd Friend as this gentle Prince—Verily I say they lye in their Throats, were the gravest of 'em in my condition, and thought it shou'd never be known, they wou'd rouze up the Spirit, cast the dapper Cloak, leave off their humming and haing, and fall too like a Man of Honour" (4.3.14–19).

But here, in Nemours's echoing of biblical phrasing and his perversion of the concluding phrase, we see that, like Count Rosidore's, Nemours's most potent weapon is his tongue, as he appropriates the language of trust, friendship, and constancy merely to obtain the objects of his desire. He *trusts* his Ganymede, Bellamore, with the secret of his adulterous desire for the Princess of Cleve (1.1.20–35). How can there be trust in such a decadent world of lubricious sexual thieves and perverts? He calls "glorious" his supplanting the Prince in the Princess's heart (2.3.218). And he perverts religious language throughout, as in the hilarious exchange in Calvinistic cant between Nemours and Tournon, who is disguised as a Huguenot (4.1.35–49), or in this outrageous exchange between the disguised Nemours and Marguerite as they accomplish their tryst during the masquerade:

> *Nemours.* For the forward brisk she that promis'd me the Ball Assignation, that said, there was nothing like slipping out of the crowd into a corner, breathing short an Ejaculation, and returning as if we came from Church— . . .
> *Marguerite.* [Clapping him on the shoulder.] I love a man that keeps the Commandment of his word.
> *Nemours.* And I a Woman that breaks hers with her Husband, yet loves her Neighbour as her self. (4.1.30–55)

Nemours's most frightening appropriation of language occurs when he postures as friend and lover. As the jealous Cleve approaches to demand satisfaction from him, Nemours prays, "Hypocrisie and Softness, with all the Arts of Woman, / Tip my Tongue" (4.1.272–73), and he pours forth all the blank verse rhetoric of friendship and trust. Begging "by the name of Friend" that Cleve desist, he draws his sword as reluctantly "As if I were to fight against my Father" (4.1.354–55). This last statement is extremely significant, for indeed Nemours, as dangerous sexual supplement, is rebelling against the patriarchal superego. Finally, Nemours deploys all the pseudo-religious rhetoric of Platonic, transcendent love to attempt to win the Princess. Lee emphasizes the purely rhetorical nature of Nemours's discourse by having him slip into heroic couplets (see Brown 1983, 398–99). When the Princess appeals to Heaven to help her resist him, Nemours appropriates the religious rhetoric:

> The Heavenly Powers
> Accept the poorest Sacrifice we bring,
> A Slave to them's as welcome as a King.
> Behold a Slave that Glories in your Chains,
> Ah! with some shew of Mercy view my Pains;
> Your piercing Eyes have made their splendid way,
> Where Lightning cou'd not pass—
> Even through my Soul their pointed Lustre goes,
> And Sacred Smart upon my Spirit throws;
> Yet I your Wounds with as much Zeal desire,
> As Sinners that wou'd pass to Bliss through Fire.
> Yes, Madam, I must love you to my Death,
> I'll sigh your name with my last gasp of Breath.
>
> (4.3.93–105)

Astonishingly, apparently convinced by his rhetoric, she offers him a kind of hope as she exhorts him to abide by the code he articulates: "Fix to your word, and let us trust our Fates" (4.3.108).

But of course, Nemours no more means these words than those to Cleve. Like the husband of the famous Widow of Ephesus, he sardonically goes to seduce the Princess on the very "Tomb" of her husband, dressed in the full panoply not of Platonic but Libertine rhetoric: "I mean a Visit by the way of Consolation, not but I knew it the only opportunity to catch a Woman in the undress of her Soul; nay, I wou'd choose such a time for my life, and 'tis like the rest of those starts, and one of the Secrets of their Nature—Why they melt, nay, in Plagues, Fire, Famine, War, or any great Calamity—Mark it— Let a man stand but right before 'em, and like hunted Hares they run into his lap" (5.2.16–22). Knowing he has Marguerite in reserve, he is undaunted, and Tournon gives him his just character: "Go thy ways Petronius, nay, if he were dying too, with his Veins cut, he wou'd call for Wine, Fiddles and Whores, and laugh himself into the other World" (5.2.31–33).

From the beginning Nemours has blasphemously defied that other world and its putative gods. When Tournon playfully taxes him with damning both his own soul and those of his victims, he pledges to her a fidelity not of the soul but of the body and its sexual performance: "by Heaven I'm thine, with all the heat and vigorous Inspiration of an unflesh'd Lover—and so will be while young Limbs and Lechery hold together, and that's a Bond methinks shou'd last till Doomsday"

(1.2.1–50). When the disguised Marguerite, protesting aside that Nemours is a "Fiend, and no Man," pretends she might indeed be a devil herself, a succubus, Nemours insouciantly and defiantly proclaims, "But be a Devil and thou wilt, if we must be Damn'd together, who can help it" (3.1.52–63). In Tirso's, Molière's, or Shadwell's plays, such defiant rhetoric constantly reminds the audience of the sure divine vengeance that awaits Don Juan, who commits rampant rape, murder, and incest. And in Lee's play, the audience's expectations of a similar divine justice are aroused when Marguerite announces she plans a revenge that will conclude with Nemours's contemplating "the Horror of his Soul" (3.1.107), or when the mortally wounded Cleve warns his wife, "There is a Power that can and will revenge" (4.3.130).

But the problem with the ending (see esp. Weber 1986, 76–78) is that Nemours is brought to no such contemplation, nor is he punished by some Power that protects the conventional morality. Instead, he enacts his last posture, that of the reformed rake, a posture so successful that even Lee's modern editors believe it (Lee 1955, 2:150). Exhorting the couples of the low plot to "Swear a whole Life's Constancy," he proclaims, "For my part, the Death of the Prince of Cleve, upon second thoughts, has so truly wrought a change in me, as nothing else but a Miracle cou'd—For first I see, and loath my Debaucheries—Next, while I am in Health, I am resolv'd to give satisfaction to all I have wrong'd; and first to this Lady [Marguerite], whom I will make my Wife before all this Company e'er we part" (5.3.289–99). With an obvious reference to the recent death of Rochester, we are supposed to believe in the "Ingenuity" of Nemours's "Repentance" because, unlike Rochester, Nemours "had the power to go on," that is to continue in iniquity:

> He well Repents that will not Sin, yet can,
> But Death-bed Sorrow rarely shews the Man.
>
> (5.3.300–303)

But how can we believe the conversion of this extreme libertine, when moments before he has predicted he will bed the Princess, naming the very minute? How can we believe him when he has parodied the very notion of "Conversion" by telling Tournon to use it to win back Marguerite from the Dauphin, threatening that the Prince's death has caused him to repent and resolve "to leave off Whoreing and marry" not Marguerite but the Princess (5.2.8–11)? How can we believe him when he has repeatedly stated that Marguerite is merely his "reserve" to fall back on if the Princess refuses him (act 5 passim)? Unlike the case of Dorimant as I have argued it

(Canfield 1989, chap. 3), Nemours has not been led to the gradual awakening of something in his soul, a different kind of passion from what he has experienced before. True, he rediscovers Marguerite's wit, but he also loves and pledges to serve always that of Tournon, and he still intends to seduce the Princess.

Thus, it would seem, the ending of the play defies three possible conventional endings: a poetical justice that takes the Don Juan off to hell, as in Tirso's, Molière's, or Shadwell's plays; a poetical justice that leaves him contemplating "the Horror of his Soul"; or a socialization that causes him truly to repent his sexual excesses and marry. Instead, we are left with the Dangerous Supplement still on the loose, the champion of the antimorality of the unpunished libertine wits both male—Bellamore, the Vidam—and female—Tournon, Celia. He masquerades behind the rhetoric of reformation, but he lurks there to ultimately supplant the Prince, his father, and all the males so ill-protected by the patriarchal code of words. He is pure Will to Sexual Power and cannot be socialized.

* * *

Dryden's *Amphitryon* is the most disturbing of all these plays, for a Christian spectator *could* still leave the theater after Howard's or Lee's plays confidently muttering, "Yes, but they'll get theirs in the end, at least at the Final End" (as Armistead argues [1979, 162], to me, overconfidently, concerning *Princess*). But Dryden's play removes the comfort of any final, providential justice. It is as if, after God's failure to support the right cause in the Glorious Revolution, Dryden availed himself of the traditional story of Amphitryon in order to depict a universe where the Rhetoric of Order is mere rhetoric, for its regnant deity is not the Logos of Saints John, Augustine, and Thomas Aquinas and the rationalist theologians but the sheer power of Hobbes (see his reading of the Book of Job in Hobbes n.d., 234–35) and the voluntarists. Dryden's Jupiter is a combination of Howard's and Lee's dukes, but he is infinitely more dangerous, because he is supposed to represent the Logos that underwrites the code of word as bond, yet he is the arch-perverter of words. He is a Dangerous Supplement who supplants by doubling, by duplicity, by the destruction of identity and integrity. And there are, there can be, no bounds to his arbitrary Will to Power.

In a scene added by Dryden to his main sources in Plautus and Molière (see Dryden 1976, 554) Jupiter's sons, Phoebus and Mercury, comically discuss their father's transgressions (which, of course, have resulted in their own bastardy). Juno has tried to take Jupiter to the "Spiritual Court" over those transgressions, but Jupiter has stood upon his royal "Prerogative" (1.1.22–25). That is, Jupiter holds himself above the law, as Mercury brings home to him, comically and submissively, by inquiring what form he will take to seduce yet another mortal woman, this time Amphitryon's chaste wife, Alcmena: "I was considering into what form your Almighty-ship would be pleas'd to transform your self to night. Whether you wou'd fornicate in the Shape of a Bull, or a Ram, or an Eagle, or a Swan: What Bird or Beast you wou'd please to honour, by transgressing your own Laws, in his likeness; or in short, whether you wou'd recreate your self in Feathers, or in Leather?" (1.1.73–79). Phoebus more seriously disputes with Jupiter, asking why he must commit what he himself confesses to be a "Crime" and dissecting the speciousness of Jupiter's recourse to "the Fates" (1.1.87–101). Jupiter is forced to proclaim,

> Fate is, what I
> By vertue of Omnipotence have made it:
> And pow'r Omnipotent can do no wrong:
> Not to my self, because I will'd it so:
> Nor yet to Men, for what they are is mine.
> This night I will enjoy *Amphitryon*'s Wife:
> For, when I made her, I decreed her such
> As I shou'd please to love. I wrong not him
> Whose Wife she is; for I reserv'd my Right,
> To have her while she pleas'd me; that once past,
> She shall be his again.
>
> (1.1.102–12)

Once again his sons call a spade a spade, the one comically, the other seriously:

> *Mercury.* Here's Omnipotence with a Vengeance, to make a Man a
> Cuckold, and yet not to do him wrong. . . .
> *Phoebus.* If there be no such thing as right and wrong,
> Of an Eternal Being, I have done—
> But if there be— (1.1.113–21)

If "pow'r Omnipotent can do no wrong" then there is no such thing as right or wrong but thinking makes it so, as Hamlet would say. Jupiter is forced to the last, desperate stratagem of theodicy, cloaking himself in the incomprehensibility of his providence, which he explains as the good that will emerge from this evil, the hero Hercules, who "shall redress the Wrongs of injur'd Mortals, / Shall conquer Monsters, and reform the World" (1.1.121–27). Mercury explodes such theodicy by pointing out that Jupiter himself made all the monsters and vices Hercules is supposed to conquer; that is, God

himself is the origin of evil. Yet Jupiter's sons—and all his subjects—
are finally forced to submit:

> *Phoebus.* Since Arbitrary Pow'r will hear no Reason, 'tis Wisdom to be
> silent.—
> *Mercury.* Why that's the Point; this same Arbitrary Power is a knock-down
> Argument; 'tis but a Word and a Blow; now methinks our Father speaks
> out like an honest bare-fac'd God, as he is; he lays the stress in the right
> Place, upon absolute Dominion: I confess if he had been a Man, he
> might have been a Tyrant, if his Subjects durst have call'd him to
> account. (1.1.131–38)

That Dryden is glancing at his contemporary situation, as James D.
Garrison has ably argued (1980), becomes even more obvious when
Jupiter, disguised as Amphitryon, beseeches Alcmena to consider
him not her husband but her libertine lover, adding to Molière's
similar sentiments (1956, act 1, scene 3) the analogy to succession:

> In me (my charming Mistris) you behold
> A Lover that disdains a Lawful Title;
> Such as of Monarchs to successive Thrones.
>
> (2.2.83–85)

Right no longer makes might; might makes right. And thus *a fortiori*,
all supplanters are justified, those on thrones as well as those in beds.
Dryden calls attention to the political implications of the sexual by
having Amphitryon complain that Alcmena's favors have been
"usurp'd" from him (3.1.294), by directly confronting Jupiter as "base
Usurper of my Name, and Bed" (5.1.144; see Garrison 1980, 194), and
by using that loaded word again in the epilogue to describe what
Jupiter has done, *"usurp'd the Husband's name"* (13). And when Sosia
anachronistically charges others "in the King's name" (4.1.253), we
must ask to whom does the appellation refer. There is no king in the
play. But if Dryden's world is being reflected, there is no real king
there, either, and therefore no one to whom to appeal for justice.

In other details added to the story by Dryden, before Jupiter
arrives to usurp Amphitryon's place, Alcmena's clever lady-in-waiting,
Phaedra, exacts from her a promise that she be her lady's bedfellow
that night. Phaedra insists that Alcmena "swear by *Jupiter*," and when
Alcmena asks why, Phaedra explains: "Because he's the greatest: I
hate to deal with one of your little baffling Gods that can do nothing,
but by permission: but *Jupiter* can swinge you off; if you swear by
him, and are forsworn" (1.2.42–51). In other words, the whole system
of word as bond works only if there is an underwriting Word, a

Supreme Being that punishes those that break their words—their pledges of allegiance and coronation oaths, their vows of marital fidelity, their promises, their judicial oaths. But Dryden raises the question, what happens when God is nothing but power, will, desire. At one point Jupiter blames his inconstancy of purpose on "Almighty Love . . . Who bows our Necks beneath her brazen Yoke" (3.1.525–27). That is, Jupiter himself is ruled by his desire. So when Alcmena explains that she cannot sleep with the disguised Jupiter because she has given her word to Phaedra, he proclaims in exasperation, "Forswear thy self; for *Jupiter* but laughs / At Lovers Perjuries" (1.2.146–47). Phaedra complains comically in response, "The more shame for him if he does: there wou'd be a fine God indeed for us Women to worship, if he laughs when our Sweet-hearts cheat us of our Maidenheads: No, no, *Jupiter* is an honester Gentleman than you make of him" (1.2.148–51). But when God is not a gentleman but a libertine himself, Dryden's play forces us to reason, then the binding force of words is lost. Dryden has made one of his lecherous, lawless emperors (as in *Aureng-Zebe* or *Don Sebastian*) into a god who sacrifices everything to his pleasure, including his providence:

> For what's to be a God, but to enjoy?
> Let human-kind their Sovereign's leisure waite;
> Love is, this Night, my great Affair of State:
> Let this one Night, of Providence be void:
> All *Jove*, for once, is on himself employ'd.
> Let unregarded Altars smoke in vain;
> And let my Subjects praise me, or complain.
>
> (1.2.191–97)

Christian Providence implies not only foresight and provision but justice, vindication of the word by the Word, the Logos. In the world of the play, both word and Word are void.[5]

If the law and the Logos do not restrain God himself, then *a fortiori* lesser figures may have the same license. Despite his comic objections, as in Dryden's sources Mercury himself proceeds by the same law(lessness). Just as Jupiter duplicitously doubles Amphitryon to take away his rights, Mercury doubles Sosia to take away his. Just as Jupiter justifies himself by his power, Mercury dominates Sosia throughout the play by the right of his cudgel. Abetting Jupiter in duping Amphitryon, Mercury comically explains (with the cynical last line added by Dryden to Molière, 3.2.1–8), "This is no very charitable Action of a God, to use him ill, who has never offended me: but my Planet disposes me to Malice: and when we great Persons do but a little Mischief, the World has a good bargain of us" (4.1.137–40).

Again in details added by Dryden, just as Jupiter bribes Phaedra out of her bond with Alcmena, Mercury bribes her into fornication with him. And just as Jupiter makes a mockery of word as bond, Mercury threatens Sosia with recalling his "word" of truce and beating him anew (2.1.292–93), and he affects to "pass" his "word" that Gripus will agree to relinquish his pretensions to Phaedra because he, Mercury, carries a sword (5.1.34–36). In a seduction song Mercury articulates the triumphant antitrust code of the play:

I.

Fair Iris I love, and hourly I dye,
But not for a lip, nor a languishing Eye:
She's fickle and false, and there we agree;
For I am as false, and as fickle as she:
We neither believe what either can say;
And, neither believing, we neither betray.

II.

'Tis civil to swear, and say things of course;
We mean not the taking for better for worse.
When present, we love; when absent, agree:
I think not of Iris, nor Iris of me:
The Legend of Love no Couple can find
So easie to part, or so equally join'd.

(4.1.482–93)

Like Jupiter and Mercury, Dryden's creation, Phaedra, is more than willing to be a sexual trickster. While she appropriates the language of the traditional code when it is to her advantage, holding Alcmena to her word in order to gain a bribe or calling Sosia a "perjur'd Villain" because he fails to produce the bribe his double promised her (3.1.412), in their hilarious proviso scene Phaedra answers Mercury's demand that she be "always constant" to him and "admit no other Lover" with the witty rejoinder, "unless it be a Lover that offers more: and that the Constancy shall not exceed the Settlement" (5.1.352–55). As opposed to the idealistically constant Alcmena, who is duped by the god who is supposed to reward that constancy, Phaedra is a figure for inconstancy. She is "Woman," as Mercury says, "and your minds are so variable, that it's very hard even for a God to know them" (4.1.498–99). He describes the billet-doux hidden in her pocket thus: "full of fraudulence, and equivocations, and shoeing-horns of Love to him; to promise much, and mean nothing; to show, over and above, that thou art a mere Woman" (4.1.454–56). As Jupiter in exasperation bribes her to relinquish Alcmena from her word, he exclaims, "this is a very Woman: / Her Sex is Avarice, and she, in One, / Is all her Sex" (1.2.182–85). So Woman is a sign of the radical inconstancy of the world that results from unbridled desire. It is tempting to speculate that Dryden adds to his sources this misogyny and its embodiment in Phaedra because of his anger at James II's daughter, Mary, who was so inconstant as to betray her father and usurp his throne.

Dryden's variations on the traditional theme darken the implications of doubling in the story. If the only Absolute is Desire and even God subverts the law by doubling, by a supplementation that is at once a repetition and a supplanting, then integrity and identity are radically threatened, as is comically played out in the Two Sosias subplot. Sosia's identity has been supplanted, usurped by Mercury, and he no longer knows who he is or what name to take. Jupiter and Mercury's doublings have destabilized not only word as bond but word as name, as unique identity. Expanding on Molière (3.6), Dryden's Sosia pleads with Mercury, "May it please you, Sir, the Name is big enough for both of us: and we may use it in common, like a Strumpet" (4.1.374–75). The name that is supposed to fix and hold reality is a whore—unfaithful, inconstant to one identity or meaning, susceptible to endless metonymy. When Dryden's Amphitryon repeats to Sosia twice, "To Repetition, Rogue, to Repetition" (3.1.35–36, 40), he gives us a figure for a world where the Dangerous Supplement destroys societal institutions, from thrones to marital beds to language itself, by denying the possibility of a single, constant state(ment).

When Mercury reveals his divinity to Phaedra in order to complete his seduction and promises to be "secret" and assist her in her petty theft, he justifies himself wittily, "for thou and I were born under the same Planet." Her reply, "And we shall come to the same end too, I'm afraid," indicates a traditional fear of retributive, providential justice. But Phaedra's—and the audience's—expectations of such a justice are not to be fulfilled in the world of this play. Mercury rejoins, "No; no; since thou hast wit enough already to couzin a Judge, thou need'st never fear hanging" (4.1.471–76). Mercury refers, of course, to Judge Gripus, whom Dryden invents and portrays as corrupted by bribes, sex, and physical threats. Thus when the nobles turn to him to be "Umpire of the Cause" between Jupiter and Amphitryon, we know his corruption frustrates such a charge. His immediate response is to turn to Mercury, who has bullied him, and ask, "On whose side wou'd you please that I shou'd give the Sentence?" (5.1.167–70).

But Dryden's real point is not the traditional theme of corrupt human justice. It is that there can be no human when there is no divine justice. When, as Mercury characterizes him, "Our *Jupiter* is a great Comedian; he counterfeits most admirably: sure his Priests have coppy'd their Hypocrisie from their Master" (5.1.129–31); when God himself, because of his omniscience, knows all the right answers to the questions designed to distinguish the true from the false Amphitryon; when the Logos becomes mere self-serving rhetoric, as Jupiter dupes the distraught Alcmena with soothing lies, "Follow no more, that false and foolish Fire, / That wou'd mislead thy Fame to sure destruction!" (5.1.262–63); then Amphitryon's desperate pathetic appeals, "Good Gods, how can this be! . . . To this [his sword]—and to the Gods I'll trust my Cause" (5.1.246, 276), are absurd. And at the end, Amphitryon and Alcmena are simply silenced by sheer power: making even darker Molière's Jupiter's appeal to the silencing power of his name (3.10), Dryden's Jupiter cynically says,

> Look up, *Amphitryon*, and behold above,
> Th'Impostour God, the Rival of thy Love:
> In thy own shape, see *Jupiter* appear,
> And let that sight, secure thy jealous fear.
> Disgrace, and Infamy, are turn'd to boast:
> No Fame, in *Jove's* Concurrence can be lost:
> What he enjoys, he sanctifies from Vice.
>
> (5.1.393–99)

Desire, when omnipotent, can sanctify whatever means it takes to obtain its end. The witty exchange at the conclusion of the Mercury-Phaedra proviso scene underscores the ramifications:

> *Sosia*. Now I wou'd ask of Madam *Phaedra*, that in case Mr. Heaven there, shou'd be pleas'd to break these Articles, in what Court of Judicature she intends to sue him?
> *Phaedra*. The fool has hit upon't:—Gods, and great Men, are never to be sued; for they can always plead priviledge of Peerage. (5.1.379–84)

Dryden has provided no poetical justice with its underwriting providential justice because he has portrayed God as amoral Desire and Power. Jupiter's promise of a Hercules provides no real consolation, for he, too, is a figure of Absolute Force, who would bring "Peace" and "Happiness" only by compulsion (5.1.419–21). As Amphitryon and Alcmena "stand mute, and know not how to take it" (5.1.409–10), while the others attempt to congratulate them, Dryden's Mercury adds to Molière's Sosie's injunction to silence (3.10) this strange comment: "Upon the whole matter, if *Amphitryon* takes the favour of *Jupiter* in patience, as from a God, he's a good Heathen" (5.1.425–27). On the one hand, the comment frees Dryden from a charge of blasphemy: his Christian audience knows Jupiter is not really God, and only a heathen would justify his abuse of power. But on the other hand, Dryden has portrayed the cosmos as heathen, where there is no recourse against political and sexual usurpers, for God himself is a tyrant and a Don Juan. Dryden's Sosia, sounding like the Wife of Bath, closes the play with a final expression of the triumph of desire over the Rhetoric of Order:

> For, let the wicked World say what they please,
> The fair Wife makes her Husband live at ease:
> The Lover keeps him too; and but receives,
> Like *Jove*, the remnants that *Amphitryon* leaves:
> 'Tis true, the Lady has enough in store,
> To satisfie those two, and eke, two more:
> In fine, the Man, who weighs the matter fully,
> Wou'd rather be the Cuckold, than the Cully.
>
> (5.1.437–44)

So much for the code of the word, underwritten by a Divine Word. Supplementarity is the only rule.

* * *

Perhaps an orthodox Derridean (he would be amused at the concept) would want to read all Restoration drama—indeed, all drama—as meaning the same thing as these three disturbing plays. But the plays are so disturbing, it seems to me, precisely because they are so different from most Restoration drama and its reaffirmation of the Rhetoric of Order or at least its general treatment of the subversive in an embracing, celebratory closure. These plays defy such closure. They deliberately eschew poetical justice, with all its metaphysical ramifications. They leave us with successful villain-tricksters who have nothing but cynical contempt for the world and its hypocrites (in Dryden's play, see Mercury's characterization of worldlings as self-interested throughout). They are a sign that, as Hobbes would agree, behind our codes lurks only Naked Desire, the only Transcendental Word signified by all our words.

Notes

1. See Williams 1979, which reprints the essence of a series of articles beginning in 1968. For recent critiques of Williams's position, see Hughes 1986 and Scouten 1987. Without citing me, although he reviewed the book (Hughes 1980), Hughes (1986) belabors two points I made some years ago (Canfield 1977, chap. 1), that *distributive* poetical justice was an innovation in Restoration *tragedy* and tragic theory and that theologians took the overwhelming absence of distributive justice in this life as a sign of its necessity in the next. Although Hughes is correct in

insisting that theologians generally took a dim view of interpreting events in individual lives as instances of Providence, he nevertheless admits that many divines catalogued such instances. And he neglects the fact, cited often by Williams, that theorists (like Dennis) called on dramatists to imitate not reality, that is, the common injustice of historical life, but Reality, that is, the ideal pattern of eschatalogical justice. Primarily by implying that the trope of Providence was the sole property of the Puritans, Scouten accuses Williams and his followers (explicitly including me) of being unhistorical; he also accuses us of failing to acknowledge that *providence* (according to the *OED*) can also be a secular term. The rhetoric of Providence (almost always implying divine agency when capitalized) was employed ubiquitiously by Royalist preachers and sympathizers as well as Roundhead, and it is ubiquitous in Restoration drama. The real difference between Williams and his critics is interpretive. Except by implication from their citations of dramatists defending themselves against charges of blasphemy for using the term Providence casually, Hughes and Scouten never really address the question of how we are to read specific instances of religious language in Restoration comedy. To sweep such language under the rug of mere convention is a critical failure. To accept at face value contemporary condemnations of such comedy as profane is naive. And to take previous critics' neglect of the issue as restrictive is illogical. Critics must interpret specific instances of religious language with regard to their function in individual texts, especially with regard to endings. Nobody's generalizations, neither Williams's nor Hughes's nor Scouten's nor mine, can relieve us of that responsibility. Both Hughes and Scouten employ the rhetoric of scandalized morality at Williams's (or my) supposed errors in scholarship (mostly minor errors in citation or really just disagreements in interpretation). Such carping seems professionally inappropriate. Let us agree to meet on the field of hermeneutics.

2. For the best readings of Otway's play and its cynicism, see Hume 1976a, 92–97, and Weber 1986, 82–89; for the best reading of Southerne's, see Weber, 162–71. For my reading of the Vanbrugh play, see Canfield 1980, 394–99.

3. Howard 1722. When the act or scene number is followed by a comma, the following numbers are page numbers in editions that do not number lines.

4. For the best readings of the play and its satire, see Hume 1976b and Weber 1986, 69–78. See also Armistead 1979, chap. 11, and Brown 1983, 397–400.

5. Garrison reads the play as portraying a world void of justice and faith. As such, our readings dovetail, though I hope mine comes in at an angle sufficiently different to supplement his. See also Milhous and Hume's appreciative reading of the play as satire (1985, chap. 7), following Garrison.

Works Cited

Armistead, J. M. 1979. *Nathaniel Lee.* Twayne's English Authors Series, no. 270. Boston: Twayne.

Brown, Richard E. 1983. "Heroics Satirized by 'Mad Nat. Lee.'" *Papers on Language and Literature* 19:385–401.

Canfield, J. Douglas. 1977. *Nicholas Rowe and Christian Tragedy.* Gainesville: University Presses of Florida.

———. 1979. "The Significance of the Restoration Rhymed Heroic Play." *Eighteenth Century Studies* 13:49–62.

———. 1980. "Religious Language and Religious Meaning in Restoration Comedy." *Studies in English Literature* 20:385–406.

———. 1984. "The Ideology of Restoration Tragicomedy." *ELH* 51:447–64.

———. 1985. "Royalism's Last Dramatic Stand: English Political Tragedy, 1679–89." *Studies in Philology* 82:234–63.

———. 1989. *Word as Bond in English Literature from the Middle Ages to the Restoration.* Philadelphia: University of Pennsylvania Press.

Derrida, Jacques. 1976. *Of Grammatology.* Trans. Gayatri Chakravorty Spivak. Baltimore: The Johns Hopkins University Press.

Dryden, John. 1976. *Amphitryon*. In *The Works of John Dryden*. Vol. 15. Ed. Earl Miner, George R. Guffey, and Franklin B. Zimmerman, 221–318. Berkeley and Los Angeles: University of California Press.

Garrison, James D. 1980. "Dryden and the Birth of Hercules." *Studies in Philology* 77:180–201.

Hobbes, Thomas. n.d. *Leviathan; or, The Matter, Forme and Power of a Commonwealth Ecclesiasticall and Civil*. Ed. Michael Oakshott. Blackwell's Political Texts. Oxford.

Howard, Sir Robert. 1722. *The Dramatic Works of Sir Robert Howard*. 3d ed. London.

Hughes, Derek. 1980. Review of Canfield, *Nicholas Rowe and Christian Tragedy*. *Modern Language Review* 75:854–55.

———. 1986. "Providential Justice and English Comedy 1660–1700: A Review of the External Evidence." *Modern Language Review* 81:273–92.

Hume, Robert D. 1976a. "Otway and the Comic Muse." *Studies in Philology* 73:87–116.

———. 1976b. "The Satiric Design of Nat. Lee's *The Princess of Cleve*." *Journal of English and Germanic Philology* 75:117–38.

Lee, Nathaniel. 1955. *The Princess of Cleve*. In *The Works of Nathaniel Lee*, ed. Thomas B. Stroup and Arthur L. Cooke, 2:147–227. Reprint. Metuchen, N.J.: Scarecrow, 1968.

Milhous, Judith, and Robert D. Hume. 1985. *Producible Interpretation: Eight English Plays 1675–1707*. Carbondale and Edwardsville: Southern Illinois University Press.

Miller, Nancy K. 1981. "Emphasis Added: Plots and Plausibilities in Women's Fiction." *PMLA* 96:36–48.

Molière. 1956. *Amphitryon*. In *Œuvres complètes*, ed. Maurice Rat, 2:217–95. Bibliothèque de la Pléiade. Paris: Gallimard.

Scouten, Arthur H. 1987. "Recent Interpretations of Restoration Comedy of Manners." In *du Verbe au geste: mélanges en l'honneur de Pierre Danchin*, 99–107. Nancy: Presses Universitaires de Nancy.

Weber, Harold. 1986. *The Restoration Rake-Hero: Transformations in Sexual Understanding in Seventeenth-Century England*. Madison: University of Wisconsin Press.

Williams, Aubrey L. 1979. *An Approach to Congreve*. New Haven: Yale University Press.

The Late Seventeenth-Century Dilemma in Discourse

Dryden's Don Sebastian *and Behn's* Oroonoko

ROSE A. ZIMBARDO

On the last step of his long, arduous journey home, Odysseus is washed ashore on the Edenic kingdom of Phaeakia. The king of that island, Alkinoos, before he even knows the stranger's name, invites him to a feast where the poet, Demodocus, sings the Trojan War. Alkinoos is surprised by Odysseus's response to the poet's song (he hides his head and weeps), for the wise king knows that true poetry, imitating the perfect balance of the universal order in the perfect articulation of its parts, should elicit an impersonal rapture in the hearer, should lift him out of himself and attune his soul to the cosmic harmonia. Odysseus's complaint, however, is that the song is *too* true, too perfect a reflection of the cosmic concord. Demodocus, he says, has sung "too much according to order." He wants instead a story about himself and the craftiness that enabled him to devise the trick of the wooden horse. He asks Demodocus to sing not *kata kosmon*—following the order of the whole, but *kata moiran*—giving to each part its full and proper due (8:496).[1]

The paradox in poetic imitation has existed in our literary tradition, it would seem, for as long as we have had one. Which is poetry to imitate: the whole order of truth or specific human truths? auctoritee or experience? the distant, elevated Idea of human being or the near, dear, distracting fever of being human? How should poetic discourse operate upon the reader? Should it "elevate the mind" to metaphysical revelation by its *"Harmony of words,"* as Dryden proposed in his preface to *Tyrannick Love* (1970, 109) or, to keep faith with truth, must all discourse "return back to the primitive purity and shortness when men delivered so many *things,* almost in an equal number of *words,"* as Bishop Sprat advised (1667, 2:20)? Should the relation between word and mind be defined as Theophilus Gale defined it in 1669: "as in the *Mind* there is a certain *Character* or *Idea* of things; so likewise in the oration or speech there is a *Character* or

Idea of the Mind" (1:52)? Or should the motto of the Royal Society be adopted as a guide: "There are no Ideas but in Things"?

What for ages had been a pleasing, if perplexing, paradox in poetic imitation became a vexing problem in the last two decades of the seventeenth century. Dualism, indeed pluralism, of perspective had been quite amenable to embrace within the complex *lusus* afforded by the classical generic forms, and multileveled perception and understanding of a text were *required* by the critical canons of the Middle Ages and the Renaissance (*littera gesta, moral, allegoria, anagogia,* and so forth). However, at the end of the seventeenth century what had been a paradox in poetic mimesis became an irreconcilable problem in epistemology. For example, in 1692 one writer asks, if Aeneas never *in fact* went to Italy, if the record of his exploits there is no more than the product of Virgil's imagination, then what is the use of our reading the *Aeneid?*

> M. Bouchart asserts that *Eneas* never went into Italy. If this be true the *Eneis* of *Virgil* is a Fiction much exceeding what we call Poetical License. . . . at least the ground of a Poem ought to be founded on Truth; . . . though the Circumstances may be feign'd 'tis somewhat too much for the chief Subject to be so too . . . our mind takes no interest in a relation where we are sensible that we are imposed upon in every particular, since we love at least to see the Image of Truth. . . . if the Hero never went out of *Asia* his achievements in Italy seem too Romantic.[2]

What had been a matter of perspective earlier in the tradition became a problem of truth in the 1690s.

There has been awareness for some time that in the last decade of the seventeenth century, drama became "novelistic."[3] Conversely, there is an awareness that one of the major difficulties in distinguishing the origins of the novel in formal, as opposed to sociological, terms rests in inability to grapple with the generic contours of a form as elusive as the novel. In my judgement that is because in considering the climate of ideas that bred the novel, "What we are witnessing," as Gabriel Josipovici puts it, "is the emergence of a new way of thinking, or if not a new way of thinking at least a new model of the mind" (1978, 141). Evident in the reassessment of the *Aeneid* just quoted, for instance, is a clear opposition in the writer's mind between "truth" and "fiction." Once such an opposition is established,

> poetry in general comes to be taken as merely ornament, decoration, simply that which makes palatable a truth which can be more simply expressed in logical terms. And if poetry and truth are thus opposed to

each other, so too are rhetoric and logic. The mind comes to be seen as a
space in which logic and rhetoric jostle each other for position. The more
space can be filled up by logic, the closer to truth will we be; rhetoric, on
the other hand, like poetry, belongs to the field of illusion. (Josipovici
1978, 141)

The proposition that I should like to entertain here is this: What if
in dealing with the end of drama and the beginning of the novel as
serious forms critical theory is dealing not simply with a competition
between two literary genres for primacy in the popular imagination,
nor yet with a sociological phenomenon (the emergence of a newly
literate bourgeoisie), but is instead faced with a far more interesting
aesthetic problem: a conflict between genre and antigenre, the condition wherein a *formal discourse,* the regnant ordering rhetoric,
which traditionally had been subordinate to the requirements of
whatever generic design it served, found itself in opposition to a
generically indeterminate form that was in the process of shaping
itself to the demands of a polyglossic, extraliterary discourse? As I
have argued elsewhere, I believe that the evolution of literary history
in the late-seventeenth and early-eighteenth centuries centered on
the problem of how "imitation of nature" was understood (Zimbardo
1986). The course of development in England between 1660 and 1732
is a transition that runs from imitation of nature as *idea* (heroic),
through imitation of the interplay between ideational and experiential
"reality" (satiric), to imitation of the experiential actual (novelistic).
My argument finds support in the theoretical speculations of M. M.
Bakhtin, especially in his essay "Epic and Novel," which discusses the
"novelization" of classical generic forms—though Bakhtin's treatment
is not confined to a single national literature nor to a strictly specific
historical period (1981, essay 1). To test the validity of my proposition
I shall examine two works that I believe are landmarks at the
crossroads of the transition; one, Dryden's *Don Sebastian,* is the
product of a mind particularly sensitive to theoretical problems; the
other, Behn's *Oroonoko,* is the product of a theoretically unsophisti-
cated mind that was, nevertheless, an almost infallible barometer of
popular understanding and taste.

Don Sebastian presents a particularly interesting example because
Dryden's sources were a historical novel and the extensive, remarkably factually detailed seventeenth-century traveler's accounts of Bar-
bary. Dryden turns these "novelistic" materials into a heroic tragedy;
yet, as he tells us in his preface, he is acutely aware that his problem
in poetic mimesis was to present in a drama a complexity, variety, and
irregularity of vision that strained the limits of dramatic form:

"Whether it happen'd through a long disuse of Writing, that I forgot the usual compass of a Play; or that by crowding it, with Characters and Incidents, I put a necessity upon my self of lengthning [*sic*] the main Action, I know not; but the first days Audience sufficiently convinc'd me of my error" (1976, 65, italics reversed throughout citations from the preface). What he has written, he says, is more suitable for the study than the stage, for "there is a vast difference betwixt a publick entertainment on the Theatre, and a private reading in the Closet: In the first we are confin'd to time . . . ; in the last, every Reader is judge of his own convenience; he can take up the book, and lay it down at his pleasure; and find out those beauties of propriety, in thought and writing, which escap'd him in the tumult and hurry of representing" (66). What is found in *Don Sebastian*, to use Bakhtinian terminology, is a classical genre in the process of "novelization."

> What are the salient features of this novelization of other genres . . . ? They become more free and flexible, their language renews itself by incorporating extraliterary heteroglossia, . . . they become dialogized, permeated with laughter, irony, humor, elements of self-parody and finally—this is the most important thing—the novel inserts into these other genres an indeterminacy, a certain semantic openendedness, a living contact with unfinished, still-evolving contemporary reality (the open-ended present). (Bakhtin 1981, 6–7)

Anticipating twentieth-century criticism, as he so often does, Dryden hits upon precisely these points in justifying his practice in the preface: that is, the heteroglossia of his language—"There [are] . . . some newnesses of *English*, translated from the Beauties of Modern Tongues, as well as from the elegancies of the *Latin;* and here and there some old words are sprinkled, which for their significance and sound, deserv'd not to be antiquated" (67); the freedom and flexibility of his form—"I must farther declare freely, that I have not exactly kept to the three Mechanick rules of unity . . . ; for the Genius of the *English* cannot bear too regular a Play; we are given to variety, even to a debauchery of Pleasure. My Scenes are therefore sometimes broken" (69–70); the variety and indeterminacy in his characterization— "a more ignorant sort of Creatures . . . maintain that the Character of *Dorax*, is not only unnatural, but inconsistent with it self; let them read the Play and think again, and if yet they are not satisfied, cast their eyes on that Chapter of the Wise *Montaigne*, which is intituled *de l'Inconstance des actions humaines*" (70); and, finally, his inclusion of comic and antiheroic elements, especially in the Antonio-Morayma plot—"I have observ'd, that the *English* will not bear a thorough

Tragedy; but are pleas'd, that it shou'd be lightned with underparts of mirth. . . . [And] what cou'd be more uniform, than to draw from out the members of a Captive Court, the Subject of a Comical entertainment?" (72). By the admission of Dryden himself, then, and according to the model of Bakhtin, in *Don Sebastian* the "novelization" of a classical genre—heroic tragedy as it was understood in the seventeenth century—begins. I shall restrict myself here to the nature of discourse in *Don Sebastian* and to the manner in which discourse functions to "novelize" a high heroic genre in three ways: to make the elevated and distant near and familiar; to transform the clarity and uniformity of heroic types into the complexity and indeterminacy we experience in the realm of actual human contact; and to draw valorized heroic action into the arena of the open-ended present.

In the words of Bakhtin,

> Epic discourse is a discourse handed down by tradition. By its very nature the epic world . . . is inaccessible to personal experience and does not permit an individual, personal point of view or evaluation. One cannot glimpse it, grope for it, touch it; one cannot look at it from just any point of view; it is impossible to experience it, analyze it, . . . penetrate into its core. . . . the important thing is not the factual sources of the epic, not the content of its historical events, nor the declarations of its authors—the important thing is this formal constitutive characteristic of the epic as a genre . . . : its reliance on impersonal and sacrosanct tradition, on a commonly held evaluation and point of view—which . . . displays a profound piety toward the subject described and toward the language used to describe it, the language of tradition. (1981, 16–17)

Heroic drama was, of course, the epic of seventeenth-century France and England. Its discourse was formally constitutive; its language, traditional and sacrosanct, moved to the demands of whatever generic design it served. The discourse of heroic drama—never to be confused with dialogue—was self-referential; that is, its points of reference were not in the world of experience but in the removed and self-contained world of heroic *Idea*, for "all high genres of the classical [or neo-classical] era . . . are structured in the zone of the distanced image, a zone outside any possible contact with the present in all its openendedness" (Bakhtin 1981, 19). If *Don Sebastian* is regarded as a Janus-faced marker on the path that poetic imitation took in the last decade of the seventeenth century, this idealization is the direction toward which its *backward* face looks. The play's frame is heroic tragedy, and much of its discourse is the language of classical heroic drama, for example, the opening speech of Muley-Moluch:

Muley-Moluch. Our Armours now may rust, our idle scymitars
   Hang by our sides, for Ornament not use:
   Children shall beat our Atabals and Drums,
   And all the noisie trades of War, no more
   Shall wake the peaceful morn: the *Xeriff's* blood
   No longer in divided Channels runs,
   The younger House took end in *Mahumet*.
   Nor shall *Sebastian's* formidable Name,
   Be longer us'd to lull the crying babe!

(1.1.157–65)

However, heroic discourse of this kind exists in the play only in patches. Most important, it does not *function*, as the language of the earlier heroic drama does, to structure a dialectical progress toward the refinement of an Idea. Moreover, unlike the dramatic language of the 1660s, whether comic or heroic, this language is not generically homogeneous and self-referential. Throughout the play there is a heteroglossia of discourse that violates heroic form and that creates complexity, variability, and the illusion of depth in the dramatis personae. Heroic figures, whose meanings are always determined by their *positions* within a formal design, become "characters" in our general (and, of course, novelistic) twentieth-century sense of the term.

Consider the opening speeches of Dorax, the character who posed such a problem for the original audience and whose "inconsistency" Dryden felt himself compelled to justify. Dorax's entering remarks particularly call attention to language, for they are concerned with the significance of naming:

Benducar.   Bare *Benducar!*
Dorax. Thou wouldst have Titles, take 'em then, Chief Minister,
   First Hangman of the State.
Benducar.   Some call me Favourite.
Dorax. What's that, his Minion?
   Thou art too old to be a Catamite!
   Now prithee tell me, and abate thy pride,
   Is not *Benducar* Bare, a better Name
   In a Friend's mouth, than all those gawdy Titles,
   Which I disdain to give the Man I love?

(1.1.65–73)

This style of discourse, though it is not in the high heroic mode, is quite acceptable within the boundaries of a loosely constructed heroic design because it is consistent within another of the classical genres,

formal satire, which in the seventeenth century was considered to be
a subspecies of epic. This is the language of the *honnête homme*, the
plain-spoken soldier, and while it adds texture to Dorax's type, it does
not threaten the consistency of the figure. However, further along in
these same opening speeches, Dorax's language becomes so homely
in its antiheroic strain that it falls below the style of satire into the
imagery and cadences of familiar spoken discourse. For example, in
heroic tragedy this is hardly the manner we expect even from a plain-
dealing soldier when he is describing his exploits in battle:

> *Dorax*. I spitted Frogs, I crush'd a heap of Emmets,
>   A hundred of 'em to a single Soul,
>   And that but scanty weight too; the great Devil
>   Scarce thank'd me for my pains; he swallows Vulgar
>   Like whip'd Cream, feels 'em not in going down.
>
> (1.1.79–83)

By its references to the familiar experience of stepping on ants and to
the sensuous experience of swallowing whipped cream, this discourse
not only loses any subordination it might be supposed to have to the
design of the generic form, but it overflows the boundaries of literary
language altogether and pours into the extraliterary open-ended "present" of experience.

Finally, consider how variegation in language operates within a
very short passage of Dorax's. Benducar asks Dorax whether he knows
what the fates in battle of the hero and heroine have been. Dorax's
response is:

> *Dorax*. I hope she dy'd in her own Female calling,
>   Choak'd up with Man, and gorg'd with Circumcision.
>   As for *Sebastian* we must search the Field,
>   And where we see a Mountain of the Slain,
>   Send one to climb, and looking down below,
>   There he shall find him at his Manly length
>   With his face up to Heav'n, in the red Monument,
>   Which his true Sword has digg'd.
>
> (1.1.132–39)

There are three levels of discourse woven into the polyglossic texture
of this speech. First is the obscenely vulgar strain of Dorax's hope that
Almeyda has been raped as well as killed. This is a strain that is found
in the classical genres only in the darkest of Juvenalian satire. Second
is the heroic strain that ends the speech, the reference to Sebastian's
manly form, pious ("his face up to Heav'n") and glorious ("the red
Monument, Which his true Sword has digg'd") even in death. This, of

course, is precisely the strain that would be expected in heroic tragedy. But binding these two antithetical strains together is a visually evocative, detailed description of digging through a mountain of dead bodies, which is consistent *neither* with heroic tragedy nor with satire. The words neither lift us to revelation by their harmonies—as heroic discourse does—nor lash us with their savage indignation—as satiric declamation does. Rather they force us to envision in detail a scene that is not dramatically represented before us. The words are equivalents not for ideas but for things. They operate upon us in the way that language does in the novel, making us, the readers, imagine a landscape into being. That is why, as Dryden said in his preface, his effects in this play are better appreciated when they are read than when they are heard in performance.

The effects of a complex and variegated discourse are two: first, it blurs, and finally transforms, generic design; second, it makes characterization indeterminate, creating the inconsistency and the illusion of depth that we experience in life rather than in classical art. "In the epic," says Bakhtin, "characters are bounded, preformed, individualized by their various situations and destinies," by what I would call their positions within a whole, rhetorical, generic design. "They have the same language, they all share the same world view, the same fate, the same extravagant externalization. These traits of the epic character, shared by and large with other highly distanced genres, are responsible for the exclusive beauty, wholeness, crystal clarity and artistic completedness of this image of man" (1981, 35). As I have argued elsewhere (Zimbardo 1986, chap. 2), the personae in English drama to the late 1680s are better understood as ideational counters, or changing positions, in a rhetorical design than as characters in the modern sense, that is, fictional simulations of actual people. In *Don Sebastian* not only Dorax but all the characters, including the heroic protagonists, have lost the "crystal clarity and artistic completedness" of the figures found in earlier heroic poetry. For example, consider how our first conception of Almeyda is formed. In an earlier heroic drama Almeyda would *figure* an Idea of heroic beauty, virtue, or greatness of spirit. One *aspect* of the Idea might be more prominent than another at one or another place in the play, but that would depend entirely upon the demand placed upon the figure at various points in the whole rhetorical design that constituted the form and, consequently, the meaning of the whole. Consider the difference in method of characterization here. As has been seen, the first reference made to Almeyda in the play is the savage remark of Dorax. Curiously enough, preparation for her first entrance extends upon this style, for it is rendered in a low comic dialect that, while not savagely satiric, is

inappropriate to a heroic figure in a heroic context. The language fits
neither the scene nor the position of Almeyda in the whole design of
the play. For example, Muley-Moluch is preparing a suitable human
sacrifice to celebrate his victory. In traditional heroic drama neither a
subject as serious as the sacrifice of noble Christians in a pagan ritual
nor the first occasion upon which the major heroic protagonists are
introduced would be treated comically. Here the low comic style of
Mustapha, the captain of the guards, is not only generically inconsistent, it is also gratuitous. No requirement of plot or characterization
demands this level of discourse; the satiric purpose it serves—to take
a swipe at the dishonesty and greed of highly placed clergymen—lies
outside the boundaries of the work in the playwright's own open-
ended "present." The Mufti has told Mustapha that he should hold
back Sebastian and Almeyda from deliverance into the hands of
Muley-Moluch. If he does what the Mufti says Mustapha has been
promised that he will gain paradise.

> *Mustapha.* Your Majesty may lay your Soul on't: but for my part, though I
> am a plain Fellow, yet I scorn to be trick'd into Paradice, I wou'd he [the
> Mufti] shou'd know it. The troth on't is, an't like you, His reverence
> bought of me the flower of all the Market; these—these are but Dogs
> meat to 'em, and a round price he pay'd me too I'll say that for him; but
> not enough for me to venture my neck for. . . . there was a dainty
> Virgin, (*Virgin* said I! but I won't be too positive of that neither) with a
> roguish leering eye! he paid me down for her upon the nail a thousand
> golden *Sultanins;* . . . Now is it very likely he would pay so dear for
> such a delicious Morsel, and give it away out of his own mouth; when it
> had such a farewel with it too? (1.1.217–23; 232–38)

No ideal female figure in the earlier heroic drama was ever introduced
as a "delicious Morsel" with a "roguish leering eye" and dubious
virginity by even the most lustful villain in the play. (Compare, for
instance, Maximin's descriptions of Saint Catharine, or Morat's response to Indamora.) When Almeyda reveals herself and delivers
herself into Muley-Moluch's hands, she is a figure of heroic greatness
and speaks in the language and cadences of the high heroic mode:

> *Almeyda.*   Hear me; I will be heard:
> I am no Slave; the noblest blood of *Affrick*
> Runs in my Veins; a purer stream than thine; . . .
> She whom thy *Mufti* tax'd to have no Soul;
> Let *Affrick* now be judg;
> Perhaps thou think'st I meanly hope to 'scape,
> As did *Sebastian* when he own'd his greatness.
> But to remove that scruple, know, base Man,

My murther'd Father, and my Brother's Ghost
Still haunt this Brest, and prompt it to revenge.

(1.1.428–30; 441–47)

But this speech, like the love-and-honor debate of Almeyda and Sebastian in act 2, exists in isolation. Heroic declamation does not *move* the play nor does rhetoric govern and control its design, as it did in the 1660s.

Running between the low comic style of Mustapha's description and the heroic declamation of Almeyda herself, there is a middle strain that calls upon us to visualize Almeyda in yet another way. Like Dorax's triple-strand speech quoted above, the language of Muley-Moluch as he describes his passion for Almeyda is multitextured:

> *Emp.*   Still 'tis strange
> To me: I know my Soul as wild as winds,
> That sweep the Desarts of our moving Plains;
> Love might as well be sow'd upon our Sands,
> As in a brest so barren:
> To love an Enemy, the only One
> Remaining too, whom yester Sun beheld,
> Must'ring her charms, and rolling as she past
> By every Squadron her alluring eyes,
> To edge her Champions Swords, and urge my ruin.
> The shouts of Soldiers, and the burst of Cannon,
> Maintain ev'n still a deaf and murm'ring noise;
> Nor is Heav'n yet recover'd of the sound
> Her Battel rows'd: Yet spight of me I love.

(2.1.16–29)

The speech begins in an elevated style appropriate to the type of the "hero of irregular greatness," but that elevated pitch is not maintained. The description of Almeyda's movements and gestures as she rouses her troops to battle, even the description of the sound of shouts and cannon fire, are novelistic. The style calls upon us to *visualize* detail. Not only does this language give us still another mental picture of Almeyda, but it endows Muley-Moluch's closing "Yet spight of me I love" with naturalism, an illusion of depth in the speaker that gives a new cast to an old love-and-honor commonplace.

By the beginning of the second act, then, we have three superimposed images of Almeyda (as the play progresses we shall have still more) that have been created by three mutually inconsistent modes of discourse. What effect has this method upon characterization? To use Bakhtinian terms once again, "A dynamic authenticity was introduced into the image of man [by the novel], dynamics of inconsistency and tension between various factors of this image; man ceased to coincide with himself, and consequently men ceased to be exhausted entirely by the plots that contain them" (1981, 35). Bakhtin, of course, is speaking of this as an operation effected by the finished novel, but some of the effects are present here, in the earliest beginnings of "novelization" of a classical generic form. The variegated discourse used by and about characters removes them from the distant, heroic plane and creates an illusion of familiarity and presence. The very inconsistency of the images that go into forming our apprehension of a character gives us the impression that the character is complex, and, what is more, is "internal" as we, and the people whom we encounter in experience, are. Furthermore, the "dynamic authenticity" of characters brings them to the forefront of attention. A character is no longer a position in a complex, intricate formal design; rather the design of a play (eventually of the eighteenth-century novel) *evolves* out of the often inconsistent "motives" and actions of complex, indeterminate characters. Characters, with all the fascinating details and incidents that attach to them, grow too big to be contained within a uniform dramatic design. As Dryden said in his preface, these characters, and the incidents designed to display their complexity, strain the limits of dramatic performance. They require the capacious temporal and spatial dimensions of the novel in which to move and the close scrutiny of a reader to appreciate them. Nevertheless, the characters themselves are created out of the variety and complexity in language and the "roughness of the numbers and cadences" (Dryden 1976, 66) they are made to speak. In his preface Dryden tells us that the roughness of discourse in this play is "not casual, but so design'd" and is "more masterly . . . than in most, if not any of [his] former Tragedies" (66–67). The three salient stylistic techniques that Earl Miner finds in *Don Sebastian* are (1) heavy internal pauses coupled with feminine endings, (2) deliberately broken verse patterns, and (3) "earthy, racy, and comic touches" that are not confined to a single plot line or group of characters, but are dispersed throughout (Dryden 1976, 413, n. to 66:36). All three of these devices are used to "dialogize" the play. Its speech descends from the lofty regions of the heroic style to the familiar sound patterns of spoken discourse, with the consequence that the characters speaking are further naturalized, and, breaking through the boundaries of the dramatic design that confines them, they enter the "present" of experience.

Finally, consider the function of those "comic touches" that permeate the play. Here again we find a *backward* glance to the structural design of classical dramatic satire of the kind that dominates in the 1670s and—predominantly—a *forward* look to the eighteenth-century novel. As I have argued (Zimbardo 1986, chap. 4), dramatic satire of the seventies was the design of an interplay between two *literary* perspectives, heroic and antiheroic. Like that of classical heroic tragedy, the design was rhetorically governed, self-contained, and self-referential. It was not an attempt to imitate the phenomenal actual, the "real" world of experience. Traces of this old style are present in *Don Sebastian*, but, like heroic declamation in the play, they occur in patches and they are not crucial to the play's structure of meaning. The comic interplay among Johayma, Antonio, and the Mufti, and the antiheroic commentary upon it that follows in the exchanges of Antonio and Morayma in act 3, scene 2, for example, hearken back to classical dramatic satire. The scene is designed to balance against and parody the heroic scene that precedes it. In act 3, scene 1, Almeyda pleads with her enemy, Muley-Moluch, to spare Sebastian's life. The love-and-honor formula expressed in the scene, as well as the level of discourse prevalent in it, shape the familiar patterns of heroic drama:

> *Almeyda.* Farewell the greatness of *Almeyda's* Soul!
> Look, Tyrant, what excess of love can do,
> It pulls me down thus low, as to thy feet; [*Kneels to him*]
> Nay to embrace thy Knees with loathing hands,
> Which blister when they touch thee; Yet ev'n thus,
> Thus far I can to save *Sebastian's* life.
>
> (3.1.240–45)

In the parody, scene 2, Antonio kneels before Johayma and the Mufti to save his *own* life, and he acquiesces in Johayma's plan to make him her sexual slave. The language of the exchanges between Johayma and Antonio in the presence of their prospective cuckold, the Mufti, is the double entendre of the covert contract scene familiar from earlier dramatic satire (like Harcourt's declarations of love to Alithea in the presence of Sparkish, or Horner's and Lady Fidget's mock-heroic "as perfectly, perfectly" love pledge in *The Country Wife*). Moreover, in the exchanges of Morayma and Antonio that follow, mock-heroic language pointedly parodies Almeyda's heroic style in the preceding scene:

> *Morayma.* No, now I think on't, you are already entr'd into Articles with my Enemy *Johayma: Any thing to serve you Madam; I shall refuse no drudgery;* whose words were those, Gentleman? Was that like a Cavalier of honour?
> *Antonio.* Not very heroick; but self preservation is a point above Honour and Religion too.—*Antonio* was a Rogue I must confess; but you must give me leave to love him.

Morayma. To beg your life so basely; and to present your Sword to your
  Enemy; Oh Recreant!
Antonio. If I had died honourably, my fame indeed wou'd have sounded
  loud, but I shou'd never have heard the blast. (3.2.229–39)

This kind of juxtaposition between heroic and antiheroic perspectives
is the essential form of classical satire. In *Don Sebastian* it appears as a
vestigial trace, the reminder of an earlier method of composition,
wherein discourse served the needs of a unified generic design of
contrastive perspectives.

More often in this play the target of satire lies outside the boundaries of the work. For example, the Mufti's casuistry as he juggles
doctrine to fit the desire of the tyrant who threatens him (3.1.60–110),
or the Mufti's admission that greed is the master he serves ("by this I
have got to be chief of my Religion; that is, honestly speaking, to teach
others what I neither know nor believe my self. For what's *Mahomet*
to me, but that I get by him?" [4.2.1–4]) overflows the boundaries of
the play and finds its target in the corrupt, highly placed Protestant
clergy of 1690.

One of the most interesting comic interludes in the play, to recall
the observation quoted at the beginning of this discussion—that in the
seventeenth century rhetoric and logic jostle for possession of the
human mind—is the contest in act 4 between the honey-tongued
Mufti and Mustapha, the soldier, for control of the empty-headed
Rabble. Initially even Mustapha is in repeated danger of falling under
the spell of the Mufti's enchanting rhetoric (*Mustapha*. " 'Tis excellent
fine matter indeed, Slave *Antonio;* he has a rare tongue; Oh, he wou'd
move a Rock of Elephant!" [4.3.73–74]). Antonio, however, dispels
the enchantment, and, when Mustapha rallies, he establishes in his
address to the Rabble the necessary conflict between word and act—
"Believers, he [the Mufti] only preach'd you up to it [rebellion and
plunder]; but durst not lead you; he was but your Counsellor, but I
was your Captain" (4.3.135–37). The targets of satire here are multiple—primary among them an extraliterary allusion to the Glorious
Revolution of 1688—but among the targets is fine rhetoric itself, that
arousing "harmony of words" that enraptures its listeners. In *Don
Sebastian* language is used to mock and undercut its own rhetorical
power.

For the most part, however, the use of comic interlude is quite new
in this play. For instance, in the stately friendship-and-honor debate
between Don Sebastian and Dorax/Alonzo that closes act 4, the
speakers are not characters but counters, positions in a dialectic that
change, exchange, and interchange to the refinement of an Idea of
heroic greatness. In act 5, scene 1, Sebastian, Almeyda and Alvarez

enact a similarly heroic "turn" toward the final discovery and resolution. But sandwiched between these scenes is a scene of low comic love exchanged between Antonio and Morayma that bears no functional structuring relation to the scenes that precede and follow it. The comic scene functions neither to parody the heroic scenes—as in the satire of the seventies—nor to replay high discourse in low style— as in the three-tiered comic designs of the sixties. Moreover, even the two scenes between which it is placed are not structurally necessary to one another. All three scenes are used to the end of roughening, complicating, and therefore thickening the texture of the action.

However, perhaps the best example of Dryden's new use of comic effect in *Don Sebastian* occurs at the end of act 1. The heroic matter of the first act consists in Don Sebastian's revelation of his kingly identity, Muley-Moluch's pardon of him on those grounds, and Almeyda's subsequent declaration of her identity and defiance of Muley-Moluch (quoted above). The "matter" of the act ends quite conventionally with an unmistakable clue to the audience that Muley-Moluch, the hero of "irregular greatness" hitherto untouched by love, has been struck to the heart by Almeyda's heroic beauty and courage: "Something, I know not what, comes over me: / Whether the Toyls of Battel, unrepaird / With due repose, or other sudden qualm" (1.1.470–72). Act 2 begins on the same conventional heroic note, with Muley-Moluch's recognition of and introspection upon his love for Almeyda (quoted above). Reaction to such "turns" is automatic in an audience bred to the conventions of heroic drama. However, sandwiched between these two episodes is a small comic interlude that is gratuitous, extrinsic both to the play's design and characterization. It begins with the stage direction: "*The Masters and Slaves come forward, and Buyers of several Qualities come in and chaffer about the several Owners, who make their Slaves do Tricks*" (1.1.481s.d.). The action is sheer slapstick; the slaves perform their "postures" and the audience is invited to laugh at their clowning. Any deeper comic effect is aimed at enlightening us upon the nature of our general human condition. For example, Antonio's reluctance to dance at the end of a rope is quickly dispelled by the crack of his owner's whip, which draws from him the observation: "Hold, my dear Thrum-cap: I obey thee chearfully, I see the Doctrine of Non-Resistance is never practis'd thoroughly but when a Man can't help himself" (1.1.520–22). Similarly, the satiric thrusts in the piece are, on the one hand, topical (i.e., mockery of the clergy, the army, and the "mobile," whose mindless actions are controlled by whatever propaganda expert is manipulating them at the moment) and are, on the other hand, universal, since the follies they mock obtain among us still in the twentieth century. In either case, comic and satiric effects are extrinsic to the play's design. Comedy and satire are no longer *literary* forms, having a unique generic profile; rather, they are effects or devices within an indeterminate, evolving, new generic mode. They are, in short, novelistic—no longer *parts* within a closed, removed design, which is held up for us to contemplate, but shafts designed to strike us where we live in the still-evolving "present" of our experience.

Dryden was quite right in saying that by crowding his drama with a variety of characters and incidents he had perhaps forgotten "the usual compass of a Play" (65). I should put the case somewhat differently and say that because he was the great pioneer that he was, in *Don Sebastian* Dryden, rather, anticipated the "compass" of the eighteenth-century novel.

*   *   *

Maximillian E. Novak and David Stuart Rodes, in the introduction to their edition of Thomas Southerne's play, *Oroonoko,* say of its source, Aphra Behn's novel, that "The combination of realistic action and *précieuse* style in Behn produces an effect that is grotesque." They prefer Southerne's style, wherein, they think, "No indecorous realism destroys the noble impact of Oroonoko's private sufferings" (Southerne 1976, xi). I strongly disagree with this assessment on three grounds: first, because there is no strict or undesigned separation between language and action in Behn's novel; second, because the "private suffering" of a character is inevitably better imitated in the novel, a form invented to simulate "real" people and to create the illusion of an internal arena within them, than it can be by the drama, which is always essentially an external "show"; and third, because the combination of high heroic and low realistic modes of discourse in Behn's novel is "masterly" in the same ways and to the same ends as Dryden's practice is in *Don Sebastian.* Like Dryden's play, Behn's novel is a landmark of the transition in poetic mimesis, in rhetorics of order. It is the transformation of a closed classical form, the romance, or prose epic, into the first tragic novel in English.

Behn employs two distinctly different modes of discourse, which, for clarity's sake, I shall call "high heroic" and "low realistic." She uses the high heroic style in discourse for the purpose that it served in heroic drama and romance—to elevate our minds to an appreciation of *Ideas* of heroic greatness embodied in her protagonists, who are *figures* of majesty and virtue. She uses the low realistic mode to serve the very purpose for which the novel was invented—to admit us into a fictional world that, while it is exotic, is, above all, *probable*, and to explore subtle nuances of thought and feeling in characters, and, by admitting us into their unspoken, interior lives, to force us to share their emotions and participate in their actions. In short, Behn's low realistic style opens a channel from the distant epic world of valorized action into the familiar world of the reader's experience. The technique effects a shift of perspective in time and space. Bakhtin describes the process in this way:

> The shift of the temporal center of artistic orientation, which placed on the same temporally valorized plane the author and his readers (on the one hand) and the world and heroes described by him (on the other), making them contemporaries, possible acquaintances, friends, familiarizing their relations . . . , permits the author, in all his various masks and faces, to move freely onto the field of his represented world, a field that in the epic had been absolutely inaccessible and closed. (27)

The first twentieth-century editor of Behn's *Works*, Montague Summers, describes the conflicting modes of discourse she employs, and the homogeneity of effect she achieves in their combination, rather well:

> Beyond the intense interest of the pure narrative we have passages of a rhythm that is lyric, exquisitely descriptive of the picturesque tropical scenery and exotic vegetations, fragrant and luxuriant; there are intimate accounts of adventuring and primitive life; there are personal touches which lend a colour only personal touches can, as Aphara tells her prose-epic of her Superman, Cæsar the slave, Oroonoko the prince. (Behn 1915, 5:127)

Perhaps unconsciously, Summers was aware of Behn's conflicting styles of discourse; quite consciously, he was aware of the wholeness she weaves out of them. The conflict consists in the opposition between the "exquisitely" lyrical and the "intimate account"; between the "personal touches" and the "prose-epic of . . . Superman," or, more concisely, between "Cæsar the slave" in all the realism of his condition and "Oroonoko the prince" in all the heroic elevation demanded by the Idea of Majesty that he figures.

The problem in imitation with which Behn was confronted is the very epistemological problem with which this discussion began: to reconcile ideational, or imaginative, truth with the truth of "fact" and experience. Her solution is to establish the ideal and to ground it in experience: to embed the ideal in the real and, conversely, to make the real a gloss upon the ideal.

Behn begins her novel with a cleverly contrived declaration of intention:

I do not pretend, in giving you the History of this *ROYAL SLAVE*, to entertain my Reader with the Adventures of a feign'd *Hero*, whose Life and Fortunes Fancy may manage at the Poet's Pleasure; nor in relating the Truth, design to adorn it with any Accidents, but such as arrived in earnest to him: And it shall come simply into the World, recommended by its own proper Merits, and natural Intrigues; there being enough of Reality to support it, and to render it diverting, without the Addition of Invention. (129)

The choice with which the writer declares that she is confronted is between the feigning and "Invention" of art and simple reportage, an unadorned account of "Reality" as she has experienced it: "I was myself an Eye-witness to a great Part of what you will find here set down; and what I could not be Witness of, I receiv'd from the Mouth of the chief Actor in this History" (129). What she actually does is to prepare the reader to accept the high heroic virtues and romantic adventures of a "feign'd *Hero*" as true by first admitting him or her into a fictional world so simply and realistically described that she enters into, and experiences it, and, in turn, is led by it into the "experience" of the feigned hero. Before Behn begins Oroonoko's story she brings the setting in which his sufferings as Caesar the Slave will take place home to the reader's experience. Here her mode of narrative discourse, full of accurate detail and description, is used to make the exotic landscape and native culture of Surinam familiar; and her art is to seem artless:

[The natives of Surinam] we live with in perfect Amity, without daring to command 'em; but, on the contrary, caress 'em with all the brotherly and friendly Affection in the World; trading with them for their Fish, Venison, Buffaloes Skins, and little Rarities; as *Marmosets*, a sort of Monkey, as big as a Rat or Weasel, but of a marvellous and delicate Shape, having Face and Hands like a Human Creature; and *Cousheries*, a little Beast in the Form and Fashion of a Lion . . . : Then for little *Paraketoes*, great *Parrots*, *Muckaws*, and a thousand other Birds and Beasts of wonderful and sur- prizing Forms, Shapes, and Colours: For Skins of prodigious Snakes, of which there are some three-score Yards in Length; as is the Skin of one that may be seen at his Majesty's *Antiquary's;* where are also some rare Flies, of amazing Forms and Colours, presented to 'em by myself; . . . and all of various Excellencies, such as Art cannot imitate. (129–30)

Not only does she bring her English reader into Surinam, but she reminds him that he has seen, close at hand, hard evidence of her having been in that country. Both the curiosities she has contributed to the king's antiquary and the costumes of one of the most popular plays of the sixties ("I had a Set of [clothes made of feathers by Indian craftsmen] presented to me, and I gave 'em to the *King's Theatre;* it was the Dress of the *Indian Queen,* infinitely admir'd by Persons of Quality; and was inimitable" [130]) are *things* that attest to her reliability as a witness and, consequently, to the factual truth of her tale. This manner of discourse closes the gap between the epic adventure to which the author will admit the reader and the reader's own world. Throughout the novel descriptions of the culture and conditions of Surinam are rendered in this almost excessively de-tailed, matter-of-fact, descriptive mode. Her assessment of the need for white colonists to maintain friendly relations with the natives, who so far outnumber them, is sociologically astute and sober. Her judg-ment of England's folly in giving this wonderful country forfeit in the Dutch Wars is not only politically accurate, but, far more important, it draws the fictional setting of her story into the immediate present of the reader's own political opinion. There is nothing here of the *"pré-cieuse"* style, nor, given the exotic nature of the landscape, is there even a hint of the Arcadian atmosphere of French romance. Quite the contrary, Behn's aim in employing the low realistic mode of discourse is to make the exotic familiar and the distant near.

Behn begins her novel in this familiar essay style for two reasons. In the first place she establishes a connection between narrator and reader that will later enable the reader to see characters and judge events through the narrator's eyes. In the second place, by its close, detailed description the low realistic discourse of the opening draws the reader into the landscape. By imagining the landscape into being on the inner screen of his own mind the reader becomes an inhabitant of the fictional world.

Nevertheless, even in the opening pages Behn plants the seeds that will grow into her high heroic mode. When she describes the bead-work or hunting methods of the Indians, Behn is a veritable seven-teenth-century Margaret Mead, but when her purpose is to lift the reader to the realm of Idea, her discourse is heroic and her subjects are the traditional formulas of heroic love and honor:

> I have seen a handsome young *Indian,* dying for Love of a very beautiful *Indian* Maid; but all his Courtship was, to fold his Arms, pursue her with his Eyes, and Sighs were all his Language. . . . And these People repre-sented to me an absolute *Idea* of the first State of Innocence, before Man knew how to sin. (131)

In telling Oroonoko's story Behn uses the high style when her aim is to delineate the spiritual essence of her hero: "that real Greatness of Soul, those refined Notions of true Honour, that absolute Generosity, and that Softness, that was capable of the highest Passions of Love and Gallantry" (135). She uses the "sacrosanct and traditional" language of heroic drama and romance when her aim is to shape a "Character of Mind" or figure of greatness that Oroonoko the Prince represents. For example, in the account of Oroonoko's first falling in love with Imoinda (which employs the classical formula: hero bred to the wars from infancy is struck instantaneously by heroic love at the sight of Ideal Beauty) not only does the narrator use high heroic language describing Oroonoko's state, but she shapes the hero's own expression of love in terms of heroic Idea:

> as he knew no Vice, his Flame aim'd at nothing but Honour, if such Distinction may be made in Love; . . . as he had right Notions of Honour, so he made her such Propositions as were not only and barely such; but . . . he made her Vows, she should be the only Woman he would possess while he liv'd; that no Age or Wrinkles should incline him to change: for her Soul would be always fine, and always young; and he should have an eternal *Idea* in his Mind of the Charms she now bore; and should look into his Heart for that *Idea*, when he could find it no longer in her Face. (138–39)

This discourse could appear unaltered in any of the heroic generic designs of the earlier seventeenth century. The style is directly antithetical in function to the low realistic narrative style. Words have reference not to things but to abstract essences and ideas: "his Flame aim'd at nothing but Honour"; her "Soul" would exist eternally as an "*Idea* in his Mind." We do not hear the character speak. We do not see the characters, neither their physical appearances, the actions in which they engage, nor the postures and gestures they assume. We are not in the world of experience but in the metaphysical world of mind and spirit. The effect of this high heroic mode of discourse is to *distance* the reader—in exact opposition to the low narrative's attempt to draw him into the scene. Here Oroonoko is not a person whom we are made to visualize; he is a figure of heroic majesty we are made to admire, to wonder at. Imoinda here is not a character whose griefs and fears we share, as she will be later in the novel; she is a figure of ideal beauty and virtue.

Limitations of space will not allow me the close textual analysis that would fully illustrate Behn's technique, the method whereby she asserts the ideal in high heroic, abstract narrative discourse, and the dexterity with which in a single page she can move from the high narrative style—"'twas amazing to imagine where . . . 'twas he got that real Greatness of Soul"—to novelistic explanatory gloss—"I have often seen and conversed with this Great Man, and been a Witness to many of his mighty Actions"—to low realistic, detailed description that brings the man himself into the narrator's, and thereby into the reader's, visual field—"He came into the Room, and addressed himself to me, and some other Women, with the best Grace in the World. He was pretty tall, but of a Shape the most exact that can be fancy'd. . . . His face was . . . a perfect Ebony, or polished Jet. His Eyes were . . . very piercing; the White of 'em being like Snow, as were his Teeth" (135–36).

The most that I can accomplish in a paper of this length is to suggest the purpose to which Behn puts the two conflicting modes of discourse in the larger design of her novel. Frederick Link, in his book *Aphra Behn* acutely observes that "*Oroonoko* has a two-part structure. The events in Coramantien introduce him and Imoinda, establish their love and his valor, intelligence, and *nobility* of character. The events in Surinam show him a prisoner in a world controlled by cruel, venal men whose cowardice and treachery succeed by virtue of their numbers. The result goes beyond pathos to tragedy" (1968, 139–40).

The design of *Oroonoko* is the design of heroic tragedy novelistically rendered. The narrative of Coramantien is written wholly in the high heroic style. It establishes the Idea of heroic greatness that Oroonoko the Prince figures. It is the distant, glittering height *from* which the tragic hero falls. The narrative of Surinam is written, for the most part, in the low realistic style. It is the crushing world of experience *into* which he falls. When Oroonoko falls into the world of experience, he falls into our world. When he is brought in chains to Surinam, he enters into a fictional world where we, by virtue of the low realistic style employed in the opening pages, are inhabitants. In Coramantien we see the adventures of Oroonoko from a distance, through the frosted glass of the high heroic style. In Surinam we are made to experience the changes of feeling that take place in Oroonoko as he moves in consciousness from the picture of a warrior prince to the condition of a slave robbed even of his name by scarcely human brutes whom we *know* (by virtue of the high heroic style's effect on us) to be his natural inferiors. We view Oroonoko's adventures in Coramantien as detached spectators; we *participate* in the events in Surinam, and most particularly, in the decisive event, the slave revolt. Having shared the interwoven, often contradictory emotions that lead to that event, we enter into the slave revolt on the side of Oroonoko. The low realistic narrative style has made us share Imoinda's fear and despair as she imagines the fate of her unborn child. We have felt, in response to our sympathy for Imoinda, the pressure upon Oroonoko to *do* something. We have seen the degeneracy and viciousness of the white colonists at first hand and have accepted the narrator's judgment of them—transported scum of England—as our own. Therefore the rousing speech of Oroonoko, imbedded as it is in the easy, low familiar style of the narrator, rouses us to be participants in the action. Oroonoko says, we think, *exactly what we would have said* had we been there. It is not the heroic declamation of the courtship speech; it is rather the voice of a close friend, heard in our minds as we read, expressing sentiments that we passionately share.

Oroonoko's story ends in fulfillment of the promise with which the novel began, not as the superhuman epic of a "feign'd *Hero*" but as the suffering and death of a man like ourselves. The antithetical styles of narrative discourse have worked in the service of a single, multitextured, indeterminate design: the evolving form of the novel.

* * *

Whereas in *Don Sebastian* we observed the struggle of a classical generic form to accommodate itself to an extraliterary, semantically indeterminate discourse, we find in *Oroonoko* intimations of a newly emerging form, shaping itself to the demands of a polyglossic discourse. What, then, is to be made of these two works—a late novelized play and an early, heroically informed novel? It is my contention that as critics and historians of ideas we ignore them at our peril, for what we find in them, I think, is no less than evidence of a transformation in consciousness; the dawn of a new way of thinking about the relation of literature to life; the birth of a new model of the mind that to this day determines our response to literary art and can confound our understanding of works that were written before the great epistemological divide occurred.

Notes

1. I am indebted for this example and for a brilliant discussion of the problem it raises to Walsh 1984, 9.
2. Review of a new edition of *Bocharti Opera Omnia, Gentlemans Journal*, October 1692.
3. As John Loftis puts it, in the 1690s and early 1700s plays "have a quality that may, perhaps anachronistically, be described as 'novelistic'" (1972, 46).

Works Cited

Bakhtin, M. M. 1981. *The Dialogic Imagination: Four Essays*. Ed. Michael Holquist. Trans. Caryl Emerson and Michael Holquist. Austin: University of Texas Press.

Behn, Aphra. 1915. *Oroonoko*. In *The Works of Aphra Behn*. Ed. Montague Summers, 5:125–208. London: William Heinemann.

Dryden, John. 1970. *The Works of John Dryden*. Vol. 10. Ed. Maximillian E. Novak and George Robert Guffey. Berkeley and Los Angeles: University of California Press.

————. 1976. *The Works of John Dryden*. Vol. 15. Ed. Earl Miner, George R. Guffey, and Franklin B. Zimmerman. Berkeley and Los Angeles: University of California Press.

Gale, Theophilus. 1669. *The Court of the Gentiles*. 2 vols. London.

Gentlemans Journal. October 1692.

Josipovici, Gabriel. 1978. *The World and the Book*. London and Basingstoke: Macmillan.

Link, Frederick M. 1968. *Aphra Behn*. New York: Twayne.

Loftis, John. 1972. "The Limits of Historical Veracity in Neo-Classical Drama." In *England in the Restoration and Eighteenth Century: Essays on Culture and Society*, ed. H. T. Swedenburg, Jr., 27–50. Berkeley and Los Angeles: University of California Press.

Southerne, Thomas. 1976. *Oroonoko*. Ed. Maximillian E. Novak and David Stuart Rodes. Regents Restoration Drama Series. Lincoln: University of Nebraska Press.

Sprat, Thomas. 1667. *The History of the Royal Society*. London.

Walsh, George B. 1984. *The Varieties of Enchantment: Early Greek Views of the Nature and Function of Poetry*. Chapel Hill: University of North Carolina Press.

Zimbardo, Rose A. 1986. *A Mirror to Nature: Transformations in Drama and Aesthetics 1660–1732*. Lexington: University Press of Kentucky.

Settle's *City Ramble*
A Yet Farther Defence of the Stage
JACKSON I. COPE

One begins, as Elkanah Settle did, with explicitly stated facts. Settle was an old stager fallen into relatively lean times during the competition between the two theaters that persisted from the last years of the seventeenth century into the new union of 1708. He had done opera with Gottfried Finger (*The Virgin Prophetess*) and had done the most stunning and (as its history evolved) most persistently popular show at Bartholomew Fair (*The Siege of Troy;* compare my analysis in Cope 1984, 107–11). And when Barton Booth, Betterton's unofficial protégé and Settle's junior by almost thirty years, suggested that the author of *The Empress of Morocco* should coalesce two of the plays from the Beaumont and Fletcher canon, Settle obliged with *The City Ramble.* The two Jacobean plays seem rhetorically incompatible, competing rhetorics of order, although Settle is subserviently clear about the source and wisdom of this inspiration.[1] Why, then, did Booth offer his senior the suggestion at just this crisis of the theatrical union? What did Settle see in this suggestion that could inspire him to a major effort, a reordering combining the seemingly reactionary with the contemporary? These are questions that raise issues more general than the particular circumstances of their geneses around 1710. But they may also be a reminder that the general, the generic responses are always modified by just the particular circumstances of any production.

Beaumont and Fletcher: The Sources

The Knight of the Burning Pestle was not popular on the Restoration stage,[2] but then it was a self-announced stage failure in its own time, too.[3] Like its progenitor, *Don Quijote,* Beaumont's play is one of those rare works that creates a new genre and a generic progeny whose features always offer specific homage to their original. As one consequence, these offspring, including *The City Ramble,* have not been immediately understood, either. It is a genre that depends upon the juxtaposition of so many dramatic tones and plot forms as to seem antigeneric, even formless. The preposterous is at its source of wonder; always there is the Lazarus syndrome, a literal resurrection from the grave, and always the seeming outer audience becomes the inner core of the plot.

Settle's *City Ramble* is easy to pass by as another of the self-reflexive theatrical farces that would become a popular but repetitive experience in eighteenth-century theaters.[4] But it was much more than that, much closer to the suprasatiric intent of *The Knight of the Burning Pestle*. A look at the title may alert us to complications: the last three acts of the "city" ramble are acted out in the country (as is so much of the action in Beaumont and Fletcher's tragicomedy).[5] And then there is Elkanah Settle's own articulation of the value of multiple plotting in an early response to the first wave of theatrical reform in Collier's strictures upon *The Relapse:*

> The *contriving the chief Business of our Plays single,* is so nauseous to an *English* Audience, that they have almost peuk'd at a very good Dish for no other Fault. . . . On the contrary, here must be Under-plots, and considerable ones too, possibly big enough to justle the Upper-plot, to support a good *English* Play. (Settle 1698, 36–37)

But even with this insistence upon multiple plotting, why did Settle accept Barton Booth's unlikely suggestion of *The Coxcomb*? Or, perhaps more to the point, why did the young actor-entrepreneur Booth single out what Pepys, not entirely unfairly, called "an old play and a silly one" at its only revival (1970–83, 17 March 1668–69)? It is a play nearly contemporary with the popular *Philaster* (with its own strong country setting), a play that Settle had already himself "improved upon" in 1695.[6] In 1711 Tonson was issuing the first complete edition of the Beaumont and Fletcher canon to appear since the folio of 1679, it is true. But *The Coxcomb* was not rediscovered as a hidden masterpiece then or later. However, unlike *Philaster* (from which Settle had eliminated the sexually symbolic love-wound of Arethusa, which had stirred the printer to one of those rare action woodcuts for the earliest quarto), *The Coxcomb* has a reformation scene on the part of the protagonist, Ricardo, that may have seemed potentially valuable and timely to Booth if put into the hands of a city poet who had already eviscerated the most titillating scene from *Philaster*. Ricardo, ambiguously motivated lover of the much-put-upon Viola, drunkenly assaults her (abortively) and abandons her subsequently to violent tribulations. When they are reunited, this untypical Jacobean rake reforms in a rhetorical soul-searching not to be overmatched by any projection of Steele or Cibber:

> A careless man, a breaker of my faith,
> A lothesome drunkard; and in that wild fury:
> A hunter after whores: I do beseech you,
> To pardon all these faults, and take me up
> An honest, sober, and a faithful man.
>   (5.1, in Beaumont and Fletcher 1905–12, 8:370)

Booth had had a busy few months, which had put neither himself nor the Drury Lane in a very flattering light. Ten years earlier he had come from Dublin's Smock Alley via Mrs. Mynn's dramatic booth at Bartholomew Fair to become both acting and managerial protégé of Betterton at Lincoln's Inn Fields. There he fully established himself, but the burden of operatic spectaculars brought about the theatrical union of 1708 and pressures that culminated in a dangerous and bloody house rebellion on 2 June 1710 (professional tensions were not eased by the fact that Booth's wife was dying or recently dead at the time). Young Aaron Hill had shown more precociousness than caution when he replaced Rich as manager a few months earlier. On the riotous day, Booth persuaded the actress Lucretia Bradshaw (the virtuous heroine, Viola, in *The City Ramble*) to admit him and his cohorts into the Drury Lane theater by way of her adjoining apartment. Intent upon seizing costumes and other properties, they encountered Hill and some companions, beating and stabbing them out of doors. It was a notorious affair that brought government intervention, and the reorganization of the Drury Lane management under Wilks, Cibber, and Dogget.[7] But this incident quite aside, the second, post-Collier wave of reform attack upon the theaters was fully under way, and proving much more dangerous than that which emerged in the late nineties. Ironically, its most immediate focus was Bartholomew Fair, where Booth had played at Mrs. Mynn's, which had also been the site of Settle's great triumph just a few years earlier.

The City versus the Theater: Alderman and Councilman

Beaumont had enveloped his optimistic resurgence with a citizen (a greengrocer), his wife, and his apprentice. They had reenacted perennial country rituals in the confines of the city, which masked the values of those rituals. Settle was more daring and straightforward in his confrontation with the city, for which he had been eminent spokesman in so many guises. As longtime celebrant of the Lord

Mayoral pageants, as author of patentee plays, as Bartholomew Fair's major claimant to wide fame with *The Siege of Troy*, with *The City Ramble* he yet confronted the city—his city. The dedication to Colerane is mock-humble enough, but with a little prewarning that under more reasonable circumstances "the Publick Stage had never wanted Monitors or Satirists for its Reformation. . . . Nor had the Press it self lain under the Necessity of Precepts or Regulations, either from the Throne, the Senate, or the Pulpit it self for its Correction" (A3r-v). The prologue takes the challenge a further step, being presented in the person of a London "Alderman in a Gold Chain." His opening lines extend the daring, making explicit the conjunction between London authority and London's quondam celebrant of just that authority in Settle's role as spokesman for Lord Mayoral pageants: *"This is a City-Play, and I have thought fit / T'appear Right Worshipful in Garb of Cit"* (1). The thrust of this Alderman's prologue is that merchant citizens, through their wealth, have formed and bought titled alliances:

> *Well, the Whole World 'tis Union must support,*
> *Then Let's shake Hands the City and the Court,*
> *Whilst mutually each others Help we need,*
> *We gild your Honour, and you mend our Breed.*
>
> (1–2)

Suddenly from a middle gallery box a man cries out (an echo of Beaumont's greengrocer) in challenge to the mock Alderman: *"Mr. Tattler; you think you have made a fine Speech to rally upon the Honourable City."* This is, however, no mere excited citizen, but a figure of authority: *"I am a Common Council-man, and had the Honour to pass my Religious Vote for the downfall of the wicked Drollery in* Bartholomew-Fair; *and though we can't have the Happiness of rooting up those Nurseries of Debauchery the two lewd Play-Houses, . . . since my Wife has dragg'd me hither amongst you, I am resolv'd to make a little Reformation-work with you"* (2). This opens a large set of ironies, the most immediately audible probably being the realization that Settle is mocking his own brilliant and recent success with *The Siege of Troy*. However, Settle is entering into the lists against the extremism of the new wave of antitheatrical reform, which we can best focus through the 1708 restriction of Bartholomew Fair by the Common Council. There had been a growing hue and cry against the inconveniences and immoral enormities of the fair from its residential neighbors. The time was propitious: a twenty-one-year lease with the city Sword Bearer was drawing to a close in 1708, offering an opportunity to reorder arrangements. Basically at issue was the extension of what had been a three-day commercial enterprise (scheduled for Saint Bartholomew's Day, its vigil and morrow [23, 24, and 25 August]) into a two-week affair. The longer schedule made it profitable to erect larger booths "chiefly for Stage-plays, Musick and Tipling (being so many receptacles of vicious and disorderly persons)." Originally designed for three-days' business in "the Sale of Live Cattle, Leather, and other Wares and Merchandise," the fair had come "to be a mere Carnival, a season of the utmost Disorder and Debauchery." The citations are from a petition by "a considerable Number of the Citizens and Inhabitants of this City" to "the present Right Honourable the Lord Mayor, to the Worshipful Court of Aldermen, and to the Common Council of the said City" (Morley 1880, 293–99). This new flood of reform sentiment prevailed, and the Common Council did issue an order restricting the 1708 Bartholomew Fair to three days—to what must have been extraordinary consternation for those like Pinkethman and Settle, who had practiced such a long-sanctioned trade in public playing. Immediately there were efforts to revise the order and return the fair to its old, accustomed fortnight of "carnival." But the times were against it; the Society for the Promotion of Christian Knowledge and the Society for the Reformation of Manners were riding a crest into the London Common Council chambers and into the characterization of the Common Councilman in *The City Ramble*. Settle is not simply satirizing the perennial antitheatrical prejudice, however. The "Petition" of 1708 was reissued in the weeks beore the 1711 fair. And if that year's fair remained as a three-day envelope around Saint Bartholomew's feast day, *The City Ramble* provided an envelope around the fair itself. As Settle says, the long vacation is not a propitious playing time, and he got little profit for his troubles (a far cry from the spectacular triumph of *The Siege of Troy*, when August at the fair, just before the crackdown of the authorities, had been a relative gold mine). The opening night was 17 August, repeated on the twenty-first. Drury Lane gave the traditional fair-eve performance of Jonson's *Bartholomew Fair* on the twenty-fourth, then closed for the fair's three-day run and exodus before giving Settle his benefit night of *The City Ramble* on the twenty-eighth. The effigy of the contemporary Common Councilman is talking profaneness and reform; the poet is talking profit, moral and commercial.

Reform: The Common Councilman Co-opted

Beaumont's grocer, his wife, and his apprentice, Rafe, were apparent victims of theatrical innocence; their attention span and their insistence upon bridging the stage action as though it were reality constituted their worst sins of taste. The grocer rather ruefully endorses the old figure of misrule, Master Merrythought, as a man free of the (sometimes uxorious) responsibilities of a commercial citizen, and his wife scorns this carnivalesque element in the inner play about London merchants. But Settle's Common Councilman is a more dangerous creature of the reformation; and his wife, a freer spirit of social and sexual negotiation.

The Councilman leads his wife onstage with the Alderman-prologue and continues to threaten in terms that not only burlesque Collier's (now dated) attacks, which Settle had earlier rebutted, but notorious contemporary new practices as well: "*I am a Spy upon you: Ay, not only upon the Profaness and Immorality of your Plays, but upon the Wickedness of your Players too*" (3).[8] "Spying" upon the players outside the playhouses might have been practiced as circumstances permitted, but there is little record of that form of surreptitious detection. However, audience tabulators of profaneness were visible and numerous from the turn of the century. These "spies" were an even bitterer joke than that made at their expense in Nicholas Rowe's epilogue to *Tamerlane*:

> *Time was, when busy Faces were a Jest,*
> *When Wit and Pleasure were in most request;*
> *When chearful Theatres with Crowds were grac'd;*
> *But those good Days of Poetry are pass'd:*
> *Now sour Reformers in an empty Pit,*
> *With Table-Books, as at a Lecture sit,*
> *To take Notes, and give Evidence 'gainst Wit.*[9]

Sometimes, although seldom, successful in urging the suppression or alteration of play texts, these "reporters" were—as far as records represent their activities—zealous rather than corrupt; what bounty monies they earned often were funneled back into Christian social services.[10]

Settle's effect in refocusing Beaumont's early classic from the decay of dramatic tastes and the persistence of dramatic form to the folly of the reformers was a document more effective than his earlier tractates in promoting the survival and significance of the theater in an aggressively conservative society. The grocer had been a mere pawn, neither a knight nor rook, in Beaumont's complicated game. In Settle's play his counterpart becomes central: unwitting witness to a new world that his social counterparts, the Christian reformers, had been witnessing against.

But now attention must be drawn away from *The Knight of the Burning Pestle* to *The Coxcomb*. Here, too, Settle indulged in important deviations. They dovetail with the transformation of the grocer into the reform Councilman. What Settle borrows is the tragicomic second plot, the story of the ambiguous Ricardo's courtship of Viola; her theft of her own fortune from her father's house; Ricardo's drunken exposure of himself (psychologically) and Viola (physically) to violence; the country gentleman Valerio's abortive seduction of the fleeing Viola. What he omits is the Widow of Ephesus testing plot (in this case wrongly associated, I think, with Cervantes's "El curioso impertinente") presented in the relations between "Antonio, the Coxcomb Gentleman" and his wife. What Settle retains is the resurrection coffin *lazzo* (*The Coxcomb*, 3.1) and the extraordinary insistence (developed into or from *Philaster*) upon the animal sexual corruption carried in Viola's beauty like a virus (Settle n.d., 50, 57). She attracts symbolic rape and rage from male and female alike, from gypsy thieves, and from gentlemen. Settle allows this unlikely element into his reformation play because he must make a bridge across country and city worlds. In Beaumont and Fletcher's play it had not been important that Viola's father was a citizen; in Settle's adaptation it is all-important, because the inner plot has become only a vehicle for the masquerade that at first separates, finally reconciles the London Councilman, his wife, and his daughter—with one another, with the gentry, and with the players.

The City Ramble: or, a Farther Defence of the Stage

The City Ramble (in accord with Settle's dramaturgical dicta) has a triple plot. That which both envelops and gives its deep structure to the play is, of course, the story of the Councilman, his wife, and his daughter, Jenny. This gives meaning to the subtitle, "A Play-House Wedding." The subtitle also bridges boxes, galleries, and text to include the outcome of the two other intrigues of love, marriage, money, and parental tyranny set in a vague "Verona."

Since its general outline has already been suggested, one can begin with the adaptation of the Ricardo-Viola-Valerio relationship borrowed from *The Coxcomb*, but enhanced by Settle with the addition of the sentimentalized "chevalier" Don Garcia, nephew to a merchant namesake, the elder Don Garcia. It may be sentimentalized, but also given a dimension of mystification that might have been expected from Beaumont and Fletcher rather than from Settle; from the Beaumont and Fletcher who were presumably learning elements of a Blackfriars repertoire from the aging Shakespeare of the romances: chevalier Don Garcia has a dream with a hermit's prophecy. Nothing quite so ambiguous, irrelevant to plot, and determinant of the action's suprasocial dimension is available to my memory between Antigonus's dream of the prophetic Hermione (*Winter's Tale* 3.3) and Settle's readaptation, outside of the operatic. Settle's Rinaldo (Ricardo) repents, is forgiven and embraced by Viola in marriage; Valerio repents and returns to his wife; the younger Don Garcia becomes a religious hermit like that whose prophecy he has heard. But he *is* the "chevalier," the gentleman become suprasocial, a transcendental figure abandoning class and the tragicomic genre. And this leads into the second marriage plot, another little step toward Settle's critique (so intensified from *The Knight of the Burning Pestle*) and rehabilitation of the Councilman.

In the satirist's allegiance to the inner play of *The Knight of the Burning Pestle*, titled with prescience "The London Merchant," Settle draws the plots together through adaptation of the bier-and-resurrection scene. In *The Knight of the Burning Pestle* the merchant's apprentice, Jasper, reached the conscience of the blocking senex/father-in-law by arising from his coffin as a flour-faced ghost; with Settle the interaction becomes a little more complex, owing to the "chevalier" Don Garcia. This ambiguously titled young nobleman inverts generic form upon his return from travel by threatening to disavow his namesake uncle should he (the senex "blocking" figure) insist upon a commercial marriage of his orphan-niece, Lucia, to a coxcomb count. His motive is to promote the love of Rinaldo's brother, Carlo, for the "niece." The mechanism is the old (*Knight of the Burning Pestle*) or new (Steele's *The Funeral*) resurrection from the coffin: in this case it frightens off the coxcomb pretender and converts the greedy senex. This is all old material, but brought to bear upon new attitudes toward money, civility, and class. And theater. When Rafe arises at the close of *The Knight of the Burning Pestle*, little has been learned of the city except its dependence upon old country traditions. When Carlo rises again, when the merchant is converted with the connivance of his "chevalier" nephew, Settle's Councilman is about to learn a great deal concerning class and genre. He is about to be co-opted as a representative of the "city" into a new view of the gentry and the theater. Settle's integration of this final love story was reactionary, a nostalgia for the Caroline hopes that the civil war and the immediately post-Restoration excesses had nullified.[11] But it was also realistic in confronting the possibilities of a new regime not only in national but in city and theatrical politics. Maybe, just maybe, he argued in reconstructing old plays about the theater that had been newly reformed with the rearranged management of Drury Lane—maybe, Settle fantasized, the gentry who supported the players and the councilmen who attacked them could see the possibility of a new generation, regeneration. It was this dream, I suppose, which drew Settle back to the old world of Beaumont and Fletcher and Shakespeare when they were creating what we have come to call "the romances." He was serious about that. But he did not abandon the satirist's eye. So in the third, enveloping plot, Jenny and her mother and the gentleman-player make a fourth play for the father and London Councilman.[12]

The Councilman would never have attended the theater merely to fulfill his job as censor and reporter of iniquities, had not his wife "dragg'd" him to the playhouse ostensibly to view, as she explains, "*a worthy Gentleman that does us the Honour to love our Daughter. But because he once play'd a Frolick, and acted a part upon your Publick Stage for his own Diversion, as they say, several Gentleman had often done before him, my Husband has conceived . . . an Aversion to him . . . a Man of Honour and Fortune, born to a Thousand a year.*" The Councilman is adamant, adapting not only the attitude but the very language of antiquated Elizabethan statutes: "*What had a Thousand a year to do upon the Stage! . . . Stroller, Scoundrel, Vagrant, and what not, are the best Titles he can afford him*" (B2r).

Her hopes of reforming the reformer, however, apparently desert the wife as they learn that the person in question is not scheduled to play. And she, too, seems to share the Councilman's distrust of the theater (gentleman-player apart) when, invited by the Aldermanic Prologue to the stage, she balks daughter Jenny's desire to accompany her: "*What behind the Scenes! Not, for the World! Thou a young innocent Creature, and trust thy self amongst a pack of wicked Players! I am an old Woman, Chicken, and there's no danger of me.*" Instructed, Jenny acquiesces in an ambiguous gesture: "*Nay, then I'll keep out of harm's way, I warrant. . . . They shan't so much as see my Face, I'll wear a Mask all the Play*" (B1v). While the Councilman and his wife move from the box to the stage, all ambiguity disappears: a masquerading actress flits into the box to assume Jenny's mask, and Jenny hurries "behind the scenes" to become an actress. As they exchange roles, they exchange that dialogue which promises everyone else's role reversal: "*'Well, if we can but put the Sham upon your old Daddy.' / 'Oh never fear his weak Eyes. Besides you know my Mother's in the Plot'*" (B2r). And this is what forces us to a revision of the triple-plot formula I stated earlier. Jenny has now joined her gentleman-player in the inner play as a vehicle to convert "old Daddy." But this is apparently only a mechanism toward the advancement of action in Settle's strange addition of "chevalier" Don Garcia to the history of Rinaldo-Viola-Valerio, a history that leads us from the city world of money, inheritances, and rank into the pastoral world, where the younger Garcia can bless all unions and appropriately become a hermit *religieuse*.

But something is wrong. We must listen again, recapitulate, re-member merging but confusing details. City and country (or "county," as more sophisticated recent developments would label a division of landed gentry) do not differ enough. Return to the role of the merchant-citizen Don Garcia. He is threatened with being dis-owned by the "chevalier" nephew because he wishes to offer Lucia to the coxcomb "count" rather than to the Carlo he has adopted and trained in merchandising. But the choice is for money. In the Coun-cilman's dubiety about the "gentleman" player, the same theme holds ("What had a Thousand a year to do upon the Stage!"). What are we to say, though, to the accountant's mentality, which is almost the first we hear from or of Viola except about the corruptive force of her sexual attraction in both city and country (Rinaldo boasts about how he will use her—even before his drunkenness; Valerio promises that he will use her gently even though he has a wife). She is intent, after all, on stealing her dowry from her father—a Jessica-become-Shylock—she will take no pound more or less than is her due. In the country, Don Garcia "chevalier" divides his fortune among the lovers upon turning *religieuse*.

Even earlier he has done another act of largesse, uniting love with money. Viola (axial symbol of his nexus) has been rescued from the titillating half-nude bondage in which the gypsies have left her, from the subsequent importunings of Valerio, and from her helpless isola-tion in this dangerous countryside by the pastoral lovers Damon and Phyllis. Meeting Don Garcia, she easily persuades him to return to Damon a land inheritance that will allow the lovers to marry (47ff.). It is not the pastoral world of Renaissance courtiers (in spite of the "chevalier's" presence and courtesy), of Sannazaro or Castiglione, any more than it is the city. But then Damon and Phyllis are not country lovers, masquerades aside. The City Councilman breaks partly through to exclaim: "*Look, Fubby, look,: That young* Phyllis *there and my* Jenny *are as like one another as two Eggs out of one Nest*" (47). His Jenny has, of course, emerged into the play with Damon, her player/gentleman lover, merged city and country again, merged inner and outer plays. And how can the Councilman or we now distinguish which is which: love or money, city or country, envelope or enveloped as genre and society are questioned in this adaptation of the old romances of Beaumont, Fletcher, Shakespeare, which seemed less sociologically giddy?

Settle's sin is propagandistic in retrospect, but that is the usual

myopia of hindsight. In 1711 he was hopeful of co-opting the city
authorities to save Bartholomew Fair, the theaters, the theater as
enterprise, from political instincts of reform. That meant, though, a
reordering of stereotypes that had been revived by reactionaries. So
Settle centered his play upon the conversion of the City Councilman,
with a play as vehicle. It was a little early, with Steele coming to
dominance; Fielding yet a few years off; and Garrick further from
imagination. But these historic facts make the engagement of Settle's
adaptation of earlier plays more daring, serious.

The Councilman's role becomes that of convert only through par-
ticipation as player. It develops slowly: when Rinaldo is tortured by
remorse at the close of act 3, the Councilman first sees the possibility
that theater might be an instrument rather than an object of reform:
"Well, Drunkenness, here's some good Fruit from a bad Tree, here's
Repentance going forwards apace" (43). When Don Garcia returns
Damon's land, the Councilman approves "a Marriage-bargain honestly struck for to morrow" (51). But at the close of act 1, when Don
Garcia senior was providing Lucia with the coxcomb count for his
money, the Councilman's wife had warned him of the parallel be-
tween the stage-plot and his plotting for his daughter's union with "a
Knight and an Alderman." The wife sees it as worse than the mis-
match proposed in the play: "an antiquated Piece of Mortality . . .
[you come] to reform the Vices of the Stage. / Oh, Husband, for true
Reformation-work / They who to mend the World abroad wou'd come,
/ Shou'd first begin, and correct all at home" (13).

The Councilman does so in the most ironic way when he interferes
with the plot of Phyllis and Damon, becoming Damon's advocate
against the moneyed chevalier suitor. Husband and wife get caught
up in the play as Phyllis seems to abandon her lover for rank and
money. There is a little wink at the audience, and another at expectations: "If that Baggage, my own Brat yonder, should play me such a
Prank, I'd make her whistle for her ten thousand Pound. . . . had one
of our Covent-Garden Brood play'd such a piece of Jilt-Work, it had
been a little excuseable; but a mere Country-Piece of simple Innocence" (58). And then the Councilman ceases to be commentator and
becomes playwright/director, threatening Phyllis/Jenny:

> The Reprobate Scriblers of this Age are such a sensells [sic] Pack of
> Rogues, that they bewray their own Nests, stuff so many villainous lewd
> Characters into their Plays, 'till they have almost undone the very Stage
> they live by. But look you, I'll have no such playing whilst I sit here. You
> have promis'd to marry this honest Damon, as you call him; and udz-
> ings, . . . Boy, take her, and say I give her thee: She's thy own, . . . take
> my City Word and Honour for't. (58)

Entering into the play and concluding its innermost (or outermost) plot to suit himself, the Councilman has done more than unwittingly marry his daughter to a gentleman-player; he has endorsed a marriage between "common" citizens: *"here's my Hand, before all this noble Company, my House shall by thy home. . . . An honest Brace of Players! Odsfish, Man, I thought you had all lived in Common"* (59). This is the unexpected *"glorious Work of Reformation,"* which the Councilman hopes may earn him a niche in Saint Paul's. When he learns the truth from his conspiratorial wife that this *"Play-House Plot of ours secur'd* [Jenny] *against all Dangers of an Alderman Pretender"* (70), the Councilman/player smugly acquiesces into Settle's dream, some version of which has possessed the theater's players and playwrights from the beginning, as they have incredulously marveled at the antitheatrical prejudice: *"instead of reforming the Stage, the Stage has reformed me."*

Settle's hopes were genuine, but he was too old a stager to forget the ambivalence between love and money, class and cash, which his adaptation of an older great city play had revived. Damon has the last word:

> My Side-Box Brothers, as I'm one of you,
> Do not my Trip on the poor Stage despise,
> You'd all play *Damons* for my golden Prize.
> In Loves fair Lottery with my Fortunes crown'd,
> May you all draw like me, ten thousand Pound.
>
> (71)

Notes

A long time ago Aubrey Williams told me I should read *The City Ramble*. I have tried.

1. *"I set Pen to Paper upon the Recommendation my good Friend Mr. Booth had given me of Two of the Plays of* Beaumont *and* Fletcher, *viz.* The Knight of the Burning Pestle, *and the* Coxcomb; *from whence he thought I might borrow some small Foundation, and perhaps some little Fabrick-work towards a Comedy. I took the Hint accordingly. . . . However, not to rob the Dead, ev'n of the least borrow'd Plume those celebrated Authors have furnish'd me . . . I have set this* ["] *Characteristick before every Line of the Original"* ("To the Reader," Settle n.d., sig. A4r-v). The publication presumably came quickly upon the heels of performance, as it includes a full cast list. First performance was 17 August 1711, repeated on the twenty-first and twenty-eighth (Settle's benefit day). (Avery 1960, 2:254–55.) There are no further performance records.
2. It may have had a complicated revival sometime between 1665 and 1671 with prologue and epilogue spoken by Nell Gwyn and an inserted scene parodying Dryden's *Secret Love* (Avery 1960, 1:95).
3. I present a detailed examination of *The Knight of the Burning Pestle* as an optimistic "folk" structure disguised as city satire in Cope 1973, 196–210.
4. See Smith 1936 and Smith and Lawhon 1979. Settle had offered an abortive skeleton in the freak text featuring Penkethman's confrontation, with a cameo appearance by Joe Haines, titled *The World in the Moon* (1697).

5. The heroine/victim Viola underlines the problematic title when, outcast into the countryside, she there declaims: "Believe me, tho' a Rambler, I am an honest one" (4.1, 48).

6. Wilson 1928, 47; Avery 1960, 1:455. There was a revival in October 1711 (Avery 1960, 2:260–61), possibly to make up for Settle's small profit from *The City Ramble* a few weeks earlier.

7. Milhous 1979, 189–221; "Barton Booth" and "Aaron Hill" in Highfill et al. 1973–.

8. Settle was mocking the reformers' failure to observe a distinction he had insisted upon in the earlier phase of the stage debate, when he had argued that we solidify characters when we read plays by pressing them into our imaginative projection, but when they are acted, characters cease to be real once the performance is concluded: "No sooner is the curtain faln, both the *Hero* and the *Heroine* are no more to you, than the *Betterton* and *Barry*" (Settle 1698, 54–56).

9. In 1756, 1, sig. L3v. Milhous 1979, 125–29 *passim*, gives a sophisticated updating of the "reporters" and other reform movements against the stage at the particular crisis years that led into the restriction of Bartholomew Fair and the new union of the theaters.

10. "Surprisingly, no theatre commentator accuses informers of being in the business to make money. The Societies for the Reformation of Manners always urged members to turn their 'moytie' over to charity, or not to accept it at all. No informer was ever prosecuted for taking a bribe, and it appears that none of the few convictions brought into question was reversed" (Milhous 1979, 126, citing Portus 1912).

11. We owe a great deal of our ability to rethink old problems to Butler 1984.

12. I will remark only in passing that this aspect of *The City Ramble* seems to me closer to the action of David Garrick's popular *A Peep Behind the Curtain* (1767) than *Les Femmes savantes* on earlier rehearsal plays; it is perhaps no coincidence that Garrick's piece was first performed on a double bill with Lillo's *London Merchant*. (See Garrick 1980–82, 2:329–31.) We are tasting a long tradition of the gentleman-player and its social (sometimes tragicomic) consequences. Perhaps the closest early analogue is a commedia dell'arte scenario, "la commedia in commedia" (reprinted from the Roman Loccatello collection in del Cerro 1914, 391–400). It is necessary for our purposes only to recall in this scenario a gradual revolution of roles through which the citizen Coviello becomes a commedia stock "Captain," and the player troupe's stock Captain emerges as the citizen Pantalone's lost son.

Works Cited

Avery, Emmett L., ed. 1960. *The London Stage 1660–1800. Part 2: 1700–1729*. Carbondale: Southern Illinois University Press.

Beaumont, Francis, and John Fletcher. 1905–12. *The Works of Beaumont and Fletcher*. Ed. Arnold Glover and A. R. Waller. Cambridge: Cambridge University Press.

Butler, Martin. 1984. *Theatre and Crisis 1632–1642*. Cambridge: Cambridge University Press.

del Cerro, Emilio. 1914. *Nel regno delle maschere*. Naples, Italy: Perrella.

Cope, Jackson. 1973. *The Theater and the Dream: From Metaphor to Form in Renaissance Drama*. Baltimore: The Johns Hopkins University Press.

———. 1984. *Dramaturgy of the Daemonic: Studies in Antigeneric Theater from Ruzante to Grimaldi*. Baltimore: The Johns Hopkins University Press.

Garrick, David. 1980–82. *The Plays of David Garrick*. Ed. H. W. Pedicord and F. L. Bergmann. Carbondale: Southern Illinois University Press.

Highfill, Philip H., Jr., Kalman A. Burnim, and Edward A. Langhans. 1973–. *A Biographical Dictionary of Actors, Actresses, Musicians, Dancers, Managers & Other Stage Personnel in London, 1660–1800*. Carbondale: Southern Illinois University Press.

Milhous, Judith. 1979. *Thomas Betterton and the Management of Lincoln's Inn Fields, 1695–1708*. Carbondale: Southern Illinois University Press.

Morley, Henry. 1880. *Memoirs of Bartholomew Fair*. London: Chatto and Windus.

Pepys, Samuel. 1970–83. *Diary*. Ed. L. C. Latham and W. Matthews. Berkeley and Los Angeles: University of California Press.

Portus, Garnet. 1912. *Caritas Anglicana*. London.

Rowe, Nicholas. 1756. *Works*. London.

Settle, Elkanah. 1697. *The World in the Moon*. London.

———. 1698. *A Farther Defence of Dramatick Poetry: Being the Second Part of the Review of Mr. Collier's View of the Immorality and Profaneness of the English Stage*. London.

———. n.d. *The City-Ramble: or, a Play-House Wedding*. London.

Smith, Dane Farnsworth. 1936. *Plays about the Theatre in England from the Rehearsal in 1671 to the Licensing Act in 1737*. New York and London: Oxford University Press.

Smith, Dane Farnsworth, and M. L. Lawhon. 1979. *Plays about the Theatre in England, 1737–1800*. Lewisburg: Bucknell University Press.

Wilson, John Harold. 1928. *The Influence of Beaumont and Fletcher on Restoration Drama*. Columbus: The Ohio State University Press.

Part 2
Poetry

The Rhetoric of *Kairos* in
Dryden's *Absalom and Achitophel*

MICHAEL J. CONLON

Arthur Hoffman in *John Dryden's Imagery* stresses how often Dryden "faced up to the difficult demands of *speaking* to many and speaking *once*" in times of "change, controversy, and confusion" (1962, 148). The list of Dryden's poems comprises an index to the significant occasions of his age, and the Greek conception of *Kairos*—meaning the "right time" for something to happen—defines, enlivens, and sometimes limits much of his writing.[1] In the case of *Absalom and Achitophel* (1681), the experience of crisis and the questions of timing and opportunity, identified so often with *Kairos* in classical and Christian literature, ground the poem's rhetorical design. Issues of time, the quality of the times, and the right time are confronted from beginning to end, from the "pious times" (Dryden 1956–, 2:5, vs.1) of David's early reign in Sion to the "Factious Times" (180) of Achitophel's conspiracy, from Absalom's temptation to seize the moment of opportunity to a "Series of new time" (1028) celebrated at the close of David's speech. Even the timing of the poem's composition weighs on Dryden's mind in his address to the reader: "Things were not brought to an Extremity where I left the Story: There seems, yet, to be room left for a Composure; hereafter, there may only be for pity" (p. 4). His telling the story comes while the fate of a sick "Body Politique" hangs in doubt and the satirist as physician can forestall "an *Ense rescindendum*" by prescribing "harsh Remedies" (p. 5).

The poet laureate's timing of "harsh Remedies" against unpleasant facts matches his monarch's political timing months earlier at Oxford. And if there is an assumption that the intentional effect of *Absalom and Achitophel* works to vindicate Charles II's unexpected dissolution of the Oxford Parliament, the poem's achievement depends on Dryden's recreation of the whole experience of threatened revolution with a gravity and immediacy that would validate the king's *Kairos*, or time of opportunity. From this perspective the power of Dryden's rhetoric involves more than the strategies of "disguise" and "persuasion" singled out in recent readings (e.g., Zwicker 1984, 85–103). Rather, the power of rhetoric to interpret the times and *Kairoi* for action parallels the power of Providence to direct the times through colligations of events bearing extraordinary results. In bringing his audience to recognize what the times demand, Dryden creates a structure of dynamic and dangerous imbalance that provides the occasion for the king to affirm constitutional limits within a matrix of classical and Christian conceptions of counterrevolution as the just balancing of opposite forces.

The rhetoric of *Kairos* in *Absalom and Achitophel* assumes a conception of the English constitution as a balance between the three pure forms of government—monarchy, aristocracy, and democracy. It was widely held, John Pocock recalls, that any one of these forms "existing alone would be replaced by its own perverted form and that by one of the pure forms, itself doomed to excess and replacement and so on in an unending cycle" of political crises. "Only a mixed or balanced constitution, combining the qualities of all three forms could hope to escape the doom of degeneration through excess."[2] This Polybian model had received its earliest official endorsement on the eve of the first civil war in a work called *His Majesties Answer to the XIX Propositions of Both Houses of Parliament* (1642):

> There being three kinds of government among men, absolute monarchy, aristocracy and democracy, and all of these having their particular conveniences and inconveniences, the experience and wisdom of your ancestors hath so moulded this out of a mixture of these as to give this kingdom (as far as human prudence can provide) the conveniences of all three, without the inconveniences of any one, as long as the balance hangs even between the three estates, and they run jointly on in their proper channel . . . and the flowing of either side raise no deluge or inundation.[3]

Although the republican language and provisional tone of the king's "Answer" dismayed many royalists, the model of a balanced constitution defined the context of subsequent political debate. It "provided apologists for both sides in the First Civil War with a common frame of reference, in which the King's cause or Parliament's could be pleaded in terms which were largely continuous and shared many assumptions and values" (Pocock 1977, 22). And when the ongoing struggle of Parliament to assert its independence from the crown reached the crisis stage once more in 1678 over the issue of Exclusion, both sides pleaded their cause in the normative language of balance. Whigs found the model useful, because it enabled them to argue from precedent for the greatest number of limitations on the king's power. Tories, on the other hand, used the model to resist intrusions by

Parliament on the king's prerogative, without resorting to an absolutist interpretation of kingship.

The sharpest differences between Whig and Tory versions of the
model, often ignored in readings of *Absalom and Achitophel*, arose
whenever the debate moved from Exclusion to the larger issue of
constitutional limits. The Whigs, drawing from earlier apologists for
Parliament like Charles Herle and Philip Hunton, emphasized the
limits of the king's legislative or so-called political power, insisting that
it was coordinate with the power of Parliament. Some Whigs put the
case against prerogative more bluntly. Only what the king did *in*
Parliament was supreme. And on these grounds alone, a bill to
exclude the Duke of York could be justified.[4] While moderate Tories
agreed to the idea of limits on the king's legislative powers, they
insisted on the primacy of his regal or prerogative powers, and they
drew their authority from the writings of Henry Ferne, who had
argued in 1643 that while the "two Houses of Parliament are in a sort
Coordinate with His Majesty . . . [in] the making of Lawes by Yield-
ing their consent," the king also governed by his regal or prerogative
powers. He could make treaties, command the militia, appoint
judges, and call or dissolve Parliament. Excluding or even reducing
any one of these powers, Ferne believed, would "make this government Democratical or Aristocratical" and thereby destroy the original
balance.[5] Henry Ferne's warning informs many of the statements
issued in behalf of the king during the Exclusion Crisis. While the
Whigs decried the abuses of royal prerogative and the corruptive
influences of the king's agents on members of Parliament, Tories
protested the calculated effort of Shaftesbury "to lengthen the list of
functions ascribed to the formal or political powers of the King," and
"either diminish his regal powers or so circumscribe them with parliamentary reservations that the . . . King could not make his personal
influence felt" (Edie 1964–65, 358–59). Dryden's partisan portrayal of
the opposition and final assertion of the king's power depends on this
point—the methodical reduction of royal prerogative, or the wish of
Achitophel "That Kingly power, thus ebbing out, might be / Drawn to
the dregs of a Democracy" (226–27).

Spokesmen for the king found themselves in the difficult position of
defending prerogative power within a model of government that
presumed a limit on any power. But they managed their case by
attacking the Whig version of coordinate government and by insisting
that the king's prerogative power, exercised in behalf of the people
and determined by law, insured a balance between the democratic
and aristocratic constitutencies of the government. The anonymous

author of *England's Concern in the Case of . . . James Duke of York* (1681) cited the precedent of Henry III: it is to "the wisdom of Henry the third . . . [that] we owe our present constitution of parliament. This King, perceiving the lords power . . . grown formidable . . . erected [the commons] into a lower house to counterpoise the weight of the other, that he, joining with either, as occasion of state required, might balance the other and so keep things in an equal and steady liberation."[6]

Similar sentiments appear in a work—once thought to be Dryden's—entitled *His Majesties Declaration Defended* (1681). In defending the king's power to call and dissolve Parliament, the author repeats the metaphors of Charles I's Answer to Parliament of 1642:

> Our Kings have always been indued with the power of calling Parliaments, nominating the time, appointing the Place, and Dissolving them when they thought it for the publick good: And the People have wisely consulted their welfare in it. Suppose, for example, that there be a jarring between the three Estates, which renders their sitting at the time Impracticable; since one of them can not pretend to Judge the proceedings of the other two, the Judgement of the whole must either reside in a Superior power or the discord must terminate in the ruine of them all. For if one of these encroach too far, there is so much lost in the Balance of the Estates, and so much more arbitrary power in one: Tis as certain in Politiques, as in Nature; That where the Sea Prevails the Land Loses.[7]

Regardless of who wrote these remarks, they agree with Dryden's vindication in *Absalom and Achitophel* of the king's exercise of his prerogative at Oxford on 28 March 1681, an event that provoked a new round of Whig attacks on the court in the summer months preceding publication of the poem. In a style reminiscent of the *Historiae* of Polybius,[8] Dryden conceives the *Kairoi* of his age as combinations of events tending toward political imbalance and demanding an unequivocal assertion of the king's lawful powers. While early in the poem he praises the moderates who achieve momentary stability after the Restoration and incline "the Ballance to the better side" (76), more often his language concedes the endemic instability of a nation "govern'd by the *Moon*" (216). The expected chronology of a historical report yields to the effects of Dryden's queasy, imbalanced, almost parodic conflation of English and Jewish history that, unlike earlier parallels between England and Israel, exploits accidental differences between the two histories in order to single out recurrent patterns of corruption, shifts in the balance of power, and examples of the sinful biases of human nature. In its larger units of meaning, the poem recreates the constitutional crisis as a confrontation of unequal forces, marked off and set into sharp relief by the passage on government and the narrator's description of the ancient constitution as a temple:

> If ancient Fabricks nod, and threat to fall,
> To Patch the Flaws, and Buttress up the Wall,
> Thus far 'tis Duty; but here fix the Mark:
> For all beyond it is to touch our Ark.
> To change Foundations, cast the Frame anew,
> Is work for Rebels who base Ends pursue:
> At once Divine and Humane Laws controul;
> And mend the Parts by ruine of the Whole.
>
> (801–8)

On one side of this warning not to transgress constitutional and providential limits, the narrator describes the formidable forces of the opposition. His description extends for some six hundred lines, from the portrait of Achitophel to the account of Absalom's progress through the kingdom. On the other side of the passage on government, the narrator describes in less than one hundred lines the diminished forces loyal to the king. In simple spatial terms, the poem—as Johnson recognized—is unequal. And the narrator sustains and reinforces this sense of imbalance by carefully selecting those aspects of events bewraying conspiracy and a nation on the verge of revolution: Achitophel's exploitation of the Popish Plot (200–213); Absalom's disaffection and campaign for popular favor (476–90, 682–782); the rebellious mood of the people (214–19); distrust and hatred of monarchy from a combination of factions made up of all "sorts of men" (289), from princes of the land to Levites, from the "*Solymaean* Rout" (513) to "A numerous host of dreaming Saints" (529). Selection of this sort truncates the poem's action, but makes emphatic the excesses of the king's enemies, their number, weight, and measure, and their determination to test limits.

The poem's images of physical limits tried and tested to the breaking point not only display the excesses of the king's enemies—as countless readings insist—but also amplify the *Kairos* of Charles-David's reign as a crisis of economic, political, and moral imbalance. Achitophel exploits the wealth and property concentrated in the Commons to prune the king's prerogative powers. As he boasts to Absalom:

> The Thrifty Sanhedrin shall keep him poor:
> And every Sheckle which he can receive,
> Shall cost a Limb of his Prerogative.
>
> (390–93)

Property, cost, matters of "pure good husbandry," and trade unite and inspire the opposition, threatening to turn the kingship into a pawn and thereby disrupt the balance of power: "For Soveraign power is too deprest or high, / When Kings are forc'd to sell, or Crowds to buy" (896–97). In striking contrast to the Harringtonian thesis that property is the "hinge of government,"[9] Dryden's poem turns property into a system of "Springs . . . bent, / And wound so high, [it] Crack'd the Government" (500). Such images of excessive force and pressure extend to every area of public life and beyond, for the people would even risk divine retribution by trying "th' extent and stretch of grace" (46).

Dryden's satiric portraits bring the moral source of disorder into focus as a kind of sinful "byast of Nature" (79). Achitophel's "fiery Soul" has "o'er-informed" and "Fretted" the limits of his body (156). Absalom is an overreacher, "Too full of Angell's Metal," and "too Covetous of Fame" (310). Corah's stories strain the laws of credibility, while Shemei's body—with his hand upholding the staff of justice— appears twisted and bent at the neck by a heavy "Chain of Gold" (596), a posture emblematic of the crisis in the "body politique." In the portrait of Zimri, imbalance, motion, and madness even conspire against aesthetic laws and poetic limits:

> A man so various, that he seem'd to be
> Not one, but all Mankinds Epitome.
> Stiff in Opinions, always in the wrong;
> Was every thing by starts, and nothing long:
> But, in the course of one revolving Moon,
> Was Chymist, Fidler, States-Man, and Buffoon:
> Then all for Women, Painting, Rhiming, Drinking;
> Besides ten thousand freaks that dy'd in thinking. . . .
> So over Violent, or over Civil
> That every man, with him, was God or Devil.
>
> (545–58)

As Alvin Kernan points out, "where the verse coheres, Zimri is 'various' and 'not one.' Where rhetorically one part of the poetic line balances and complements another part, Zimri's enthusiasms pull him apart. Where the couplets march evenly along the same seemly level, Zimri's frantic activities lead him down to bathos—'Chymist, Fidler, States-Man, Buffoon.' And where the couplets do not depart too far from their regular pace—only enough to provide suitable variety— Zimri is excessive in all he does, 'over Violent, or over Civil'" (1965, 18). But the forces of instability extend further than Kernan's reading allows, and in rhymes like "Moon" / "Buffoon," "Drinking" / "thinking," and "Civil" / "Devil," Dryden binds the reader to increasingly disparate terms so that human balances of any kind seem queasy and subject to the swings of fortune.

What happens in the portrait of Zimri happens in the poem as a whole. Dryden's emphasis on the pressure of opposition identifies the *Kairos* of 1681 with a wild, relentless force bearing down on the kingship and posing a grave danger to the balance and order of the realm. As Johnson says, when we come to the narrator's tribute to the loyal few at line 811, we are indeed "alarmed by a faction formed of many sects, various in their principles, but agreeing in their purpose of mischief, formidable for their numbers and strong by their supports, while the king's friends are few and weak" (1925, 1:242). From a royalist view of the constitution, this was precisely the moment in time that would command and commend the king's intervention and exercise of his prerogative. And in *Absalom and Achitophel* the king acts only when the reader must expect the whole fabric of government to crack under the pressure of "powerful Engines bent to batter it down" (917).

There is nothing novel in calling attention to the language of imbalance in *Absalom and Achitophel*. I do so, however, to emphasize its importance to the poem's rhetoric of *Kairos*. Spatial disorders, played against a widely accepted view of the English constitution as a counterpoise of powers, make issues of timing in the poem all the more vital. Clearly, the opportunity, or *Kairos*, for the king to affirm his prerogative counters Achitophel's determination to force what Dryden calls the "event of things" (835) by, first, seizing the occasion of the Popish Plot, then, manipulating economic interests in "factious times," and, finally, in his temptation of Absalom, exploiting the panic inspired by the ticking clock:

> Leave the warm People no Considering time;
> For then Rebellion may be thought a Crime.
> Prevail your self of what Occasion gives,
> But try your Title while your Father lives:
> And that your Arms may have a fair Pretence,
> Proclaim, you take them in the King's Defence:
> Whose Sacred Life each minute would Expose,
> To Plots, from seeming Friends, and Secret Foes.
>
> (459–66)

In striking contrast to the belief that God has assigned a time for all things, Achitophel convinces Absalom to take and make his own time, to be, as it were, his own providence.

Timing is all. And Dryden distinguishes the king's timing from

Achitophel's by suffusing David's speech with appeals to the law and God's distributive justice in times of rebellion. Recent readings, however, find little difference between David's rhetoric and Achitophel's. For Dustin Griffin, the king emerges as a "witty, calculating politician" who outmaneuvers his enemies in a struggle for power (1978, 36). For Steven Zwicker, the king's evocations of law and providential justice complete a strategy of rhetorical disguise that distances Charles II from personal responsibility for drawing the sword (1984, 86). For Leon Guilhamet, David is a "figure outdoing God" (1969, 407). And for George Lord, he embodies the "final cause" of an "autonomous myth of divine right" (1972, 189). For all of these readers, in short, Dryden's vindication of the king turns out to be an arbitrary use of a normative language to justify a Machiavellian program of vengeance and an absolutist form of kingship.

The king's speech invites such readings, because it makes sense to assume what Quentin Skinner calls a purely "instrumental connection" between Dryden's use of a normative language and the actions Charles II had taken in the summer of 1681 to protect his interests.[10] The king had already embarked on a program to purge the kingdom and rule without Parliament. But in doing so he wished to appear both honorable and reluctant to draw the sword of justice. It follows for many readers that Dryden's rhetoric would cast the king in the best light, using a normative language that relates to Charles II's actions ex post facto. It follows, as well, that Dryden's portrayal of the king in a matrix of constitutional checks and balances need not reflect either the king's actual intentions or Dryden's beliefs. Dryden's constitutionalism simply stops at the level of style, effectively mitigating up to the end what Zwicker interprets as Charles II's will "to act on the bold and vindictive claim for executive vengeance" that climaxes David's speech (86): "By their own arts Tis Righteously decreed, / Those dire Artificers of Death shall bleed" (1010–12). I would argue, however, that the normative language Dryden brings to David's speech has more than an instrumental connection to the king's actions. As Quentin Skinner also points out, the criteria implied by the normative language a society uses to describe its political life can be understood not simply to disguise the actions of its rulers but to limit those actions (xiii). Given the depth of corruption and the potential for revolution Dryden presents in the body of the poem, the range of just and honorable actions open to the king would have been wide indeed, but not so wide as to include any action—especially any that could be construed as arbitrary and vindictive. If the poem has shown a crisis born of breaking constitutional and providential limits, the king's actions must affirm those limits. The *Kairos* Dryden creates demands nothing less than a counterstroke tailored to the criteria implied by the normative language of law, balance, and providential justice.

The text invites this approach by capturing in the content and timing of the king's speech three related ideas of *Kairos:* the time of crisis, the opportunity for decisive action, and the time when colligations of events reveal the interpositions of Divine Providence. David begins by reviewing the pressures and stresses on natural and ordained limits that have brought both the kingship and the kingdom to its time of crisis. David's natural and godlike attributes of patience, mercy, and clemency have been tried to the limits by a people determined to "divert" his "native course" (933–50). Overindulged by his father, Absalom has rebelled against the limits of his birth and destiny: "Had God ordain'd his fate for Empire born, / He would have given his Soul another turn" (963–64). Sanhedrins incessantly petition the king's consent to suspend the laws of succession, refusing the legitimate disposition of power and the present balance between the three estates. The insatiable demands of his petitioners evoke in David's mind the image of a world reduced by excessive cravings to the final limits of "barren Womb" and "Grave" (987–88).

This crisis of limits determines the king's decision to act. And the transition at line 991 to an oracular mode signals the poem's vital turn from the fallible and embattled person of David to the *persona publica* of the king, who recognizes the right time for change and declares his intention to "sustain and prop the nations weight" (954) by the limiting power of the law: "The Law shall still direct my peaceful Sway, / And the same Law teach Rebels to Obey" (991–92). Belief that a state can be both reclaimed and sustained by wise laws complements the belief that Providence, as the Reverend Isaac Barrow preached, "hath a main stroke in all revolutions and changes of state" (1859, 1:464). Invoking a traditional emblem of providential justice and the self-destructive nature of rebellion, the king predicts his enemies will turn on themselves like vipers:

> Against themselves their Witnesses will Swear,
> Till Viper-like their Mother Plot they tear:
> And suck for Nutriment that bloody gore
> Which was their Principle of Life before.
>
> (1012–15)

From the perspective of the poem's biblical and Miltonic contexts, the prospect of "oppressors . . . welter[ing] in their own gore"[11] identifies the king's vision of time with the *Kairos* of providential justice and, as Hoffman shows, anchors the entire speech to the history of God's "acts and utterances" (88). Unlike the opportunism of

Achitophel, the king's response to the times recognizes the precariousness of all political arrangements and defers to the belief that Providence shows forth "essentially in the balancing and diverting of opposite powers" (Collinges 1678, 93):

> Nor doubt th' event: for Factious crowds engage
> In their first Onset, all their Brutal Rage;
> Then, let 'em take an unresisted Course,
> Retire and Traverse, and Delude their Force:
> But when they stand all Breathless, urge the fight,
> And rise upon 'em with redoubled might:
> For Lawfull Pow'r is Still Superiour found,
> When long driven back, at length it stands the ground.
>
> (1018–25)

This final prophecy recapitulates the poem's "event of things" as a confrontation of unequal forces, and renders the king a witness to the ways in which Providence arranges the patterns of victory and defeat.

Dryden's timing of the speech to mark the sudden turn of support to the king's side agrees with both classical and Christian accounts of *Kairos* as that time when history turns by a "kind of 'gravitational pull' . . . toward the reclamation of ordered, balanced, and morally better conditions" (Trompf 1979, 87). But what classical historians documented as the *Kairoi* of Fortune, Christian apologists like Isaac Barrow ascribed to the interpositions of Providence. And the *Kairos* of Providence Barrow described several years before the Exclusion Crisis anticipates the *Kairos* of *Absalom and Achitophel:* "When by weak forces great feats are accomplished and impotency triumpheth over might," when the "most perspicatious and profound counsellors are blinded," when "profane, malicious, subtle, treacherous politicians (such as . . . Achitophel . . .) are not only supplanted in their . . . contrivances, but dismally chastised for them," when "plots" are "brought to light," when "any pernicious enterprise levelled against the safety of prince and people, is disappointed," when "divers odd accidents do befall at a seasonable time, for the public benefit, and the preservation of princes, the maintenance of truth and piety, according to the wishes and prayers of good men; . . . such a complication . . . in one event may thoroughly suffice to raise a firm persuasion, to force a confident acknowledgement concerning God's providence."[12]

Viewed as a poem of *Kairos*, the "unpleasing disproportion" in *Absalom and Achitophel* that troubled Dr. Johnson enables Dryden to assimilate Davidic myth to the facts of English history. In this regard, the final and proper analogue to Charles II's remarkable command of the crisis after the Oxford Parliament of 1681 appears in 2 Samuel when David delivers his message to the men of Judah, after the rebellion of Absalom. Cited frequently in seventeenth-century sermons as an example of how Providence may "preserve government from dissolution by intestine Adversaries by disposing the minds of people to their duty" (Pindar 1679, 6), the passage recalls how David "bowed the hearts of all the men of Judah, even as *the heart of* one man" (2 Sam. 19:14). In a gloss of the passage, John Parker says David "inclined the hearts of all . . . and that inclination implies a bend of the mind, or heart, and the people began to lean to their King."[13] This last turn in the poem's foreground of biblical events frees the two histories to intersect. Charles II's restoration recapitulates David's, and the rhetoric of *Kairos* in *Absalom and Achitophel*, its power to interpret the times, becomes coextensive with the power of Providence to direct the times.

In the final lines of *Absalom and Achitophel*, Dryden projects a "Series of New Time": *Kairos* gives way to *Chronus* in the poet's measure of a peaceful reign:

> The mighty Years in long Procession ran:
> Once more the Godlike *David* was Restor'd,
> And willing Nations knew their Lawful Lord.
>
> (1029–31)

Despite the confidence and hope Dryden brings out of his account of the Exclusion Crisis, the restoration of order seems less than ideal, too dependent upon the threat of stern measures, and for some critics all too rhetorical an order, one so imposed that the metaphors of leverage and balance become either independent of political realities or symptomatic of deeper historical contradictions (McKeon 1987). But it is not necessary to conclude that the precarious harmony at poem's end looks either forward to a secular myth of power or backward to an age of "anointed absolutism" (cf. Lord 1972 and Zwicker 1984). Balances recovered are inevitably precarious and unstable. The stern appeals to law and justice, and the assertions of God's controlling Providence in the affairs of state curiously resist the kind of closure they invite by reflecting the growing sense of contingency in Dryden's world. This is not a world of static balance, but—as Georges Poulet observes—a world that shows "an acute sense of the discontinuity of duration, and a total dependence upon a creation continually reiterated" (1956, 14–15). In these terms, the rhetoric of *Absalom and Achitophel* speaks of and to the times.

Notes

1. My use of the Greek word *Kairos* to describe the "qualitative character of time" in *Absalom and Achitophel* depends substantially on Smith 1969 and Kermode 1967, 46–50.

2. Pocock 1971, 129. On the origins and influence of "mixed government" in England, see Weston 1965, 9–112, and Judson 1949, 65–69.

3. *Stuart* 1966, 22. On the composition and historical importance of this document, see Weston 1965, 5–28.

4. For the idea of a coordinate power between king and Parliament, see Weston 1970. Typical of the Whig arguments for Exclusion, based on the supremacy of the king in Parliament, is Hunt 1680, 4.

5. Ferne 1643, 6. John Brydall, writing during the Exclusion Crisis, repeats Ferne's argument verbatim (1681, 3–4). Similar views appear in Sheringham 1682, 73–74. For an early parliamentarian response to Ferne, see Hunton 1644, 38.

6. *Somers Tracts* 1812, 8:172. L'Estrange makes a similar point: "And yet again, admitting your Co-ordination; First, every King runs the hazard of his crown upon every Parliament he calls: For the third Estate lies at the mercy of the *Other Two:* and further, 'Tis a kind of Ringing the changes with Government, the King and Lords shall be uppermost *one day*, the King and *Commons Another*, and the Lords and Commons: For in this Scale of Constitution, whatsoever the *One* will not, the other *Two* may" (1680, 36).

7. Dryden 1956–, 17:223. For the evidence against Dryden's authorship, see Saslow 1977–78.

8. See the account of shifting balances in Polybius's *Historiae* by Trompf 1979, 88.

9. The phrase appears in *Letter* 1681, 6. Relevant, too, are the remarks of Neville [1681] 1969, 87–89. Pocock discusses the emergence of a neo-Harringtonian version of the constitution in the years 1675–81 (1971, 115–32).

10. Skinner 1978, xii–xiii. I draw the language and argument of this paragraph from Skinner's discussion of the connection between "ideology and political action."

11. The phrasing comes from Barrow: "When bloody oppressors have blood given them to drink, and come to welter in their own gore; . . . when treacherous men by their own confidents, or by themselves, are betrayed . . . by such occurences the finger of God doth point out and indicate itself" (1859, 1:468).

12. Barrow 1859, 1:465–71. A similar description of providential design in the preservation of governments, with reference to the rebellion of Absalom, appears in Pindar 1679, 8.

13. Parker 1661, 14. See also Long 1683.

Works Cited

Barrow, Isaac. 1859. *The Theological Works*. Ed. Alexander Napier. 9 vols. Cambridge: Cambridge University Press.

Brydall, John. 1681. *The Absurdity of that New Devised State Principle*. London.

Collinges, John. 1678. *Several Discourses Concerning the Actual Providence of God*. London.

Dryden, John. 1956–. *The Works of John Dryden*. Gen. ed. H. T. Swedenberg, Jr. 20 vols. Berkeley and Los Angeles: University of California Press.

Edie, Carolyn Adervort. 1964–65. "Succession and Monarchy: The Controversy of 1679–1681." *The American Historical Review* 70:350–70.

England's Concern in the Case of . . . James Duke of York. [1681] 1812. Vol. 8 of *The Somers Collection of Tracts*, ed. Walter Scott. London.

Ferne, Henry. 1643. *Conscience Satisfied that there is No Warrent for Armes Now Taken up by Subjects*. Oxford.

Griffin, Dustin. 1978. "Dryden's Charles: The Ending of *Absalom and Achitophel*." *Philological Quarterly* 57:359–82.

Guilhamet, Leon. 1969. "Dryden's Debasement of Scripture in *Absalom and Achitophel*." *Studies in English Literature* 9:395–413.

Hoffman, Arthur. 1962. *John Dryden's Imagery*. Gainesville: University of Florida Press.

Hunt, Thomas. 1680. *The Great and Weighty Considerations, Relating to the Duke of York, or, Succession of the Crown*. London.

Hunton, Philip. 1644. *A Vindication of the Treatise of Monarchy, Containing an Answer to Dr. Ferne's Reply*. London.

Johnson, Samuel. 1925. *Lives of the Poets*. 2 vols. Reprint. London: J. M. Dent.

Judson, Margaret Atwood. 1949. *The Crisis of the Constitution*. New Brunswick, N.J.: Rutgers University Press.

Kermode, Frank. 1967. *The Sense of an Ending: Studies in the Theory of Fiction*. New York: Oxford University Press.

Kernan, Alvin. 1965. *The Plot of Satire*. New Haven: Yale University Press.

A Letter from a Person of Quality to his Friend Concerning His Majesties Late Declaration. 1681. n.p.

L'Estrange, Roger. 1680. *Citt and Bumpkin*. London.

Long, Thomas. 1683. *King David's Danger and Deliverance; or, The Conspiracy of Absalom and Achitophel*. London.

Lord, George De F. 1972. "*Absalom and Achitophel* and Dryden's Political Cosmos." In *John Dryden*, ed. Earl Miner, 156–90. Athens: Ohio University Press.

McKeon, Michael. 1987. "Historicizing *Absalom and Achitophel*." In *The New Eighteenth Century*, ed. Felicity Nussbaum and Laura Brown, 23–40. New York and London: Methuen.

Neville, Henry. [1681] 1969. *Plato Redivivus or, A Dialogue Concerning His Majesties late Declaration*. Reprinted in *Two English Republican Tracts*, ed. Caroline Robbins. Cambridge: Cambridge University Press.

Parker, John. 1661. *A Sermon Presented . . . [on] the Anniversary of His Majesty King Charles the Second, his most Memorable and Happy Restoration*. London.

Pindar, William. 1679. *A Sermon of Divine Providence, In the Special Preservation of Governments and Kingdoms*. London.

Pocock, John. 1971. *Politics, Language and Time*. New York: Atheneum.

———, ed. 1977. *The Political Works of James Harrington*. Cambridge: Cambridge University Press.

Poulet, Georges. 1956. *Studies in Human Time*. Trans. Elliott Coleman. Baltimore: The Johns Hopkins University Press.

Saslow, Edward L. 1977–78. "Dryden as Historiographer Royal and the Authorship of *His Majesties Declaration Defended*." *Modern Philology* 75:261–72.

Sheringham, Robert. 1682. *The King's Supremacy Asserted*. 3d ed. London.

Skinner, Quentin. 1978. *The Foundations of Modern Political Thought*. Vol. 1, *The Renaissance*. Cambridge: Cambridge University Press.

Smith, John. 1969. "Time, Times, and the 'Right Time': *Chronus* and *Kairos*." *The Monist* 53:1–13.

The Stuart Constitution. 1966. Ed. J. P. Kenyon. Cambridge: Cambridge University Press.

Trompf, G. W. 1979. *The Idea of Historical Recurrence in Western Thought*. Berkeley and Los Angeles: University of California Press.

Weston, Corinne Comstock. 1965. *English Constitutional Theory and the House of Lords 1550–1832*. New York: Columbia University Press.

———. 1970. "Concepts of Estates in Stuart Political Thought." In *Representative Institutions in Theory and Practice*, vol. 39 of *Studies Presented to the Inter-national Commission for the History of Representative Parliamentary Institutions*, 87–130. Brussels: n. p.

Zwicker, Steven N. 1984. *Politics and Language in Dryden's Poetry: The Arts of Disguise*. Princeton: Princeton University Press.

Alexander Pope, 1688–1988
Salute to a Three-Hundredth Birthday
MAYNARD MACK

To judge from the record to date, the eighty-eighth year of a century has proved to be auspicious for the generation of poets. Eighteen eighty-eight gave us T. S. Eliot, not to mention Eugene O'Neill and John Crowe Ransom. Seventeen eighty-eight gave us Byron. And sixteen eighty-eight Pope.

My concern in this paper happens to be with Pope, whose three-hundredth birthday fell on the twenty-first of May, nineteen eighty-eight. Yet there is a general appropriateness, at least for those of us who profess literature, in honoring the anniversaries of all great writers, no matter the year. Such occasions have virtues, it seems to me. They remind us, reassuringly, of the common humanity we share with the great, since we too at least have birthdays. They prompt us to reconsider, perhaps even rediscover, the works that have given the world so much nourishment and (here I fall back on a word no longer, alas, very often associated with literature) joy. And, further, very usefully just now when the cry of post-modernism is all on our helpless entrapment in semiotic systems and on how, in Heidegger's words, "language writes, not the man," these anniversaries with their insistence on the exact opposite of that proposition restore us from metaphysics to sense, like Dr. Johnson when he kicked that stone.

A more specific appropriateness of this commemorative occasion is peculiarly American. For us in the United States, having completed in 1987 a year of homage to the Constitution, there is a particular relevance in remembering Pope. Almost to a man, the signers of that Constitution grew up in a world his poetry dominated. Some of his sentiments and his ways of phrasing them sang in their bones:

> Till jarring int'rests of themselves create
> Th' according music of a well-mixt State.

> Stuck o'er with titles or hung round with strings,
> That thou may'st be by kings, or whores of kings.

Worth makes the man, and want of it, the fellow;
The rest is all but leather and prunella.

One self-approving hour whole years outweighs
Of stupid starers, and of loud huzzas.

An honest Man's the noblest work of God.

Sentiments like these, together with the ridicule Pope everywhere showers on kings, court servilities, and retrograde bishops and peers, made him an exemplary figure for a young republic striving to make impossible on this side of the Atlantic the monarchy, state church, and hereditary patrician class it had gone to war to be free of. Pope's works (including his Homer, from which Jefferson quotes seventeen times in one early journal alone) could be had in American bookstores from the mid-1730s on. Between 1750 and 1850 the *Essay on Man* was pirated by American publishers more than 150 times, mostly in small New England towns. But Pope's readers were not confined to New England or to the affluent and established. Out close to the frontier in Indiana, Calvin Fletcher, later to be a prominent lawyer in that state, having had to give up school to earn a living, always carried a copy of Pope in his pocket to continue, as he said, his education. And at about the same time, in newly settled Ohio, young Alice Cary battled the then-usual parental obstructions to the education of women. Obliged to scrub, sweep, milk cows, and wash dishes all day, denied even a candle at night, she read and reread the *Essay on Man* along with a few other books "by the light of a saucer of lard with rag wick" (Sibley 1949, 21).

1

It is reported of Plato that in a dream he saw himself as a flying swan while beneath him dozens of archers took aim and tried to shoot him down. I am reminded of this story on Pope's tercentenary because he was thought in his time to be one of the swans of Thames in the succession that proceeds from Chaucer and because in the three centuries since 1688 so many archers have tried to shoot him down. So far he has managed to weather his demotion to the second order of poets by Joseph Warton, the aspersions cast on his character in Johnson's life, many of them unfounded, the dismissal of his poetry as prose by Matthew Arnold, and the frontal assault on his poetry and character alike by the Reverend Whitwell Elwin in the great Elwin-

Courthope edition that held the field when I was young. During the
past three decades or so, he has even weathered the attentions of
(some think) a demented Yale professor, whose name just now escapes
me.

Further fluctuations are doubtless in store. Pope's considerable
investment of poetic energy in authors largely unread today outside
the academy—Homer, Virgil, Horace, Ovid, and the rest—increasingly places one part of his achievement, as with Milton, beyond
the reach of all but a faithful few. Likewise, what I suppose modern
pundits would call his intertextuality—the continuous appropriation
and recreation in his work, again as with Milton, of the entire literary
past, joining the voices of many predecessors in a thrilling unison with
his own or sometimes in a calculated dissonance—becomes difficult to
appreciate when the sources of those voices, no longer present in
readers' minds as whole works, are withering to editorial footnotes. To
place Pope's pen, for instance ("What? arm'd for *Virtue* when I point
the Pen"), in his own imaginative scheme of things, one must recognize its connection with the sword of the knight and the spear of the
epic warrior, whose moral functions in society the poet has now
assumed. (Some may recall the picture of Pope by Michael Dahl in
which he holds his quill as if it were indeed a weapon). To place that
pen in its broadest perspective, however, one not available to Pope
himself, we must reach not only back in time to other virtuous
weapons like Excalibur, Durandal, and the many swords of Beowulf,
but forward. Forward to Blake's unsleeping sword as he, too, seeks to
build Jerusalem "in England's green and pleasant land." Forward to
Shelley's "sword of lightning ever unsheathed," the name he gives to
poetry in his *Defence of Poetry*. And forward in our own day to Yeats's
"all-destroying sword-blade Still carried by the wandering fool."

All this presupposes a kind of reading that the present populist drift
in world culture hardly encourages. Nor does it much encourage
placing a high value on some of Pope's principal strengths, such as wit
and the compressions of language that make for wit. Even in light
verse, John Updike has lately reminded us, wit died at about the same
time as Fred Astaire's dancing down a staircase in white tie and tails
ceased to be a representative image of every young man's dream. So
far indeed has urban sprawl now reached Helicon that some of our
1980s poets, having jettisoned meter, rhyme, rhythm, simile, metaphor, and whatever else might smack of artifice in order to approxi-
mate the idiom of the man in the street, are having to confront the
uncomfortable circumstance that the man actually in the street these
days is not (to quote from another recent commentator on the American scene) your Wordsworthian shepherd with "a rich vein of un-

tutored poetry" in his speech but a linguistic cripple who sounds like someone "auditioning for . . . a Lite Beer commercial" (Leithauser 1987, 27).

It could be, of course, that minimalism has outlived its usefulness— like Dada. One notes with interest that a British novelist of some stature has recently insisted that "art is rare and sacred and hard work. . . . If you want to be considered a poet, you will have to show mastery of the Petrarchan sonnet form or the sestina. Your musical efforts must begin with well-formed fugues. There is no substitute for craft" (Burgess 1986, 101). And on our side of the water, even Sunday reviewers have taken to quoting Goethe's sentiment that it is the restraints an artist consents to that show his mastery. Such outbreaks of sanity, coupled with the fact that barbers (at least in my university town) are prosperous once more and its undergraduates are taking lessons in ballroom dancing, could just possibly signify that the times they are "agin a-changin'." But whether this is true or not, I retain a certain confidence that Pope is a survivor and stands a reasonable chance of being saluted on his four-hundredth birthday by the same small but loyal audience as will continue to honor the anniversaries of the greater English and American poets generally: an audience responsive both to historical accomplishments and to the active pleasures that great poetry can bring.

2

To look at Pope's accomplishments in the chronicle of literary history is to be astonished by their variety and extent. Some of course are too complex to be canvassed in so circumscribed an essay as this. One thinks, for instance, of his involvement, especially in the *Essay on Man*, with that process of redefining human nature which is always taking place, but took place spectacularly between Calvin and Hobbes, on the one hand, and Rousseau and Adam Smith, on the other—a redefinition without which neither modern capitalism nor modern democratic government is easily imagined.

One thinks, also, of the influential part he played in the transition from a political culture focused on "right" to one focused on civic virtue. As an astute observer of this period has pointed out, after 1688 the central question in British political theory was no longer "whether a ruler might be resisted for misconduct"—a question of right—but whether a regime founded like Sir Robert Walpole's on government patronage (not to say bribery), public debt, and professionalization of the armed forces "did not corrupt both governors and governed"—a question of virtue. Hence the political thought of the period "moves decisively, though never entirely, out of the law-centered paradigm into the paradigm of virtue and corruption" (Pocock 1985, 48). The relevance of this shift to Pope's chosen persona in the poems of the 1730s and to the motto he adopted for his life at Twickenham ("To Virtue, only, and her Friends, a Friend") needs no comment.

But such matters, as I have said, lie well beyond the bounds of a single essay. Let me turn at once, then, to some of Pope's more manageable achievements, of which one surely is the sheer variety of experience he manages to encompass.

Only the greater poets, I think, combine the kind of power represented by a line like "the green myriads in the peopled grass" with the very different kind represented in "To err is human, to forgive divine." And only if they are very gifted indeed do they combine either of those powers with the power to evoke a scene, a mood, or an inward landscape with one twitch of the wand. It is when we place Pope's rendering of his Eloisa's defiant admission of her sexual past ("I have not yet forgot myself to stone") beside his rendering of a very young girl's shyness in the presence of unformed longings she does not wish to name ("Or o'er cold coffee trifle with the spoon") and both of these beside one of the most spirited openings in English poetry ("Shut, shut the door, good John, fatigu'd I said") that we understand what Johnson meant by his emphasis on the adventurousness of Pope's mind—"in its widest searches still longing to go forward, in its highest flights wishing to be higher, always imagining something greater than it knows" (1903, 3:217). As a modest case in point, one may remark that in this very opening Pope has taken up the caveat posed by his admired Dryden—who held that the heroic couplet was not suited to describing homely actions like calling a servant or shutting a door—and has blown it quite out of the sky (Tasch 1986, 499–500).

The appearance in that same line of "good John," Pope's gardener and general factotum, John Searle, points to a further reason why Pope's place in the history of English poetry seems likely to remain secure. I have in mind the degree of close-up intimacy that his chosen manner of being present in his poems encourages us to feel. We hear, for instance, of his father and mother, his dogs, a neighbor's dog, his Binfield boyhood. We learn something of his diet, of the kitchen garden where he grows broccoli, grapes, and figs, cherishes a walnut tree, and keeps chickens; and of course we find allusions to the Thames, on which his property fronted, as well as to the famous gardens that lay behind his house and the grotto through which one reached them. Of his person he tells us that he had one shoulder higher than the other, a nose too long, but a lively eye; of his costume, that his coat and breeches did not always match, nor were his white gloves and neck linen invariably spotless. Of his personal habits we discover, among many other small details, that he took snuff, said grace at meals, and, since he slept poorly, dozed off in company.

To be sure, this is a posed portrait like the many portraits he sat for to his painter friends. Yet for all its artifice, the figure impressively resembles the historical A. Pope, is deficient largely by what it leaves out, and—this is the point I wish to stress—marks a significant moment in English poetry. If one combines these biographical details with the larger questions Pope raises throughout his work concerning the rules and graces of his art, the events and deprivations that made him seek his fortune in poetry, the uncertainties he expresses, not always in complete jest, about the sources of his inspiration—is it an itch, a nervous tic, a disease, a madness (for Pope, Bedlam and Parnassus are never very far apart), a lust for fame, a gift from heaven?—if one combines these strands, it becomes very clear that his way of presenting himself is a landmark in a continuity of poetic self-presentations that stretches in one direction from Milton's austere bard (communing in his nightly vigils only with Urania) toward the introspections of Wordsworth's *Prelude*, and, in another direction, toward the demystified casual poet of our own day who lets us make what we can of his confession that *his* garden is an avocado seed in a glass of water.

3

Other innovations that deserve attention in any birthday appraisal of Pope's work are his concern for women and his victory over the patronage system. His attitudes toward women are not altogether, of course, what either a 1980s woman or a 1980s man, including especially myself, would choose; though it is easy to exaggerate his failings and easier still, as in all our dealings with the past, to preen and pirouette on the graves of those who cannot rise to defend themselves. Were they in fact to do so—and occasionally as I riffle through our trade journals or read self-confident papers such as the one I am even now presenting, I find myself wondering how much longer they will refrain—what an Armageddon might we see! what an embarrassing garage sale of second-hand mortarboards! and what silvery laughter would drift down from Parnassus!

My object, however, is not to justify Pope's treatment of women, but simply to note that in his poems women are for the first time accorded attention in contexts that, whether sympathetic, unsympathetic, or something of both, relate to the real lives of real women in his time. We hear, for instance, of the charities of his mother to the poor in the *Essay on Man,* of her old age and invalidism in the *Epistle to Arbuthnot.* We hear of his close friend Martha Blount, at length and teasingly in the epistle addressed to her, briefly and with passion in the verses sent to her on her birthday, for which the now-famous lines on how the world of amorous conquests rewards its veterans were first composed: "A Fop their Passion, but their Prize a Sot; Alive, ridiculous, and dead, forgot!"

We hear, too, of the actress Narcissa, incongruously dressing herself up on her deathbed to look pretty in the grave: "One would not, sure, be frightful when one's dead—And Betty give this Cheek a little Red." Yet under the satire, as so often with Pope, runs a complex undertone. It does indeed have some of the feelings in Hamlet's address to the skull of Yorick ("Now get you to my lady's chamber and tell her, let her paint an inch thick, to this favor she must come"); but it has, too, some of the very different feelings in Cleopatra's last address to her women: "Give me my robe, put on my crown, I have Immortal longings in me."

Likewise not to be overlooked is the strength of character Pope asks us to admire in the heroine of his "Elegy to the Memory of an Unfortunate Lady." Though her preference of suicide to a forced marriage belongs partly to romance, as with Shakespeare's Juliet, Pope's placing of the incident in a clearly contemporary frame allies it with the body of opinion that was beginning to be revolted by the merchandising of daughters and female wards. His early poem on this matter, addressed to Teresa Blount, Martha's sister, at a moment when very possibly marriage negotiations affecting her were underway, is hardly to be matched in English for its clear-eyed statement of the dilemma any well-placed nubile female then faced. Before marriage, she was bound by all the traditional constraints designed to bring her still a virgin to the altar. After marriage, freed of these "petty Tyrants," as Pope calls them, she had every chance of finding a greater one in the husband whose chattel she had now become: "Still in Constraint your suff'ring Sex remains."

The line just quoted introduces a thumbnail sketch of a young woman named Pamela (accented Pamèla by Pope, who uses the older pronunciation), who has allowed herself to be dazzled into an opulent marriage by "shining Robes, rich Jewels, Beds of State, And to compleat her Bliss a Fool for Mate"—and is now repenting at leisure: "A vain, unquiet, glitt'ring, wretched Thing." As that last word quietly announces, the logic of materialism rarely fails. She has become what she coveted, a "Thing" among the "things" she sold her body for, another trinket in her husband's collection. And, if "Thing" retains here any of the genital sense in which Pope uses it in his modernization of the *Wife of Bath's Prologue*, her new status is doubly degrading.

Of Pope's two best-known poems about women, the *Rape of the Lock* and *Eloisa to Abelard*, let me say only that their very different heroines dramatize complexities of feminine feeling that had never, apart from the stage, been so openly addressed in English poetry before. In the *Rape*, as many have observed, all encounters between men and women become charged with sexual electricity, and all hint at what could be and usually were the physical and psychological transformations imposed on women by the married state. *Hint*, to be sure, has to remain the operative word. No actual rape occurs; no marriage has been arranged; the Baron, as the poem promised from the start, has been "rejected" and is now "dejected"; and of the heroine's possible connubial future, no word is forthcoming. Even so, it is hard to believe that a narrative that begins with a young woman's awakening, takes her from boudoir and billets-doux into the grown-up world of marriage market and sexual game-playing, and looks ahead at its close to death in an absolute sense that throws the sexual sense of dying into its proper perspective—it is hard to believe that such a narrative offers no clue to the poem's intentions. However much the matronly Clarissa may be undercut by Pope, she seems to me to touch the heart of the matter when in a speech considerably tinged with resignation she advises putting the best face possible on the married woman's lot because the spinsterhood alternative under eighteenth-century conditions was likely to be worse:

> But since, alas! frail Beauty must decay,
> Curl'd or uncurl'd, since Locks will turn to grey,
> Since painted, or not painted, all shall fade,
> And she who scorns a Man, must die a Maid;
> What then remains, but well our Pow'r to use,
> And keep good Humour still whate'er we lose.

I call attention to her final word.

Pope's Eloisa, by contrast, is a woman who has already known sexual passion and in whom that passion revives with increasing boldness as the excitement kindled by Abelard's letter courses through her body as well as her mind. It would be difficult, I think, to find any English poem earlier than Pope's time, not excluding the *Wife of Bath's Prologue*, so frank in dismissing the Petrarchan convention that nice women know nothing of such passion and would never, never entertain erotic images as explicit as those that flood

Eloisa's consciousness as she recapitulates their tragic past and the brutal mutilations of Abelard by her uncle's agents, which forced them into a convent life:

> Cut from the root my perish'd joys I see,
> And love's warm tyde for ever stopt in thee.

My object, let me say again, is not to claim that Pope writes either well or badly about women or to inquire from what personal experiences or impulsions his attitudes may spring. I wish simply to register that he is something of a pioneer in this matter, as he is also in self-presentation.

4

In a famous—some would say infamous—review of a new edition of Boswell's *Life of Johnson,* Macaulay named with envious gusto the men of letters and learning who were benefiting from one or other device of government patronage during the years shortly before Johnson came on the scene. "Never," he remarks, were the rewards of literary merit "so splendid."

> Congreve . . . was rewarded for his first comedy with places which made him independent for life. . . . Rowe was not only Poet-Laureate, but also land-surveyor of the customs in the port of London, clerk of the council to the Prince of Wales, and secretary of the Presentations to the Lord Chancellor. . . . Locke was Commissioner of Appeals and of the Board of Trade. Newton was Master of the Mint. . . . Steele was a commissioner of stamps and a member of Parliament. . . . Addison was secretary of state. (Macauley 1903, 1:372–73)

It is against this picture that Pope's encounter with the patronage system and the book publishers must be seen. He was born into a literary establishment that still cherished the Renaissance myth of the courtly- or gentleman-poet for whom writing is one of the adornments of the well-rounded life, a pastime to be indulged whenever one is not better occupied with service to the church or the crown. It was a myth with very long roots—even the early Roman poet Ennius liked to claim he wrote poetry only when he had the gout—and some of its characteristic values stayed with Pope to his dying day. The ideal of the grace beyond the reach of art, for instance, which has its origins in the courtier's *sprezzatura,* and his unfailing stress on "ease" in writing, which springs from the same origins and is revealingly associated in his mind, as it was in the courtier's, with a corresponding physical agility such as he could never hope for from his own twisted carcass:

> True Ease in Writing comes from Art, not Chance,
> As those move easiest who have learn'd to dance.

Pope's poetical career begins, in fact, with a manuscript containing his four "Pastorals," written out in the most beautiful printing hand ever commanded by a writer, which was then passed around among a circle of gentlemen and noblemen in much the same way as were, in their own time, the poems of Sidney or Donne. When he comes before the world more maturely in the preface of his collected *Works* of 1717, his conformity with Renaissance courtly conventions remains: "I writ because it amused me; I corrected because it was as pleasant to me to correct as to write; and I publish'd because I was told I might please such as it was a credit to please." No mention of filthy lucre *here*. Never during his lifetime does Pope entirely give over his habit of referring, not altogether jocularly, to his poetry as "this idle trade," "The rhymes and rattles of the Man or Boy," "Songs for Fools to get by heart," and so on.

On the other hand, as every reader of his poems knows, expressions precisely the reverse of these recur regularly and reflect more accurately his settled views. Vanity and ambition, the expectations of the surrounding culture, the fact that he was in truth a merchant's son, no gentleman by birth, and possibly as well some occasional genuine misgivings about the efficacy of his calling might prompt him to assume the courtly poet's postures of nonchalance. Nothing, however, ever dampened his zeal to be a poet not in the Castiglione manner but in the great tradition coming down from Virgil and Milton, and behind that from the Hebrew prophets—one of that line of seers whom Wordsworth would later describe as "each with each connected in a mighty scheme of truth," and to whom Joyce in a famous flourish assigns the task of forging in the smithy of their souls the uncreated conscience of their race. With something of that same sense of poetry's high destiny, Pope rejected from the start the galling dependencies imposed on authorial freedom by the older forms of patronage. Far better risk its newer forms, tersely summarized by the third Earl of Shaftesbury in the very next year after Pope's *Pastorals* found their way to print. "In our Days," said Shaftesbury, *"the Audience* makes *the Poet;* and *the Bookseller the Author"* (Shaftesbury [1711] 1732, 1:264).

The only good thing about that formula, Pope seems to have understood at once, was that it could be turned upside down. Let the poet create the audience, and the author make the bookseller. By 1714, aged twenty-six, he had come close to accomplishing both. He had pleased the classically educated with the intricate music of his *Pastorals* and the appropriation of Roman themes and Roman patriotism to the British scene. With his *Essay on Criticism* he had astonished the pundits of the coffeehouses while incidentally making the case for a literary criticism less ideological and more humane—an achievement that has impelled some in our own time to exclaim: "Pope! thou shouldst be living at this hour." *Windsor Forest*, his next major publication, used the coming Peace of Utrecht to shape for his readers, Tory and Whig alike, a vision of England as it might become in a world freed of wars and colonial exploitation. The climax in this process of audience formation—a process surely more stumbled on than planned—was, of course, the *Rape of the Lock*. This attracted all parties, women as well as men, sold three thousand copies in four days, three thousand more within a few months, and appealed (if we may believe Gay) even to seamstresses, who stood at bookstalls and read it standing up.

With this success as leverage, Pope persuaded the ambitious publisher Bernard Lintot to buy the rights to his proposed six-volume translation of Homer's *Iliad* on terms never before approached. The translator was to receive an outright fee of two hundred guineas for each volume. Far more important, he was to be given gratis by the publisher an edition of 750 copies of each in the fashionable quarto size. These copies, entirely at his own disposal, would be available to subscribers at a guinea a volume, making a hypothetical total just short of five-thousand pounds—always provided, of course, that he could attract that many subscribers for a handsome but admittedly expensive book. In this way, for the subscribers' quarto, Pope became his own publisher, hiring Lintot in return for the copyright to serve him as agent. With the help of friends and the obvious quality of the book both poetically and bibliographically, he produced the necessary subscriptions and made a killing. So did Lintot. The author *had* made the publisher, and both had reason to be gratified.

In later years, Pope extended his innovations. He set up publishers and even printers with grants of money. He brought authors to them and gave them exclusive rights to some of his own pieces, but always for limited periods and in return for what amounted to royalty concessions. How much money he made from his poems throughout his lifetime it is impossible at this late date to say. Substantial sums, obviously, since he was able to lease a villa on the Thames, live and entertain there comfortably, and give away annually (Swift tells us) sums that would have allowed him to keep a coach had he abandoned his charities. Small wonder that he was hated by many of the dunces long before the *Dunciad* was written. *They* remained where Shaftesbury had predicted they would: in hock to the booksellers and sometimes so literally in hock as to be kept like prostitutes in a brothel, paid only when they performed and stingily at that. How could they not hate a little hunchbacked Roman Catholic who had broken the bank at Monte Carlo?

The truth that emerges from these facts is simple. In this department as elsewhere Pope was a pioneer. One may still, if one chooses, take Johnson's proud letter to Lord Chesterfield on 7 January 1755 as the symbolic moment of defeat for the old forms of patronage, provided one understands that the actual moment came forty years earlier with Pope's contract for the *Iliad*. So, too, if it amuses, one may consider the famous interview between Johnson and George III in the King's Library in February 1767 to be a great symbolic enactment of the transfer of moral power from the throne to the pen; but only, again, if one understands that this transaction was more tellingly enacted thirty years before in Pope's epistle to George II.

5

Much else survives in the historical record to keep Pope's reputation green. But it is time for the other half of my topic: the pleasures to be found in the poetry itself. Readers will appreciate, I hope, that what follows is of necessity personal (since what one finds in poems is always, in part, though only in part, what one brings to them), and will consider themselves warned by the association of poetry with pleasure that the views about to be aired are considerably archaic. Speaking then only for myself, and in the dodaic idiom that elderly dodos are prone to use: what pleasures *does* Pope's poetry offer?

Some small effects first, I would suggest. Effects that call no attention to themselves, yet are so ideally "right" that they send tremors up the spine. (My spine, at least; though I am told it could be osteoporosis.) I think, for instance, of the word "inherit" in the line from the *Essay on Man*: "Each home-felt joy that life inherits here." Appearing in a context that stresses the mutual wants and weaknesses that help bind humanity together, how appropriately it reminds one of one's unpayable debts to those who have gone before. First, to one's home, where "home-felt" joys are presumably first experienced; but next to one's forebears and their forebears and all those dying generations who by their art or craft or ingenuity or decency or love have endowed one's "world-home," one's "here" (as Pope's line puts it), with their gifts. This sense of commutuality, of the interdependence of nations, generations, social classes, the dead and the living, and even animals and human beings, runs deep in Pope and is one of the more distinctive characteristics of his mind. As he puts it in another place, "the strength" one "gains" is from "the embrace" one "gives." Whether one speaks of predecessors, neighbors, friends, lovers, books, or simply of understanding poems, it is a thought worth meditating on—and, I would add, worth inheriting.

Or again, I think of the line in the same poem that Pope uses to describe the so-called Golden Age, or state of nature, when "Man walk'd with beast joint tenant of the shade." "Shade," of course, indicates a time when the earth was primeval forest, but the more arresting term, obviously, is "joint tenant." The application of a legal concept hammered out through centuries of litigation over the trans-mission of landed property to a state of nature that knew no property is plainly designed to provoke a smile. Yet before the smile has faded, one realizes that the incongruity carries a cutting edge. For the operative fact about a "joint tenancy" is that the property in ques-tion—in this case, the earth itself—devolves on an ultimate survivor only when all others sharing the joint-tenancy have died. Under his little joke, in short, Pope, who was well read in law and had extremely strong feelings about animals, has planted a comment on the rights of other species that we in the late-twentieth century are even better situated to appreciate than he.

These of course are trifles. Their interest lies in the fact that they are also samples, routine samples, of hundreds, even thousands of triumphant small exactitudes and minute surprises that make Pope's poetry, taken line by line, continuously gratifying. Even if judged by Emerson's standard that "Every poem should be made up of lines that are poems" (1909–14, 7:523) Pope's work scores high. What seems to me particularly pleasing, however, is that his poetry is as comprehen-sive overall as it is scrupulous in the individual detail. To rove at random through the six stout volumes of his original poems is to go on a formidable tour of early-eighteenth-century England in all its color-ful variety. Topographical specifics abound: "Lincoln Fen," "fat E'sham," "Saperton's fair Dale." Augustan London sprawls in a hun-dred named localities from "Bloomsb'ry Square" and "Hyde-Park-Corner" to Temple Bar and the Royal Exchange, not forgetting the then-surrounding villages: Tottenham, Tooting, Deptford, Earls Court, Woolwich, Wapping. From Pope's dietary allusions alone, one could make up a week of eighteenth-century menus. On the flesh and fowl side: mutton, beef, ham, chicken, guinea hen, peacock, lark, pigeon, woodcock, hare, and rabbit; on the fish and shellfish side:

salmon, gudgeons, flounders, crawfish, and oysters (not to mention the perch, eel, carp, trout, and pike for which in *Windsor-Forest* the "patient Fisher" casts his line); plus cabbage, broccoli, turnips, beets, and lettuce in the way of vegetables, and strawberries and custard for desserts.

Yet more expressive, perhaps, in bringing the very age and body of the time before us are the glancing references that exhibit the people of the day in their normal routines, habits, mind-sets, idioms. One thinks of the East End clerk, precursor of Dickens's Bob Cratchit, "whose quills stand quiver'd at his ear," a moment not easy to forget. One listens to the current bits of slang and patois—as to have one's bribe from the government "rug," meaning "secret and secure"; or, to take one's "chirping," meaning one's "cheering" pint; or, to win one's way to a married woman's bedroom with "*Two* or *Three* Squeezes, and *Two* or *Three* Towzes" (the latter used as a noun by Pope some eighty-odd years earlier than its first *OED* citation), which "Can never fail Cuckolding *Two* or *Three* Spouses." One hears also of contemporary hostility to turnpike tolls and standing armies, of plans to build the new bridge across the Thames that will later become the subject of one of Wordsworth's finest sonnets, of embezzlements by the rich from the Charitable Corporation (primitive version of our Department of Welfare). One meets with the comfortable delusion of self-made men—no less in our time than in Pope's—that poverty is a mark of God's disfavor: "God cannot love" (says Blunt, with tearless eyes) "The wretch he starves." And of course, since it is one of Pope's major concerns in the later poems, one hears a great deal about the world of adolescent capitalism, with its national debt, interest rates, bankbills and bankrupts, paper currency, subscriptions, stocks, market manipulations, and suchlike—without, however, ever losing track of such ephemera of the common life as the new habit of "japanning," which is to say, of putting shoeblack on one's shoes. Few poetries bring an entire age so sharply into focus as that of Alexander Pope.

6

I single out in closing two features of Pope's poetry that, for me at least, never fail to supply what Johnson calls in his own estimate of that poetry "overpowering pleasure."

First off, there is the all-but-inexhaustible versatility of his command of sound and movement. Though not all readers seem aware of this, Pope is one of the must musical of poets. In his earliest work, predictably, the effects are sometimes broad, notoriously so in the

couplets of the *Essay on Criticism* exemplifying his simplistic youthful
"rule" that the sound of a verse "must seem an Eccho to the Sense."

> When *Ajax* strives, some Rock's vast Weight to throw,
> The Line too *labours*, and the Words move *slow;*
> Not so, when Swift *Camilla* scours the Plain,
> Flies o'er th' unbending Corn, and skims along the Main.

As he matures, however, he applies this principle in subtler and
subtler ways—in fact, to the vanishing point. Here, for instance, is his
rendering of the fairies' dance in "January and May" (1709), miming
the movement of dainty feet by the placement of dentals and metrical
speed:

> So featly tripp'd the light-foot Ladies round,
> The Knights so nimbly o'er the Greensword bound,
> That scarce they bent the Flow'rs, or touch'd the Ground.

Enchanting, but one-dimensional. Here for contrast is his evocation
eight years later (1717) of Eloisa's rebellious consciousness after
Abelard's letter has stirred her blood:

> Relentless walls! whose darksom round contains
> Repentant sighs, and voluntary pains:
> Ye rugged rocks! which holy knees have worn;
> Ye grots and caverns shagg'd with horrid thorn!
> Shrines! where their vigils pale-ey'd virgins keep,
> And pitying saints, whose statues learn to weep!
> Tho' cold like you, unmov'd, and silent grown,
> I have not yet forgot myself to stone.

Sound participates here, to be sure. The suggestive linking of the
initial words of the first two lines alerts us to the support that hard
consonants and short vowels are giving to sense in "rugged rocks,"
"grots," and "shagg'd," and the two effects together throw into high
relief the astonishing incidence of plaintive *m* and *n* sounds (some
twenty-six in eight lines), which tie the passage together and set its
tone. Yet the decisive agents here are surely syntax and pacing. Pope
has made them flexible enough to accommodate, in the first six lines,
the recoil of sensible warm flesh from contacts that in the glow of
rekindled passion have become confining, harsh, unyielding, cold,
lifeless, and, in the last two lines, the recovery of that same flesh as it
clenches to the controlled defiance registered in the steady iambic
beat. Some poeticisms linger in "darksom" and the Renaissance con-

ceit about weeping statues, but we have plainly come a long way from "Eccho."

In the later poetry, the musical dimension is further absorbed. Now it largely serves as obbligato or continuo to a consensus of effects, its role readily visible in the five characteristic samples (see p. 114). To clarify some of the relationships from which Pope builds his phonic structures, I have indicated internal rhyme by R (with a number intended to facilitate location of the matching sound); partial or off-rhyme by R in round brackets (again with number); repetition, itself a form of rhyme, by Re (with number); and significant recurrence of consonantal sounds by C (likewise with number). Alliteration as such, and assonance, both often extremely subtle in Pope, I have left unindicated for fear of making the illustrations tediously confusing.

This is Pope's norm, formed with the sensitivity to sound crudely illustrated in the samples and with an equal sensitivity to sound in interaction with rhythm that can never be illustrated, only heard. From this norm he occasionally departs to add a phonic wit to verbal, as in the emphatically feminine rhyme and rapidly shifting recombinations of the letter *c* found in this couplet from his *Epistle to a Lady* (1735), both devices humorously simulating the mobility that the poet affects to be unable to describe:

> Chuse a firm Cloud, before it fall, and in it
> Catch, ere she change, the *Cynthia* of this minute.

Or again, as in this more complex couplet from his first Horatian imitation, where he resists the suggestion of his Whiggish friend, Fortescue, that he devote his poems to praise of George II and the royal family:

> Alas! few Verses touch their nicer Ear;
> They scarce can bear their Laureate twice a Year.

It is difficult to imagine a more intricate arrangement of consonance, assonance, alliteration, and internal rhyme than this, consciously overdone (one presumes) in parody of the court's alleged preference for surface over substance. Yet the musical aspects are so diffused into the ironic thrusts at royal taste and Cibber's selection to be laureate as well as in the general derisive tone climaxing in an almost-grinning triple rhyme that considerable conscious effort is required to sort them out.

In the final *Dunciad* (1743), where the sonorities of the early work are oftener allowed to surface that in the poems of the Thirties, the

C^1 $\quad$ R^1Re^1 $\quad$ R^1Re^2 $\quad$ C^1 $\quad$ Re^3
Top-gallant he and she in all her Trim,

R^1Re^1 $\quad$ Re^4 $\quad$ Re^3 $\quad$ R^1Re^2 $\quad$ Re^4 $\quad$ C^1
He boarding her, she striking sail to him.

(<u>The Impertinent</u> 1733, 230-31)

$(R)^1$ $\quad$ R^1 $\quad$ R^2 $\quad$ C^1 $\quad$ C^1 $\quad$ Re^1
Shall burning AEtna, if a sage re quires,

R^2 $\quad$ R^1 $\quad$ Re^1 $\quad$ $(R)^1$ $\quad$ R^1
Forget to thunder, and recall her fires?

(<u>Essay on Man</u>, 1734, 4: 123-24)

R^1 $\quad$ Re^1 $\quad$ Re^4 $\quad$ R^2 $\quad$ Re^3 $\quad$ Re^1
Born to no Pride, inheriting no strife,

R^1 $\quad$ R^2 $\quad$ Re^3 $\quad$ R^1 $\quad$ Re^2 $\quad$ Re^1
Nor marrying Discord in a Noble Wife.

(<u>Epistle to Dr. Arbuthnot</u> 1735, 392-93)

Re^1 $\quad$ R^1 $\quad$ C^1 $\quad$ R^2 $\quad$ C^2 $\quad$ C^2
But thanks to Homer, since I live and thrive

Re^1 $\quad$ R^1 $\quad$ R^2 $\quad$ C^1 $\quad$ C^1
Indebted to no Prince or Peer alive.

(<u>Imit. Hor.</u> 1737, Ep.2.2.68-69)

R^1Re^1 $\quad$ R^1Re^2 $\quad$ R^1Re^2 $\quad$ R^1
Would he oblige me, let me on ly find

R^1Re^1 $\quad$ $(R)^1$ $\quad$ Re^3 $\quad$ R^1Re^2 $\quad$ $(R)^1$ $\quad$ R^1Re^1 $\quad$ Re^3
He does not think me what he thinks mankind.

(<u>One Thousand Seven Hundred and Thirty-
Eight</u> 1738, Dial. I:33-34) marriage of sound to sense of which Pope had given so crude a sketch in his *Essay on Criticism* is wholly consummated. Like the souls of the lovers in Donne's "The Ectasy," they flow together into something "abler" and integral.

> To happy Convents, bosom'd deep in vines,
> Where slumber Abbots, purple as their wines.

> To where the Seine, obsequious as she runs,
> Pours at great Bourbon's feet her silken sons.

e first quotation, the heavy incidence of the labials *b*, *m*, *p* and of the fricatives *s*, *v*, *z* produces a texture of sound that, to my ear, accords superbly with the rich central mix of comic imagery in which whole convents of abbots, the color of ripe grapes and bursting with the juices of good living, slumber after a vinous nursing like infants on the maternal bosom. Yet the precise manner in which the phonic element invades (?), enlarges (?), supports (?), relates to (?) all the other elements remains, I think, impervious to analysis.

So, too, and more so, with the second quotation. Here the image of the Seine conveying to the Sun King's court all the young noblesse of France to make up his gallery of subservient idlers seems to carry within itself a possible further image of some immense baroque bronze or marble depicting the Seine as river-goddess pouring tribute from her urn beneath a figure of Louis XIV enthroned; or, alternatively (an analogy that has always appealed to kings), as the goddess Plenty showering riches from her cornucopia on the lucky land a Bourbon rules. In either case, as Pope's staunchly British rendering insists, the offerings are questionable because they are French silks, not honest English kersey, and because they are also sons, raising the possibility that somewhere here, in the deep background, lurks the idol Moloch (French casualties in Louis's wars had been appalling), whose cult involved child sacrifice and whom Pope perhaps remembers opportunely now from *Paradise Lost*. Some such reading of the passage strikes me as acceptable. The lesson, however, that leaps out at us on listening to it is that it is impracticable, perhaps impossible, to sunder what a great poet at the top of his form has joined.

The foregoing paragraphs do scant justice to one of the great masters of the sounds and rhythms of words. And, yes, their feel and taste, too, as they are shaped on the lips, teeth, tongue, palate and propelled into being by the muscles of mouth and jaw. Like all true poetry, Pope's is composed to be read aloud. Not with the rocking lurch from rhyme to rhyme that one so often hears today from readers

insufficiently attentive, but with a thoughtful alertness to their aural
and kinetic as well as to their semantic powers. So read, they can
sound as exquisitely on the ear—in their own verbal mode, of
course—as Mozart.

7

I come last to the quality in Pope's poetry that seems to me not only
to give delight, but—taken in all its manifestations—differentiates his
work from that of other non-dramatic English poets. I have in mind its
distinctive ways of expressing dramatic energy. This feature shows
itself most visibly in the sheer number of invented "characters" who
crowd his pages: Belinda, Eloisa, Atticus, Sporus, Atossa, Cloe, to
mention only six of some sixty-odd, including perhaps his greatest
character creation: himself.

No less visibly, but this time in a manner altogether his own, Pope's
dramatic instinct colors the occasions from which his poems spring.
Wordsworth's poems, one remembers, usually assert as their incen-
tive some aspect of the speaker's subjective state: "I wandered lonely
as a cloud," "My heart leaps up when I behold," "A slumber did my
spirit seal"—an emphasis altogether appropriate since the poet's "I"
and "eye" are among Wordsworth's themes. Dryden, on the other
hand (to glance back at the previous century), launches at least his
major works with some sort of unexceptionable generalization addressed to an audience undefined. Thus *Mac Flecknoe* begins with
"All human things are subject to decay," *Absalom and Achitophel* with
"In pious times, ere priest-craft did begin," and *Religio laici* very
beautifully with

> Dim as the borrow'd beams of moon and stars
> To lonely, weary, wandering travellers
> Is Reason to the soul.

The speaker as an "I" does not regularly appear in Dryden's more
serious poetry, nor does the addressee as a "you."

Pope's practice contrasts sharply with these. His typical poetic
occasion is a conversation, an exchange of views, often in the last
poems a confrontation. Always there is some immediate evocation of
an "I" and a "you." "Yes, you despise the man to Books confin'd," he
says by way of openers to his friend Lord Cobham. "Nothing so true
as what you once let fall, 'Most Women have no Characters at all,'" he
says to Martha Blount. "Who shall decide," he says to Bathurst,

"when Doctors disagree, And soundest casuists doubt, like you and me." Always, too, some polarity is startled into view. Pope never forgets the proposition he had put forward in his *Essay on Criticism*— that aimless force converts to creative energy only when contained or opposed: "The wingèd Courser, like a gen'rous Horse, Shows most true Mettle when you *check* his Course." Nor does he ever long forget the *concordia discors* principle, which offered his century its comforting perspective on political as well as cosmic phenomena; which persists in the motto our own eighteenth-century forebears chose for their currency *(E pluribus unum);* and which seemed exemplified to the young Pope even in the Windsor Forest landscape in which he grew up: "Where Order in Variety we see, And where, tho' all things differ, all agree."

Within the dialogue and implicit dialogue of his poems, therefore, ideas, ideals, personalities, life-styles, values, voices, even styles of speech are made to clash dramatically, yet always along lines and within limits that the poet as designer prescribes. For him, a poem, a painting, a garden, a landscape, a society, a nation, a world, or a cosmos is invariably a plan imposed on random elements and energies, as at the first Creation. And such, too, as he sees it, is the human personality.

For men, the task of self-fashioning requires becoming fully alert to the conflicting elements in the individual makeup as well as in human nature generally and then striving to achieve in both an equipoise of jarring interests, a "full consent of things." To succeed takes the same sort of serious labor—so Pope's language implies—as the composition of poems. One must try continually to "smooth and harmonize" one's mind, as one would smooth and harmonize the materials of a stanza. One must work to "keep the equal Measure of the Soul," as one would struggle to get right the measure of a line. Essential to this undertaking, as always in Pope's scheme of things, is a paradox that must somehow be resolved: how to live in the world without giving in to it.

> Soon as I enter at my Country door,
> My mind resumes the thread I dropt before;
> Thoughts, which at Hyde-Park-Corner I forgot
> Meet and rejoin me, in the pensive Grot.

For women, the task of self-fashioning is similarly arduous. The object is to arrive at an exquisite inner stability: not the unimpassioned void or stasis that Pope's Cloe knows; not the whirlwind of discordant furies that constitute Atossa; not the single-minded sexual appetite that drives Philomedé. The desideratum is a poise as vibrant

as the poise of a dancer, creating a personality so secure in its integrity
that it needs neither intimidate nor dazzle on that ancient field of
battle where the world rewards its veterans with "A Youth of frolicks,
an old Age of Cards."

> For foreign glory, foreign joy they roam;
> No thought of Peace or Happiness at home.

From both sexes only those succeed who have learned to be gen-
uinely "at home" in that deep sense in which Pope here and
elsewhere uses the word "home," meaning the security of an ideal
self-possession. Like the poise of the dancer, however, or the peace he
imagines for himself at the end of the *Epistle to Arbuthnot*, or the
condition he alludes to when he says in a letter of 1726: "One's chief
business is to be really at home," or the triumph he describes in his
verse letter to Bolingbroke a dozen years later: "At home tho' exil'd,
free, tho' in the Tower," it is a self-possession that has always to be
rewon. In Pope's understanding of the human situation, for men as
well as women, there are few permissible flaccidities.

Nor—if I may end where I began—are there many flaccidities in
his poetry. Here and there a line is slack, a rhyme forced; but in the
main the variety and drama of the large structures is exuberantly
reinforced by the small. Everything in Pope's verse, as he once said of
Homer's, moves. Strong verbs march down the paragraphs like parish
beadles, marshaling the order of our perceptions, while weak verbs
qualify and color them. Proper names bring specificity. Antitheses
attack our stock responses and make us think again ("At home, tho'
exil'd, free, tho' in the Tower"). Paradoxes set up road blocks and
make us look for unfamiliar exits ("All Nature is but Art, unknown to
thee"). Everywhere, imperatives alert us to behold, look, see, listen,
hear, consider, judge, stay, come, go, awake—especially awake, since
to be in Pope's sense "awake" is our best protection from the Great
Surrender against which poets have been warning us since Homer
imagined Circe's palace; Spenser, the House of Busirane; Milton, the
temptations of Comus, Satan, and Dalila; Pope, the all-enveloping
yawn that concludes the *Dunciad;* and Wordsworth, the getting and
spending that lays waste our powers.

Meantime, at the very core of this dazzling infrastructure, the
systole and diastole of the closed pentameter couplet, with its con-
tainment-under-pressure of opposing grammatical and syntactic
forces, supports, or even, if we wish to see it that way, acts out in
miniature those larger but equally strenuous reconciliations of nature
with art, wit with judgment, passion with reason, action with con-

templation, ancient rules with modern graces that the great world of everyday experience requires of each of us but to which we are ill-equipped to rise unless—as is also necessary for reading Pope—we are "awake" and "at home."

And so—I hope with the good will of all his readers—I may wish the little chap Godspeed on his journey into century number four.

Notes

This paper originated in a talk given at Yale University on 9 April 1988 to open an exhibition of books and manuscripts in honor of Pope's three-hundredth birthday.

Works Cited

Burgess, Anthony. 1986. "A Deadly Sin—Creativity for All." *But Do Blondes Prefer Gentlemen?* New York: McGraw Hill.

Emerson, Ralph Waldo. 1909–1914. *Journals*. Ed. E. W. Emerson and W. E. Forbes. 10 vols. Boston: Houghton Mifflin.

Johnson, Samuel. 1905. *Lives of the English Poets*. Ed. George Birkbeck Hill. 3 vols. Oxford: Clarendon Press.

Leithauser, Brad. 7 June 1987. "Light Verse: Dead but Remarkably Robust." *New York Times Book Review*, 27.

Macaulay, Thomas Babington. 1903. "Samuel Johnson." In *Critical and Historical Essays*. 3 vols. 1:343–96. London: Methuen.

Pocock, J. G. A. 1985. *Virtue, Commerce, and History*. Cambridge: Cambridge University Press.

Pope, Alexander. 1939–69. *The Twickenham Edition of the Poems of Alexander Pope*. Gen. ed. John Butt. 11 vols. London: Methuen; New Haven: Yale University Press.

Shaftesbury, Anthony Ashley Cooper, third Earl of. [1711] 1732. *Characteristicks of Men, Manners, Opinions, Times*. 3d ed. 3 vols. London: J. Darby.

Sibley, Agnes M. 1949. *Alexander Pope's Prestige in America, 1725–1835*. New York: King's Crown Press.

Tasch, Peter A. 1986. "Pope and Dryden on Shutting Doors." *Notes and Queries* 231 (New Series 33):499–500.

Pope's *Unfortunate Lady* and Elegiac Form
JAMES THOMPSON

In 1756, Joseph Warton wrote of Alexander Pope's *Elegy to the Memory of an Unfortunate Lady*: "if this *Elegy* be so excellent, it may be ascribed to this cause; that the occasion of it was real; for it is certainly an indisputable maxim, that nature is more powerful than fancy; that we can always feel more than we can imagine; and that the most artful fiction must give way to truth" ([1782] 1973, 401). Having concluded that the Unfortunate Lady was not real, but rather a fictitious invention of Pope's, twentieth-century readers have had considerable difficulty with the poem. Unable to read the poem as a sincere and passionate response to a particular death, recent studies can be glossed as a series of strategies for overcoming the egregious insincerity of a poem that, at least through its earlier history, had successfully elicited an emotional response.[1] These problems cannot be explained away simply as latent romanticism and the problem of sincerity (especially since later-eighteenth-century and early-nineteenth-century readers favored this poem above the satires that are now favored), because there is no difficulty approving of earlier elegies for which sincerity is not an issue (see Perkins 1964). That John Donne never knew Elizabeth Drury or that John Dryden never met Eleonora does not seem to detract from what are otherwise regarded as splendid elegies. On the contrary, Pope's never having known an Unfortunate Lady seems all the more deceptive because he exploits a sincerity that is immaterial to the earlier poems; that is, the poet claims and capitalizes on a sense of great personal loss.

I shall argue that Pope's poem differs both from previous and from subsequent funeral elegies sufficiently to disorient the response to it, and so the difficulty this poem presents can be ascribed, at least in part, to changing concepts of the elegy as an ordering rhetoric.[2] In differing from earlier elegies, the poem has shifted away from traditional poems of praise of the dead and consolation and has shifted, however faintly, toward the later elegy of memory, as in "Surprised by Joy," "Tintern Abbey," or the Lucy poems—that is, toward interiorized, psychological explorations of grief and memory. Elegies, in short, pass from collective to individualized expressions of grief. In this respect, the problem of form must be seen in terms of the relation between the subject and the object of elegy. For despite its apparently universal nature—acknowledgment of death, the great leveler—the elegy should be regarded as one of the most historical of forms because its presuppositions rest on social relations: are these relations understood as conventional or constructed? are they presented in public or private terms? what, in short, can one person mean to a community or to a single other? The fact that in this poem Pope has taken as his subject the most problematical of subjects, a vulnerable and victimized woman, should indicate that this is a narrative in dire need of historicizing.

*   *   *

Pope's *Elegy to the Memory of an Unfortunate Lady* is in many ways an anomalous work in his canon. Included in the last sheets of the 1717 *Works* along with *Eloisa to Abelard*, the *Elegy* appears to have been composed at a time when the poet was almost entirely preoccupied with his translation of *The Iliad*, a period in which Pope composed very few original poems (Russo 1972, 84, 136). In June 1717, Pope published volume 3 of *The Iliad*, which included books 9–12, covering, among other things, the Embassy, Dolonia, Agamemnon's *aristeia*, the battle of the wall, and the episode of Sarpedon: that is to say, the very heart of the cult of the warrior in the masculine battle epic. To find Pope working on both the *Elegy* and *Eloisa to Abelard* at the same time suggests that the poet sought diversion in the most antithetical poetry possible: lyric poetry of feminine desire.[3] These two poems are coupled by their female subjects, as well as by some shared lines: six lines from the *Elegy* (that is, the verse paragraph beginning "So peaceful rests, without a stone, a name" [69–74]) appear in one manuscript of *Eloisa to Abelard* (Mack 1983, 322–23). In addition, most contemporary readers seem to agree that these two poems are unusually passionate for Pope, in that the emotions they engender are not Pope's more typical righteous indignation, anger, or disgust, but rather feminine desire and pathos, emotions with which Pope is not usually connected.[4] The *Elegy* is also Pope's only formal elegy, though for many earlier poets, such as Jonson, Donne, or Dryden, the elegy is something of a stock-in-trade. Pope's preferred funereal form is plainly the epitaph, of which he wrote some twenty-seven; short (between two and twenty lines), epigrammatic, and often satiric pieces, these epitaphs are closer to what we might think of as his norm.[5]

What is perhaps most noticeable about the *Elegy* is its unusual mixture of forms and elements, for it is both an elegy and a narrative, with homage to the Lady set side by side with satiric condemnation of her uncle and family. To explore Pope's use of elegiac form, it should not be thought of in terms of pure, unmixed form, but rather, as Ralph Cohen has argued, in terms of an interrelation of forms (1974, 33–78).[6] The proportion of the mixture of praise to blame, satire to panegyric, distinguishes this poem from other elegies. While the poet expends a good deal of effort extolling the virtues of the Lady's soul, he spends an almost equal effort condemning her hard-hearted relatives. The material/ideal (or male/female) opposition at work in the second verse paragraph sets up the governing contrast between the "purer spirits" of the Unfortunate Lady and the dross of the world below (Pope 1939–69, 2:364, 25–26). The rapacity of the uncle exaggerates the viciousness of this lower world in order to elevate the aspirations of the Lady. More muted satire is, of course, often found in such earlier elegies as *Eleonora, Lycidas*, or *The Anniversaries*.[7] As Barbara Lewalski argues, English funeral elegies have their origin in epideictic or display oratory, such that praise is necessarily demonstrated by means of contrast with the less worthy. Renaissance funeral elegies of nobility and gentry, Lewalski writes, "assume the didactic function of praise, they identify moral virtue as the proper object of praise, and they portray their subjects as ideal types rather than as peccable individuals" (1973, 38). As in *The Anniversaries*, Jonson's "Elegie on the Lady Jane Pawlet" (which is apparently Pope's immediate source for the beckoning ghost with which the poem opens) or Dryden's ode "To the Pious Memory of Anne Killigrew" or *Eleonora*, "the most common of the conventional topics of praise, [is] the virtuous lady" or the "divine lady" (Lewalski 1973, 53–63). Celebration of the virtuous lady is most clearly seen in *Eleonora: a Panegyrical Poem*, which Dryden originally intended to call *The Pattern;* as he writes in the preface, "*Eleonora* is still the Pattern of Charity, Devotion, and Humility; of the best Wife, the best Mother, and the best of Friends" (1970, 467).

In contrast to his predecessors, Pope's most significant change in the panegyrical elegy is to take as his subject a woman of debatable merit. In so doing, even while he extravagantly praises her in the traditional style, Pope complicates the public, panegyrical elegy, for the Unfortunate Lady is arguably unworthy of the praise Pope gives her. Samuel Johnson, for one, was decidedly offended by Pope's distortion of the form from which he takes his language, for Johnson's harsh strictures on the *Elegy* are based on the inadequacy of the subject to the form. His memorable condemnation of the *Elegy* in the *Life of Pope* concludes, "Poetry has not often been worse employed than in dignifying the amorous fury of a raving girl" (n.d., 173). In this dismissal of the poem, Johnson asserts that funeral elegies are designed to praise exceptional virtue: "from this account [Owen Ruffhead's *Life of Pope*], given with the evident intention to raise the lady's character, it does not appear that she had any claims to praise, nor much to compassion. She seems to have been impatient, violent, and ungovernable"—far from the best wife, the best mother, and the best of friends (*ibid.*).

Another generic complication involves the relationship of this elegy to prior and subsequent pastorals. Pastoral was arguably on Pope's mind since his "Discourse on Pastoral Poetry," which describes the origin and progress of the pastoral from Theocritus, Virgil, Tasso, and Spenser through his own time, though written earlier, was first published, along with the *Elegy to the Memory of an Unfortunate Lady* in the 1717 *Works*. While this is not a formal elegy, nonetheless Pope has combined some elements of the pastoral with those of the panegyric. For example, if her uncle inhabits the public world of the great and the powerful, the Lady is too sensitive to survive in the world, like many a shepherd and shepherdess in Theocritus, Virgil, Spenser, Milton, and Pope's own pastorals. Pope arranges his poem around the difficulties that his subject presents, making the claim that the Lady is too pure, too fine, too feeling for this world, and therefore she is indeed deserving of the compassion Johnson would, and her family did, deny her: "into air the purer spirits flow, / And sep'rate from their kindred dregs below" (25–26).

Though Pope does draw on pastoral tradition in his poem, this form is distorted or deformed as well, for his *Elegy*, with its crowds, streets, and "frequent herses" (38) is a distinctly urban, social, and satiric pastoral, of the sort his friend John Gay was to write. In these urban and satiric pastorals, social conflicts and complications remain, with nothing of the simplicity William Empson emphasizes as the key feature of the pastoral (1960). To see the ways in which this poem differs from more conventional pastoral elegy, it is instructive to compare Pope's *Unfortunate Lady* with his earlier "Winter" pastoral to discover how he has altered the inherited form.[8] The 1704 elegy exhibits a substantially more straightfoward confidence and consolation of traditional Christian pastoral, affirming faith and a belief in an eternal life that dispel grief. The world weeps for Daphne, yet she rises and grief is no more: "While Plants their Shade, or Flow'rs their Odours give, / Thy name, thy Honour, and thy Praise shall live!" (Pope 1939–69, 1:94, 83–84). In her study of pastoral convention, Ellen Lambert observes, "the basic thrust of the pastoral elegy is to affirm continuity; life, albeit in new forms, goes on," and it is just this sense of continuity in natural process that Pope emphasizes in the

"Winter" pastoral (Lambert 1970, xxv). By 1717, however, the analogy between individual and landscape by which the pastoral represents regeneration and continuity is not asserted with the same confidence, such that in the *Elegy* continuity is only questionably affirmed (on the complexities of continuity, see Patterson 1979, 449–58).

More important is the difference in subject. Mrs. Tempest, the figure memorialized in "Winter," was not apparently personally known to Pope, but, according to Aubrey Williams, became the subject of Pope's elegy through the suggestion or mediation of his friend William Walsh (Pope 1939–69, 1:47). As such, Mrs. Tempest is much closer to the impersonal figuration of the "virtuous lady" in Renaissance elegy. In both *Eloisa to Abelard* and the *Elegy*, however, the distance as well as the relationship between the poet and the figure he memorializes is unclear, making it necessary for the poet to intrude into his poem to discuss and explain his role as memorializer These intrusions point up the problematics of close identification with passive women, as the poet is drawn in by his sympathy and identification with those who suffer rather than with those who act.[9] With its formal strategies of distance and commemoration, the "Winter" pastoral of 1704 is a much more traditional poem; in the *Elegy*, however, as in many of the memorable elegies after Pope, the stance of the poet and his relationship to the dead is privatized. When this happens, the distance between subject and object collapses, as, for example, in Gray's "Sonnet on the Death of Richard West," his "Elegy Written in a Country Churchyard," or Wordsworth's Lucy poems. In these later elegies, the focus shifts from consolation and commemoration of the qualities of the dead to the examination of the relationship between the dead and living and finally to the poet himself. That is to say, later eighteenth-century and romantic elegies become more private, psychological, and interiorized. The focus of later elegy, in short, shifts from virtue and faith to memory, elegized to elegizer, object to subject.

The tenuous relationship drawn between poet and Unfortunate Lady at the close of the *Elegy* suggests the uncertainty of the place of Pope's poem in the history of the funeral elegy, drawing on both the public panegyrical and pastoral elegies that precede it, while differing from the private and interior elegies that follow. Earlier elegies, even successful and moving ones such as Dryden's "To the Memory of Mr. Oldham," do not focus on the pain of memory in the way Gray's "Sonnet" or Wordsworth's "Surprised by Joy" do.[10] In such poems as "Oldham," it is memory that provides consolation, but in "Surprised by Joy," Wordsworth claims that because we can remember only what has been forgotten, *re*membering doubles loss and makes it all the more painful. Jonson's "On My First Son" and Wordsworth's "Surprised by Joy" deal with the same putative subject, the death of a child, but Jonson's poem is more about the son, and Wordsworth's is more about the father. Gray's "Sonnet" tells us absolutely nothing about West—West's name is not even mentioned—only about how the poet feels, just as the Lucy poems tell us next to nothing about Lucy, only about the poet's foreboding and his response to her death (on the absence of Lucy, see Ferguson 1977, 174–76).

On this crucial matter of the relation between subject and object, Pope's *Elegy* again falls somewhere in between, for though he does not fully enter into the poem either to personalize or to personify grief for the Lady, he also tells us remarkably little about the Unfortunate Lady herself, so little that much of the eighteenth- and nineteenth-century commentary on this poem was taken up with biographical or narrative speculation about her, attempts to unearth her character and story (as Ruffhead and Johnson tried to) from the meager details available in the poem. What these readers appear to have been after are the domestic details of a distressed or pathetic maiden story, as found in Otway or Rowe or eventually, in somewhat altered form, in Richardson.[11] Such lurid stories, drawn from drama or fiction, seem quite out of place in an elegy. But again, readers' expectations point to the mixture of forms at work in the *Elegy*, as if the poet in effect offers to treat us to the story of the Unfortunate Lady but then reneges. There is an inevitable frustration here as the poet indicates that, by virtue of her exemplary life, the Lady is due homage, but we have to take that exemplary life on faith, for what we are treated to here is not a life story but only a foreclosed death story.

Despite the interest that he manages to generate in the sparse details of her life story, Pope nonetheless concentrates upon the Lady's death. The emotional power of elegy often turns on this essential contrast of presence and absence, as, for example, in Spenser's November eclogue, where such essential difference is starkly expressed: "Waile we the wight, whose presence was our pryde: / Waile we the wight, whose absence is our carke" (Spenser 1912, 461, 64–65). Pope's *Elegy*, too, works self-consciously on difference, by foregrounding difference in the figure of his initial beckoning ghost, a sign of the Lady that is neither fully present nor absent, for the ghost serves to mark what was once present; bleeding and damaged, the ghost is not the Lady, but a sign that both differs and defers from the true presence, the once-living Lady.

The ghost works quite differently in Pope's source, Ben Jonson's "An Elegie on the Lady Jane Pawlet," where the beckoning ghost merely serves as a device to bring the poet news of her death: Pope's ghost is rather more like Hamlet's, a powerful ghost with some sense of threat, as in Keats's "This Living Hand." Pope's *Elegy* should also be contrasted with the almost beatific vision of Milton's sonnet "Methought I saw my late espoused saint." In Pope, the ghost functions as a kind of phantasmagorical image of woman, wounded and bleeding, yet compelling. After Sacks's very suggestive discussion of elegy and castration, it is difficult not to connect this initial beckoning object with the Lacanian formulation of desire, of some initial lack. Where ordinary psychoanalysis focuses on object relations, as Anthony Wilden has argued, Lacan focuses on the lack of the object, which Lacan represents with the term *phallus* (commentary in Lacan 1968, 186–92). That is to say, the phallus marks the lack, the presence of absence. Or, to put it another way, the signifier of the phallus, which no one possesses (Lemaire terms it the "Mythical Phallus" [1977, 59]) initiates or marks the desire for plenitude and presence; it is the signifier that comes to indicate what is absent. The lack of the object has several aspects: castration, frustration, real separation from the mother, and, ultimately, the law that insists on lack—you cannot possess the original object of your desire. The phallus then in some sense comes to signify the original desire for the mother: "The phallus is the privileged signifier of that mark in which the role of the logos is joined with the advent of desire" (Lacan 1977, 287).

Pope's ghost haunts the memory, exacting some remembrance that is owed to her in the form of the rites, the pity, the love, the fulfillment denied to her in life and in death. Yet this is a debt that the poet seems to suggest cannot finally be paid; her neglect can never be rectified, because the poet has no lasting power. Poetic recognition cannot return a life lost, and, worse, subsequent readers will never be able to remember a life that they never knew in the first place. The poem can serve only to mark her lack, her unfulfilled desire, by representing her, through the ghost, as an emblem of unsatisfied desire. In the last verse paragraph, then, the object of the poem comes to be not so much a commemoration of a specific life or death as a lament for that which is always slipping away and being lost—life, passion, and memory.[12] Just as in *Eloisa to Abelard*, where the dead letter is a distressingly inadequate supplement for the beloved, this poem also denies the efficacy of substitutes, poems, elegies, belated rites, and remembrances for a life lost.

The close of the *Elegy* examines what is owed to and what can be paid to the dead. The poem opens with a whole series of questions directed toward the Unfortunate Lady, questions that are condensed and restated in the central question which the poem poses: "What can atone (oh ever-injur'd shade!) / Thy fate unpity'd, and thy rites unpaid?" (47–48). Several answers are offered and rejected. The regeneration of natural process, the traditional device of solace in pastoral, here leads only to dust. The characteristic reversals, by which this poem proceeds, such as kind Lady/cruel uncle, proud family/ruinous family, neglected burial/remembered death, lead to the expected regeneration of nature, "The ground, now sacred by thy reliques made" (68). But this gesture or process is not reciprocal, for the ground in turn does not make her relics sacred: "A heap of dust alone remains of thee; / 'Tis all thou art, and all the proud shall be!" (73–74). The cycle of natural regeneration continues but is indifferent to her remains; Pope makes no explicit affirmation of eternal salvation for his suicide, leaving it only suggested in the form of the unanswered question: "Is there no bright reversion in the sky / For those who greatly think, or bravely die?" (9–10). And finally, the last source of eternal remembrance, the permanence of art, is most surprisingly abandoned: memory survives not in the inert poetry, but in the sentient tongue and tear, such that when the poet dies, the Lady will be "belov'd no more!" (82). The poem unexpectedly concludes in denying the expected claim that art preserves and sustains, for the *Elegy* concedes that memory cannot be permanently fixed in language: memory, too, is human and therefore subject to death. Though we might expect the poetic tribute to supply the canonization that both family and nature have failed to supply, the poet also dies, and with him the last memory of what is owed to the unquiet ghost: both praised and praiser end deaf and mute. The most obvious answer to the question "What can atone (oh ever-injur'd shade!) . . . ?" which ought to be "this poem," of course, turns out to be the least adequate. The correct answer, it would seem, is "nothing," in a state where, unlamented or lamented, all must die and turn to dust.

The *Elegy* closes in questioning the purpose and efficacy of elegiac poetry in general, particularly its grandest claims of consolation. It is not simply that Pope is hobbled by his suicidal subject, and so his appeal to religious affirmation must be muted or at least put forward with great care (notice, for example, the qualifications in "From these perhaps (ere nature bade her die) / Fate snatch'd her early to the pitying sky" [23–24]). Rather, the *Elegy* fully partakes of neither Christian consolation nor of later internalization of grief, as in Wordsworth's "Elegiac Stanzas on Peele Castle," for example, because Pope is unsure of his relationship with the subject. That relationship is not defined socially (he never knew the Lady, nor does he pretend to be the one she might have preferred) or professionally (she was neither his patron nor the wife nor the daughter of his patron), as relationships are defined in Donne's or Dryden's elegies on patrons or public

figures, nor is the relationship purely personal, as those are in Gray's
"Sonnet on the Death of Richard West" or Johnson's "Lines on the
Death of Dr. Levet." As a consequence, the grief that the *Elegy* is
supposed to manage is handled neither as a religious nor a social
phenomenon, nor as a personal burden. Pope employs fiction in order
to create a relationship—any sort of relationship—to supply a proper,
or at least a traditional, subject, a lack of subject caused by a disin-
tegrating patronage system for professional poetry. In this respect,
without the formally defined professional relationships, like those
clearly delineated in *Eleonora* or "To the Memory of Mr. Oldham,"
the poet is forced to explain what the dead person means to him,
making elegy increasingly difficult to write. This very difficulty of the
unestablished or unconventional relationship between subject and
object in elegy is nicely captured at the close of Theodore Roethke's
"Elegy for Jane":

> Over this damp grave I speak the words of my love:
> I, with no rights in this matter,
> Neither father nor lover.

$$(1975, 98)$$

Elegy to the Memory of an Unfortunate Lady can settle easily on
neither traditionally communal nor on more modern private responses to grief, for it tries to have it both ways, though they are
incompatible. Is the Unfortunate Lady to be retained or remembered
or immortalized by the poet's heart and memory, by his poem, or by
eternal salvation? Though these three solutions have not been incompatible before—in earlier elegies such as *Lycidas* all three paths are
reconciled—in Pope's *Elegy*, personal, poetic, and religious immor-
tality are starting to pull apart and war with each other. The entire
drift of this poem is away from social and communal obligations, and
toward personal, private, individual solutions. Consider the standard
fleshing-out of the narrative: the Unfortunate Lady wished to marry
another but was forced to marry someone of the uncle's choosing for
familial and/or financial aggrandizement (the *Clarissa*, or enforced-
marriage, narrative), a plot and pattern of ideas concerning marriage
and personal fulfillment that are appropriate to what Lawrence Stone
presents as a later phase of affective individualism. The Lady wishes
to marry none but of her own choosing, not the one the family has
chosen for its benefit. The family will not be corrected or improved,
but instead Pope predicts that it will be destroyed; society at large is
pictured only as a jeering crowd, as unconcerned as the family ever
was at the Lady's suffering and death. In some sense, Samuel Johnson

may be correct in his evaluation of the poem: the elegy recommends antisocial behavior, because it is flight and refuge that are approved here. Such conduct is not limited to the Lady, for the poet, as well, celebrates her in a thoroughly privatized fashion: I alone am sensitive enough to feel the Unfortunate Lady's pain. Only the single individual, the solitary shade, and the solitary mourner have any real presence or purpose here. The poet is unable or unwilling to communicate the burden of grief to others, even to his readers, as he asserts that we who never knew can never properly remember.

Samuel Richardson's *Clarissa* provides a somewhat anachronistic though suggestive analogy to these issues in Pope's *Elegy* on a number of fronts. It is not just that the two works share the narrative of the besieged young woman who is tragically forced by her family into an unthinkable match. But as Richardson's more recent commentators, including Warner (1979), Castle (1982), and Eagleton (1982), have argued, the whole of *Clarissa* dramatizes a struggle for control over the nubile female. What is most intriguing about both of these works is that the struggles for control continue long after the woman's death. In the novel, the Harlowe family and Belford contest over the right to execute Clarissa's will (and so, by indirection, to become her editor); in the poem, Pope, in effect, plays the role of Belford, executing the Unfortunate Lady's "will," by serving as the preserver and defender of her true memory while, like Belford, establishing his authority to the lady's memory by vilifying her family. Like *Clarissa*, as well, Pope's *Elegy to the Memory of an Unfortunate Lady* skirts the problem of self-determination for women, for the dead can have no autonomy. The struggle between the uncle and the Lady is, in this sense, replicated in the proposed fate of the *Elegy* itself, as Pope appoints himself to the role of guardian, a role that the uncle has abdicated. And just as *Clarissa* can be seen and glossed as a document about the control or traffic in women, so, too, the *Elegy* replicates male claims to guardianship or control in the economy of women, to use the suggestive terms of Gayle Rubin (1975).

*   *   *

In the great seventeenth-century elegies, the source of consolation is almost always communal, as the burden of grief is distributed socially. In Pope's *Elegy,* however, social relations, dependence, and obligation all pointedly fail: the Unfortunate Lady's family casts her into a pauper's grave, disowning her in death as in life. The poet heroically offers to shoulder the burden of the community, to mourn in place of an indifferent family and society. Again, this offer prefigures the private stance of romantic elegies, which are located squarely within the ideology of the individual subject, in which grief is personalized and privatized, absorbed inward (in Freud's term, fetishized), and not distributed communally because the community is now perceived as indifferent at best to individual grief and hostile at worst. Such indifference is the burden of Thomas Gray's "Sonnet on the Death of Richard West," where nature as a whole, in its continuing cycle of regeneration, is completely unconcerned with his private loss; in the "Elegy Written in a Country Churchyard" as well, society at large is unconcerned with the private sufferings of the individual villagers, just as the poet in his turn remains separated and alienated from the villagers. In both poems, the poet is unable to share the burden of grief, which then becomes solitary and private. So, too, in the *Elegy*, a private individual offers to perform what the family and society have failed to do, for the poet alone is willing to bear the burden of maintaining the Unfortunate Lady's memory.

Pope's *Elegy to the Memory of an Unfortunate Lady* is a difficult poem to recuperate, for it is not a particularly successful elegy, and in studies of Pope the *Elegy* has always been overshadowed by its companion poem, *Eloisa to Abelard*. Maynard Mack concludes that the *Elegy* is "a pastiche of motifs and attitudes not very well accommodated to the whole in which they find themselves" (1985, 315). In part, its failure can be ascribed to the fact that it is caught between social and individual responses, as well as between responses or solutions to the task of mourning. Works such as *Lycidas, Eleonora, The Anniversaries* are, in their way, just as fictional as Pope's elegy, for Donne invents his vision of Elizabeth Drury as Pope invents his vision of a bleeding ghost. The crucial difference would seem to lie in the fact that Donne has his excuse for writing—the situation, the death, and the patron—and Pope does not. Both Dryden's and Wordsworth's elegies should, of course, provide inappropriate standards by which to read Pope's *Elegy*: Pope consciously experiments with his inherited forms without any clear anticipation of later, romantic elegiac poetry. At best, we could try to accommodate a form betwixt and between, in a poem that can rely upon neither the public, impersonal, and stylized relationship of earlier elegy, nor on the personal, private, and internalized relationship of later elegy.

Notes

1. For a history of the *Elegy*'s reception, see Jack 1978, 69–83, and Vieth 1983, 425–34 What little comment the poem has received recently—this is one of Pope's currently unpopular poems, with only about half a dozen discussions over the last twenty years—is characterized by unusual disagreement. In addition to Jack and Vieth, discussions of the *Elegy* include: Gillie 1955; Weinbrot 1971; Mell 1974, 29–42.

2. As is well known, the term "elegy" became solely identified with death poetry well after Pope's time: in the Renaissance, "elegy" still referred to any poem written in elegiac meter: Donne's bawdy elegy 19, "Going to Bed," is hardly funereal. See Lambert 1970, xix.

3. In a letter to Parnell, Pope wrote of his forthcoming 1717 *Works,* "I shall very soon print an entire collection of my own madrigals"; the primary definition of madrigal then was love lyric, and perhaps Pope composed these two love poems against the death poetry of the epic (Pope 1956, 1:396). From another perspective, *The Iliad* and the *Elegy* represent two separate strands that Pope had entangled for satiric effect in *The Rape of the Lock* three years earlier; the satiric composition of the *Rape of the Lock* is compounded of a confusion between a high norm of the masculine battle epic and a low norm of femininity. It may stand to reason, then, that at just the time when Pope was involved with producing a pure, nonsatiric version of the battle epic, he found distraction in a pure, nonsatiric version of feminine desire.

4. These three poems, the *Elegy, Eloisa,* and *The Iliad* (in such figures as Hecuba and Andromache), are linked by the fact that they are Pope's only poems that display unrestrained passion. Along this same line, the Unfortunate Lady and Eloisa are celebrated for just the excess for which Belinda in *The Rape of the Lock* is derided, largely because Belinda's passion is narcissistic, whereas the Unfortunate Lady and Eloisa more appropriately expend their passion, however doomed, on men. For a thorough analysis of Pope's portrayal of women in terms of this ideal of "cultivated passivity," see Pollak 1985, 42; most applicable to the *Elegy* is Pollak's discussion of *Eloisa to Abelard,* 183–86.

5. The epitaph on Sir Isaac Newton is typical of the wit of Pope's epitaphs, but they range in subject from a moving tribute to John Gay to pithy dismissals of Francis Chartres and James Moore Smythe. The wit of Pope's epitaphs provoked nothing but contempt from Wordsworth; in his *Essays on Epitaphs,* Wordsworth finds Pope's "Epitaph on Mrs. Corbet" feeble, objectionable, vicious, and unfeeling: "why was this not simply expressed; without playing with the Reader's fancy, to the delusion and dishonour of his understanding, by a trifling epigrammatic point" (1966, 119).

6. If Pope wrote only one formal elegy, the elegiac mode can be found throughout his poetry. Earlier in his poetic career, the "Winter" pastoral is a highly traditional pastoral elegy, and later we find elaborately heightened evocations of pathos in *The Iliad*—see, for example, Hecuba's and Andromache's laments in book 22—as well as in the later satires, where a nostalgic, elegiac voice at times contrasts with the present state of corruption, as it does in Epistle 2.2:

> Years foll'wing Years, steal something ev'ry day,
> At last they steal us from our selves away;
> In one our Frolicks, one Amusements end,
> In one a Mistress drops, in one a Friend:
> This subtle Thief of Life, this paltry Time,
> What will it leave me, if it snatch my Rhime?
> If ev'ry Wheel of that unweary'd Mill
> That turn'd ten thousand Verses, now stands still.
>
> (Pope 1939–69, 4:171, 72–79)

7. Sacks observes that elements of anger, resentment, and desire for revenge are common to the expression of grief and to the elegy, even if the particular poem is not overtly satirical (1985, 64–89).

8. One might do well here to remember Raymond Williams's strictures on the notion of inheriting the pastoral (1973, 13–34): apparent similarities in traditional forms need careful scrutiny and historicizing. Sacks, whose study is primarily concerned with the pastoral elegy, argues that the form was in disrepute and decline, such that Pope's "Winter" and Dryden's "On the Death of Amyntas," among others, assert "the general powerlessness of the pastoral elegy throughout this period" (118).

9. To both Vieth and Weinbrot, this problematic identification is supposed to signal to the reader the inadequacy of the speaker's response, leading to entrapment for Vieth or to rejection of the speaker's authority for Weinbrot; assuming that the poem embodies some sort of ruse, neither will grant any straightforward sympathy to the Lady.

10. It might be argued that this is a consequence of a pervasive secularization; Gray's

"Sonnet" offers no spiritual consolation at all, leaving the death all the more inconsolable. In addition, Lawrence Stone argues that declining death rates in the eighteenth century made death far less of an everyday occurrence, which, paradoxically, made it more frightening and less bearable (1977).

11. Brown's discussion of victimization and passivity in defenseless female protagonists in late Restoration and early eighteenth-century tragedy from Otway and Southerne through Rowe is relevant here: "The defenseless woman, then, is the preferred protagonist of a form which is governed neither by the aristocratic ideal of chivalric magnanimity nor by the didactic bourgeois ideal of moral worth. . . . Pathetic tragedy serves, in effect, to bridge the gap between intrinsically irreconcilable forms" (1982, 442).

12. For a suggestive connection between Freud's essay on "Mourning and Melancholia" and the strategies of elegy in Gray, see Manning 1982.

Works Cited

Brown, Laura. 1982. "The Defenseless Woman and the Development of English Tragedy." *Studies in English Literature* 22:428–43.

Castle, Terry. 1982. *Clarissa's Ciphers: Meaning and Disruption in Richardson's Clarissa.* Ithaca: Cornell University Press.

Cohen, Ralph. 1974. "On the Interrelations of Eighteenth-Century Forms." In *New Approaches to Eighteenth-Century Literature,* ed. Phillip Harth, 33–78. New York: Columbia University Press.

Dryden, John. 1970. *The Poems and Fables of John Dryden.* Ed. James Kinsley. Oxford: Oxford University Press.

Eagleton, Terry. 1982. *The Rape of Clarissa.* Minneapolis: University of Minnesota Press.

Empson, William. 1960. *Some Versions of Pastoral.* Norfolk, Conn.: New Directions.

Ferguson, Frances. 1977. *Wordsworth: Language as Counter-Spirit.* New Haven: Yale University Press.

Gillie, Christopher. 1955. "Elegy to the Memory of an Unfortunate Lady." In *Interpretations,* ed. John Wain, 77–85. London: Routledge and Kegan Paul.

Jack, Ian. 1978. "The Elegy as Exorcism: Pope's 'Verses to the Memory of an Unfortunate Lady.'" In *Augustan Worlds: New Essays in Eighteenth-Century Literature,* ed. J. C. Hilson, M. M. B. Jones, and J. R. Watson, 69–83. New York: Barnes and Noble.

Johnson, Samuel. n.d. *Lives of the Poets.* Garden City, N.J.: Doubleday.

Lacan, Jacques. 1968. *The Language of the Self.* Ed. and trans. Anthony Wilden. Baltimore: The Johns Hopkins University Press.

———. 1977. *Ecrits.* Trans. Alan Sheridan. New York: Norton.

Lambert, Ellen Zetzel. 1970. *Placing Sorrow: A Study of Pastoral Elegy Convention from Theocritus to Milton.* Chapel Hill: University of North Carolina Press.

Lemaire, Anika. 1977. *Jacques Lacan.* Trans. David Macey. London: Routledge and Kegan Paul.

Lewalski, Barbara. 1973. *Donne's Anniversaries and the Poetry of Praise.* Princeton: Princeton University Press.

Mack, Maynard. 1983. *Collected in Himself.* Newark: University of Delaware Press.

———. 1985. *Alexander Pope: A Life.* New York: Norton.

Manning, Peter J. 1982. "Wordsworth and Gray's *Sonnet on the Death of Mr. Richard West.*" *Studies in English Literature* 22:505–518.

Mell, Donald. 1974. *A Poetics of Augustan Elegy.* Amsterdam: Rodopi.

Patterson, Annabel M. 1979. "'How to load and . . . bend': Syntax and Interpretation in Keats's *To Autumn.*" *PMLA* 94:449–58.

Perkins, David. 1964. *Wordsworth and the Poetry of Sincerity.* Cambridge: Harvard University Press.

Pollak, Ellen. 1985. *The Poetics of Sexual Myth: Gender and Ideology in the Verse of Swift and Pope.* Women in Culture and Society. Chicago: University of Chicago Press.

Pope, Alexander. 1939–69. *The Twickenham Edition of the Poems of Alexander Pope.* Gen. ed. John Butt. 11 vols. London: Methuen.

———. 1956. *The Correspondence of Alexander Pope.* Ed. George Sherburn. 5 vols. Oxford: Clarendon Press.

Roethke, Theodore. 1975. *The Collected Poems of Theodore Roethke.* New York: Doubleday.

Rubin, Gayle. 1975. "The Traffic in Women: Notes on the 'Political Economy' of Sex." In *Towards an Anthropology of Women*, ed. Rayna R. Reiter, 157–210. New York: Monthly Review Press.

Russo, John Paul. 1972. *Alexander Pope: Tradition and Identity.* Cambridge: Harvard University Press.

Sacks, Peter M. 1985. *The English Elegy: Studies in the Genre from Spenser to Yeats.* Baltimore: The Johns Hopkins University Press.

Spenser, Edmund. 1912. *The Poetical Works of Edmund Spenser.* Ed. J. C. Smith and E. de Selincourt. Oxford: Oxford University Press.

Stone, Lawrence. 1977. *The Family, Sex and Marriage in England 1500–1800.* New York: Harper and Row.

Vieth, David M. 1983. "Entrapment in Pope's *Elegy*," *Studies in English Literature* 23:425–34.

Warner, William. 1979. *Reading Clarissa: The Struggles of Interpretation.* New Haven: Yale University Press.

Warton, Joseph. [1782] 1973. Extracts from *An Essay on the Writings and Genius of Pope.* In *Pope: The Critical Heritage,* ed. John Barnard, 508–521. London: Routledge and Kegan Paul.

Weinbrot, Howard. 1971. "Pope's 'Elegy to the Memory of an Unfortunate Lady.'" *Modern Language Quarterly* 32:255–67.

Williams, Raymond. 1973. *The Country and the City.* New York: Oxford University Press.

Wordsworth, William. 1966. *Literary Criticism of William Wordsworth.* Ed. Paul M. Zall. Lincoln: University of Nebraska Press.

Part 3
Prose

About Wit
Locke, Addison, Prior, and the Order of Things
JOHN SITTER

> For thee explain a thing till all men doubt it,
> And write about it, Goddess, and about it.
> —Alexander Pope, *Dunciad*

Sooner or later in any discussion of neoclassical literature the word *wit*, if not the spaniel, splashes its way back to the hunter's side. That major authors of the Restoration and early eighteenth century prized and practiced wit is perhaps the one thing every succeeding generation has agreed on, although with widely differing evaluations of that achievement. Each retrospective estimate of Dryden or Pope seems, interestingly, to approach Dryden's view of one of his predecessors: "if we are not so great wits as Donne, yet certainly we are better poets." As Dryden's usage and the work of many modern scholars remind us, the value and definition of wit have been complex all along. Wit is Nature in ambiguity dressed—and so is Nature.[1]

Despite the broad problems of historical semantics, readers continue to agree that Restoration repartee, *The Rape of the Lock*, Fielding's asides and prefaces, most of the poetry of Swift and Prior, and *The Beggar's Opera* all are witty. Whatever neoclassical wit is taken to be, it is likelier sought in Gay than Gray. It is not sought everywhere in the period—rarely in Defoe, scarcely in Richardson, for example—but wherever it is found the impression is generally one of hearing a shared language of the age, a shared rhetoric, rather than a clever ideolect. The examples mentioned range greatly but call to mind a familiar mixture of "common" sense, unconventional perspective, quickness, economy, and irreverence, to which no single writer (no Austen or Wilde, for example) has a unique claim in the period. This historical impression might be focused by looking for a moment at what might be called the epitaph of neoclassical wit, the couplet John Gay wrote for his tomb, and at the reaction it provoked in a young writer of a later generation, Samuel Johnson. The lines Gay asked Pope to put on his grave and that duly appeared in Westminster Abbey are these: "Life is a jest; and all things show it, / I thought so once; but now I know it" (Gay 1974, 1:253). Writing for the *Gentle-man's Magazine* in 1738, Johnson finds this "trifling distich" more proper for the "window of a brothel" than for a monument. All people, he argues, do or do not believe in a future state of rewards and punishments. "In one of these classes our poet must be ranked. . . . If he was of the latter opinion, he must think life more than a jest, unless he thought eternity a jest too; and if these were his sentiments, he is by this time most certainly undeceived. These lines, therefore, are impious in the mouth of a Christian, and nonsense in that of an aetheist" (1984, 52–53). Nothing suggests that Gay saw any contradiction between making a good end and making a jest, or that friends such as Pope, Arbuthnot, and Swift found the epitaph trifling. Johnson's objections have their reason, but not the reason of his predecessors. The encounter is a reminder again of how often neo-classical wit plays upon mortality and how often it laughs at the oppositional logic of either/or. The common language Gay counted on was quickly disappearing.

While this episode suggests wit's passage, the more closely this ordering rhetoric is looked for the less explicit it seems to have been. Not only does "wit" itself have an array of meanings, as even the casual reader of *An Essay on Criticism* soon suspects, but it has its own oppositional story through the late-seventeenth and early-eighteenth centuries. The best-known version is that of true wit versus false wit in Addison's series of *Spectator* essays (nos. 58–63), but Addison builds on Locke's earlier opposition of wit and judgment. Locke in turn was probably influenced by Malebranche, almost surely by Hobbes, perhaps by Boyle, and possibly by Bacon.[2] Locke is a good place to begin not only because his oppositions seem to have been the most influential but also because a careful reading of *An Essay Concerning Human Understanding* shows that behind the desire to derogate or dignify wit lie issues far different from cof-feehouse decorum. At stake are conflicting notions of intellectual coherence and competing versions of reality. After exploring Locke's dichotomy and its implications in his theory of knowledge, I shall turn to its subversion, respectively genteel and raucous, by Addison and Prior. Less suspicious of language than Locke, both Addison and Prior are more deeply sceptical of individual aspirations to an unmediated agreement of thinking and things.

Wit and Judgment in Locke

I shall imagine I have done some service to Truth, Peace, and Learning if, by any enlargement on this Subject, I can make Men reflect on their own

Use of Language; and give them Reason to suspect, that since it is frequent for others, it may also be possible for them, to have sometimes very good and approved Words in their Mouths, and Writings, with very uncertain, little, or no signification. And therefore it is not unreasonable for them to be wary herein themselves, and not to be unwilling to have them examined by others. (Locke [1975] 1979, 438)

In a later chapter of the same book Locke would attend to wit under the rubric "Of the Abuse of Words," but he had in fact discussed it at some length before deciding to take language as his province. This earlier passage from book 2 ("Of Ideas") is the one Addison put into broad circulation the morning of 11 May 1711 by quoting most of it in the fifth of six *Spectators* on wit:

If in having our *Ideas* in the Memory ready at hand, consists quickness of parts; in this, of having them unconfused, and being able nicely to distinguish one thing from another, where there is but the least difference, consists, in a great measure, the exactness of Judgment and clearness of Reason, which is to be observed in one Man above another. And hence, perhaps, may be given some Reason of that common Observation, That Men who have a great deal of Wit, and prompt Memories, have not always the clearest Judgment, or deepest Reason. For *Wit* lying most in the assemblage of *Ideas*, and putting those together with quickness and variety, wherein can be found any resemblance or congruity, thereby to make up pleasant Pictures, and agreeable Visions in the fancy: *Judgment*, on the contrary, lies quite on the other side, in repeating carefully, one from another, *Ideas* wherein can be found the least difference, thereby to avoid being misled by Similitude, and by affinity to take one thing for another. This is a way of proceeding quite contrary to Metaphor and Allusion, wherein, for the most part, lies that entertainment and pleasantry of Wit, which strikes so lively on the Fancy, and therefore [is] so acceptable to all People; because its Beauty appears at first sight, and there is required no labour of thought, to examine what Truth or Reason there is in it. The Mind, without looking further, rests satisfied with the agreeableness of the Picture, and the gayety of the Fancy: And it is a kind of affront to go about to examine it, by the severe Rules of Truth, and good Reason; whereby it appears, that it consists in something, that is not perfectly conformable to them. (Locke, 2.11.2)

This pasage is worth considering more carefully than has been the modern habit. Kenneth MacLean, in what is regrettably still the standard work on Locke and eighteenth-century literature, points to the influence of the dichotomy but refers to it as a "detached bit of psychology" of "obviously little significance" in Locke's philosophy (1936, 63), a view more recent commentators seem to endorse by

passing on in silence. Even literary critics as alert to Locke's metaphorical valences as is Paul de Man (1979) tend to proceed directly to
book 3 and the explicit remarks on language. My view is that this
piece of psychologizing is thoroughly attached to the tensions in
Locke's argument throughout the *Essay* and that understanding those
tensions can help in the reading of several neoclassical works of wit in
something more of the spirit their authors writ.

Since Locke's account is clearly on the side of judgment—itself
finding differences rather than resemblances—it may help to underscore just what is "quite contrary" to what. We can make the following
lists of constituents or qualities:

Wit	*Judgment*
assemblage of ideas	discrimination of ideas
quickness	care
variety	clarity
entertainment and pleasantry	truth and reason
immediate picture	labor of thought
gaiety of fancy	severity of truth and good reason
metaphor	[distinction?]
allusion	[?]

Although Locke does not provide an opposing term to metaphor, it
is clear that metaphor marks the appetite of wit for similarities, while
judgment patiently seeks out differences. The place of allusion may
seem less obvious, however, first because it is not necessarily associated with wit in particular (as distinguished, for example, from scholarly writing or sermons), and secondly because Locke gives no plain
counterpart to it other than judgment's "whole way of proceeding."
But it is clear that allusion is still on Locke's mind when he discusses
wit again in book 3. This section is again long, but I quote it whole in
the interests of care rather than quickness:

> Since Wit and Fancy finds easier entertainment in the World, than dry
> Truth and real Knowledge, *figurative Speeches*, and allusion in Language,
> will hardly be admitted as *an* imperfection or *abuse* of it. I confess, in
> Discourses, where we seek rather Pleasure and Delight, than Information
> and Improvement, such Ornaments as are borrowed from them, can
> scarce pass for Faults. But yet, if we would speak of Things as they are, we
> must allow, that all the Art of Rhetoric, besides Order and Clearness, all
> the artificial and figurative application of Words Eloquence hath invented,
> are for nothing else but to insinuate wrong *Ideas*, move the Passions, and
> thereby mislead the Judgment; and so indeed are perfect cheat; and
> therefore however laudable or allowable Oratory may render them in

Harangues and popular Addresses, they are certainly, in all Discourses that pretend to inform or instruct, wholly to be avoided; and where Truth or Knowledge are concerned, cannot but be thought a great fault, either of the Language or Person that makes use of them. What, and how various they are, will be superfluous here to take notice; the books of Rhetorick which abound in the world will instruct those who want to be informed: Only I cannot but observe, how little the preservation and improvement of Truth and Knowledge is the Care and Concern of Mankind; since the Arts of Fallacy are endow'd and preferred. 'Tis evident how much Men love to deceive, and be deceived, since Rhetorick, that powerful instrument of Error and Deceit, has its established Professors, is publickly taught, and has always been had in great Reputation: And I doubt not but it will be thought great boldness, if not brutality in me, to have said thus much against it. *Eloquence*, like the fair Sex, has too prevailing Beauties in it to suffer itself ever to be spoken against. And 'tis in vain to find fault with those Arts of Deceiving, wherein Men find pleasure to be Deceived. (3.10.34)

The opposition of "truth" and "rhetoric," it has been argued, has been essential to philosophy's self-definition since Plato's attack on the Sophists; philosophy is distinguished by not being rhetoric or poetry. Locke's particular "plain-style" aversion to the "arts of fallacy" is familiar.[3] This passage emphasizes the values implicit in Locke's earlier distinction, since the quasi-psychological opposition of wit and judgment now becomes the openly ethical contest of wit and fancy on one side (the syntax of the first sentence merges them) against knowledge and truth on the other. Keeping the "sides" in the same order as before, we can extend the list of oppositions partially but significantly.

Wit and Fancy	*Knowledge and Truth*
pleasure and delight	information and instruction
rhetoric and eloquence	speech of "things as they are"
artificial and figurative application of words	[?]
allusion	[?]

Before trying to fill in the blanks it is necessary to consider the dramatic entrance from the right of "things as they are." The phrase entails a claim to full knowledge of the world, which contradicts countless reminders of epistemological limits in every major part of the *Essay*. Many of these are familiar and prudential (for example, "Our Business here is not to know all things, but those which concern our Conduct" [1.1.6]); the point behind them is that we do not, generally speaking, have knowledge of things but knowledge of "things" as they appear in the mind, that is, knowledge of ideas. If we look back to the distinction between wit and judgment in book 2 we find Locke attempting to be more careful in describing the operations of the mind that assemble and that separate as both being operations upon *ideas*. But we also find there a brief lapse important enough to suggest that the recurrence to "things as they are" in book 3 may be unguarded but not exactly accidental.

The first sentence of the earlier passage associates wit with "having our *ideas* in the memory ready at hand" but judgment with "having them unconfused and being able nicely to distinguish one *thing* from another" (my emphasis). This silent slide from ideas to things is crucial to Locke's dichotomy and, as I shall try to show, a clue to greater problems within the *Essay*. The attribution to wit of the "artificial and figurative application of words" and of "allusion" implies, of course, contrary ways of proceeding in the world of judgment, knowledge, and truth. What exactly are these contraries? Presumably the first would be the natural and literal application of words, and the second would be unallusive language.

In short, Locke's charged opposition of wit and judgment entails three major claims: (1) we can know and speak of things as they are; (2) we can (and should) speak naturally and literally; (3) we can (and should) speak without allusion. The question is whether there is really any space in Locke's *Essay* for any of the three assumptions. Put another way, in light of Locke's rigorous contributions to epistemology, to the study of language, and to ethics, what are we to make of his supposition that we can and should seek an unartificial language free of allusion and illusion? The boundaries between the epistemological and linguistic-ethical claims Locke makes in attacking wit are less clear than my listing of them may suggest, but I shall try to consider them in the order enumerated above.

I have already suggested that the general difficulty behind Locke's claim that judgment distinguishes *things* or that it guides us in speaking of "things as they are" stems from the commitment of the *Essay* as a whole to the view that what we know are (only) our ideas. Since able readers of Locke from Thomas Reid to the present have commented on the tension between that commitment and Locke's equally strong belief that our senses give knowledge of the external world, it is possible to concentrate selectively on a few of the *Essay*'s moments of attempted reconciliation in order to see the range of Locke's ideas about ideas. Seeing that range may help in understanding Locke's occasional vehemence, because it stretches, sometimes awkwardly, from ideas as "mental Draughts" or "Pictures of Things" (2.29.8) to ideas as barely legible signs.

In his discussion of "clear and obscure, Distant and Confused Ideas," Locke launches at once into visual metaphor—"the Perception of the Mind, being most aptly explained by Words relating to the Sight"—in order to argue that "our *simple ideas* are *clear*, when they are such as the objects from whence they were taken did or might in a well-ordered sensation or perception, present them" (2.29.2). This painstakingly worded statement seems to offer more certainty than it provides. It sounds as if clear ideas are visual copies ("taken") of objects viewed in the way a normal person perceives them. But if in place of the words Locke italicizes we attend to *as* and *might*, we find that what seemed a generic or causal account of the origin of clear ideas is a conditional description of them based on a simile: Ideas are clear when they are kinds of mental images *like* those that normal viewers *might* have registered had they been there.

The fate of *simple* ideas is noteworthy because while Locke is habitually ready to grant that *complex* ideas are things we make up to think and talk with ("fictions of the mind") rather than direct perceptions, he is understandably less willing to sever the mimetic link between simple ideas and the external world. At his most scrupulous, however, he does sever most of it. Not only is "likeness" to things in the world restricted to simple ideas, it is narrowed still further to simple ideas of "primary qualities" of body (solidity, extension, figure, motion, and number as opposed to colors, sounds, tastes, and so on). It would seem that only Newton spent most of his time having ideas "like" the world. Such ideas *are resemblances* of bodies and "these patterns do really exist." The rest *have no resemblance* of them at all. There is nothing like our *Ideas* existing in the bodies themselves" (2.8.15). It is in this chapter that Locke's "idea" becomes more like the response to a sign than like a picture. Most simple ideas of sensation are "no more the likeness of something existing without us than the names that stand for them are the likeness of our *ideas*, which yet upon hearing they are apt to excite in us" (2.8.7).

Our experience, in other words, is closer to reading or listening to speech than to looking at things. We have, with the exception of primary qualities, access not to objects but to signifiers. Had Locke pursued this model of experience consistently, rather than the complex of visual metaphors noted earlier, the *Essay* would be a very different book.[4] As it is, the linguistic analogy surfaces at several revealing points, often in negative terms, as in the remarks on wit or rhetoric. Before going further it is necessary to underscore the significance of the analogy here by recalling that Locke is perhaps the first major analyst of language to stress that the relation of signifier to signified is not divinely instituted or mimetic but "perfectly arbitrary"

(3.2.8). What the linguistic analogy implies, then, is a functional, convenient but wholly ungrounded relation of idea and world.

At this point we can begin to see Locke's denigration of figurative expressions and allusions in the context of his uneasiness about language in general. There are moments in Locke, as will be seen, where words alone are certain truth, but many more, and more explicit ones, of linguistic skepticism: "For he that shall well consider the *Errors and Obscurity, the Mistakes and Confusion, that is spread in the World by an ill use of Words*, will find some reason to doubt whether Language, as it has been employ'd, has contributed more to the improvement or hindrance of Knowledge amongst Mankind" (3.11.4). Locke's suspicion of what he terms the "cover of wit and good language" runs deeper than the currents of plain-style Puritanism or scientific polemic. The tension between Locke's thinking of ideas as pictures or as interpretations of signs (or correspondingly of objects available to us as things or as signifiers) is played out at large in the *Essay* as a tension between truth as residing in perceptions or in propositions. The explanation I want to try to illustrate is this: having reached the uncomfortable insight that our experience of "things" is in fact the experience of signifiers, Locke seeks to manage the radical implications of the linguistic analogy by reverting to the model of perceptions and pictures and by stipulating impossibly strict standards for proper language. If experience may just be a language, then language itself had best be kept determinate. It should (against all odds) speak of things as they are.

Locke's treatment of language in book 3 of the *Essay* strikes most readers as remarkably free of theories of origin and (and perhaps therefore) surprisingly consistent on the arbitrariness of the relation between signified and signifier. Hans Aarsleff claims more than chronological priority for Locke (1982). To be sure, language is God's gift to humanity, but the terms remain general: language is defined as the totality of all natural languages and as their use by the totality of speakers. Unlike vast numbers of his contemporaries and many later writers, Locke nowhere in the *Essay*'s chapters on language speculates about how Adam and Eve communicated, the Tower of Babel, or, except dismissively, mysterious or mystical connections between names and things named. However pious his intentions at large (the "main end of these inquiries" being "knowledge and veneration" of the "Sovereign Disposer of all things" [2.7.6]), for purposes of philosophic discussion there is no linguistic paradise lost. Where an Adamic myth surfaces instead is in Locke's notion of a language of judgment that names things as they are, without figure and, as only Adam could, without allusion.

Locke's contradictions on the subject of figurative language in book 3 have been brilliantly illustrated by de Man, and the issue of metaphor in the *Essay* as a whole can best be considered in connection with the responses to Locke of Addison and Prior. For now at least a partial answer emerges to the question of what allusion has to do with figurative speech in Locke's opposition of wit and judgment. Like "eloquence" and other "artificial" uses of language, allusions lack original innocence, are in fact the most emphatic figure of this lack, of having fallen into time. Return briefly, then, to the question of how an ideal of an unallusive language fits so uneasily with Locke's arguments elsewhere in the *Essay*.

The two arguments that run counter to the unallusive norm are linguistic and epistemological, although again the boundaries are not always distinct. The linguistic is relatively simple. When discussing language directly Locke argues, consistently, that since words have "naturally no signification" the "*idea* which each stands for must be learned and retained by those who would exchange thoughts and hold intelligible discourse with others" (3.9.5). What such learning and retention of common usage amounts to is a continual series of allusions, namely to the usage of past and present speakers. Most of these allusions are of course unconscious, and any conventional notion of language implies the ability to make them, even the inability to *not* make them most of the time. But Locke goes further to recommend conscious allusions. If we would seek "propriety of speech" as indeed we should since words are "no man's private possession by the common measure of commerce and communication," we will find propriety by studying and imitating the usage of our linguistic predecessors: "The proper signification and best use of Terms is best to be learned from those, who in their Writings and Discourses, appear to have had the clearest Notions, and apply'd to them their Terms with the exactest choice and fitness" (3.11.11).

Let me acknowledge at once that my use of "allusion" may well be broader than Locke intended and that he might have been thinking not of the shared use of words but of distinctive phrases and sentences—something closer to quotation. But it is also clear that in the attacks on wit in books 2 and 3 he is not criticizing the citation of authorities, something he does attack elsewhere but as characteristic of Scholasticism rather than of wit, fancy, or eloquence. It may be that he means something close to what allusion usually means in modern literary discussion, that is, intentional reference to previously used phrases or verbally established contexts for the complication of present meaning. And if it may be added that allusion often complicates by suggesting at least a fleeting parallel, it may be seen why Locke repeats the word in the same breath with "figurative speeches" and "similitude." But when all of this has been granted, it remains true that Locke's notion of a wholly direct and unallusive discourse belongs to a less sophisticated theory of language than to the secular one he works out. While we can speak of some writers, for example, as more allusive than others, there is no logical place for a use of language "quite contrary" to allusion. In view of Locke's account of language as the sum of common conventions, a speech that is the opposite of allusive speech would seem to belong to a world of neither wit nor judgment but desire.

If the allusiveness Locke denigrates is in fact central to his theory of language, is it also central to his theory of knowledge? Much of the *Essay* can be read as a succession of attempts to answer no to this question, to put the knower and the known in a direct relation, unmediated by community or language. Before considering a few of the efforts to find extralinguistic certainties in book 4, let us turn to a final episode in the discussion of language that seems already an epistemological episode as well. Locke is discussing the names of "mixed Modes," that is, several ideas of "sorts or Species of Things" (3.5.1), and arrives at the interesting observation that, unlike simple ideas, these complex ideas usually become known to us *after* we have learned the words for them.

> I confess, that in the beginning of Languages, it was necessary to have the *Idea*, before one gave it the Name: and so it is still, where making a new complex *Idea*, one also, by giving it a new Name, makes a new Word. But this concerns not Languages made, which have generally pretty well provided for *Ideas*, which Men have frequent Occasion to have, and communicate: And in such, I ask, whether it be not the ordinary Method, that Children learn the Names of mixed Modes, before they have their *Ideas*? What one of a thousand ever frames the abstract *Idea* of *Glory* and *Ambition*, before he has heard the Names of them? (3.5.15)

With the rare exceptions, then, of new coinages, the large range of ideas that make converse of any complexity possible are learned by a process of allusion. The vocabulary of these ideas exists first as a vocabulary.

I have been arguing that Locke's criticism of the figures and allusions of wit is part of an uneasiness about language at large and that his criticism was sharpened by the suspicion that knowledge and language are inseparable. Locke would not concede their inseparability. What he says instead, explaining how he came to write book 3, is that he found that knowledge and words had "so near a connexion" that "very little" could be "said clearly or pertinently" about

knowledge without first observing the "face and manner of signification" of words. Because knowledge is, in Locke's suggestive phrase,
"conversant about truth," it has "constantly to do with propositions."
While it ends "in things," it arrives there "so much by the intervention of words" that they seem "scarce separable" from general knowledge. "At least they interpose themselves so much between our
Understandings, and the Truth, which it would contemplate and
apprehend that, like the *Medium* through which visible Objects pass,
their Obscurity and Disorder does not seldom cast a mist before our
Eyes, and impose upon our Understandings" (3.9.21). The progress of
actions attributed to words is striking: words intervene, then interpose, and finally impose.

In a landscape so populated or where, to take a later metaphor, so
many have wandered "lost in the great Wood of Words" (4.3.30),
mathematics often looks like the safest way out of allusion and illusion.
"By abstracting their Thoughts from Names, and accustoming themselves to set before their Minds the *Ideas* themselves . . . and not
sounds instead of them," mathematicians have escaped most of the
"perplexity, puddering, and confusion" of other fields (ibid.). If we
would "but separate the *Idea* under consideration from the Sign that
stands for it" moral knowledge would be "as *capable of real Certainty,*
as Mathematics" (4.4.7, 9). I shall return to Locke's admiration for
mathematical method in discussing Prior's response to the *Essay,* but
the general point is simply that the main appeal of mathematics for
Locke seems to be that it offers not a world of symmetry unencum-
bered by matter, or (as one might expect), more direct access to
primary qualities, but an escape from words.

Locke's desire for extralinguistic certainty shows forth even when
he argues more fully the point that truth resides in propositions. The
chapter in which he does so, "Of Truth in General" (4.5), is one of the
most curious in the *Essay,* primarily because of Locke's insistence on
a distinction between mental and verbal propositions, "truth of
thought" and "truth of words." For it turns out that when he begins
by defining truth as "nothing but *the joining or separating of Signs, as
the Things signified by them, do agree or disagree one with another,*"
Locke is not at all making the same definitional move that Hobbes had
made in declaring that "*true* and *false* are attributes of speech, not of
things. And where speech is not, there is neither *truth* nor
falsehood. . . . Truth consisteth in the right ordering of names in our
affirmations" (Hobbes n.d., 1.4). For Locke, on the contrary, the
"signs" joined or separated to make propositions can be either words
or ideas: "So that Truth properly belongs only to Propositions:
whereof there are two sorts, viz. Mental and Verbal; as there are two

sorts of Signs commonly made use of, *viz. Ideas* and Words" (4.5.2).
This is a most unusual definition of "idea," I believe unprecedented in
the *Essay* to this point. (Although I have argued that some of Locke's
descriptions of ideas imply that they are like our responses to signs,
the synonyms he himself normally uses are phantasms, notions, perceptions, pictures, and so on.) This odd twist allows Locke, however,
to go on to assert the necessity of considering truth of thought and
truth of words "distinctly one from another" (4.5.2–3).

Necessary as it may be, two difficulties are conceded. The first is
that as soon as we begin to describe mental propositions in words they
become verbal propositions (a problem analogous to trying to observe
oneself without being self-conscious, say, which does not usually
lessen the belief that one has periods of unselfconsciousness). The
second, much greater difficulty Locke poses to his own distinction
appears to undo it entirely: "And that which makes it *harder to treat
of mental* and verbal *Propositions separately,* is That most Men, *if not
all* [my emphasis], in their Thinking and Reasonings within themselves, make use of Words instead of *Ideas,* at least when the subject
of their meditation contains in it complex *Ideas*" (4.5.3; cf. 4.6.2).
Having opened the possibility that all propositions of much complexity are verbal rather than purely mental, Locke vacillates in the rest of
this brief chapter between extremes, wishing at one point that those
who speak on subjects like religion, power, or melancholy (all of them
remarkably complex ideas) would "think only of the Things themselves" (4.5.4) rather than their words, and at another point restricting
his definition of truth further to only verbal propositions: "*Truth* is the
marking down in Words, the agreement or disagreement of *Ideas* as it
is" (4.5.9).

> Every one's Experience will satisfie him, that the Mind, either by
> perceiving or supposing the Agreement or Disagreement of its *Ideas,* does
> tacitly within it self put them into a kind of Proposition affirmative or
> negative, which I have endeavoured to express by the terms *Putting
> together* and *Separating.* But this Action of the Mind, which is so familiar
> to every thinking and reasoning Man, is easier to be conceived by reflect-
> ing on what passes in us, when we affirm or deny, than to be explained by
> Words. (4.5.6)

Locke's meaning seems to be that our habit of making nonverbal
propositions can be better imagined nonverbally than explained verbally. In other words, the proposition that we habitually make tacit
propositions is most clear as a tacit proposition.

Addison, Prior, and Locke's Dichotomy

If Locke's opposition of wit and judgment involves as many problems as the previous section claims (and a few more will be suggested here), it is material to ask why it ever attracted Joseph Addison. That we cannot know Addison's motivation as he sat to the pages that would become *Spectator* 62 does not preclude some guesses. There is the general prestige of the *Essay,* and there is Addison's particular interest in bringing philosophy from the closet to the coffeehouse. Moreover, Locke's opposition has the appeal of familiar wisdom (so-and-so is "clever" but not thoughtful, or "steady" but not quick) suddenly bolstered by modern analysis ("and hence perhaps may be given some reason . . .") and looking for the moment as if it might offer an exhaustive characterological dichotomy (a recurrent fantasy neatly satirized in the quip, "There are two kinds of people: those who divide things into two and those who don't"). Neither eighteenth- nor twentieth-century intellectuals are immune to the charms of such a prospect. But it is probably safer to modify the question about Addison to *how* he found Locke's dichotomy attractive. How much of it does he accept, how does he use it, and how does it look when he has finished?

Like the rest of the series (nos. 58–63), *Spectator* 62 contrasts "true" wit and "false" wit (Addison 1965, 1:263–70). Addison begins it by referring to Locke's "admirable Reflection upon the Difference of Wit and Judgment, whereby he endeavours to shew the Reason why they are not always the Talents of the same Person." He then quotes all of the passage from 2.11.2 quoted earlier, except the first sentence, replaced by his summary, and the last sentence and a half, thus ending with Locke's observation that through metaphor and allusion wit "strikes so lively on the Fancy, and is therefore acceptable to all People." The passage, then, that Addison commends as the "best and most philosophical Account that I have ever met with of Wit" has already changed clothes for the meeting. His introduction neutralizes Locke's explanation of why men of wit are often not good judges (Locke says nothing of wit being beyond the reach of men of judgment) to a distinction of talents. And in silently ignoring the latter part of Locke's section he suppresses Locke's *regret* that wit is so "acceptable to all people," a fact due to its requiring "no labour of thought" and not being up to the rigor of "truth or reason." Similarly, there is no mention in the essay of Locke's attack on wit, figurative language, and allusion in book 3 (quoted above).

To what he does quote, Addison adds and qualifies. Locke's is the best (previous) explanation of wit, "which generally, tho' not always, consists in such a Resemblance and Congruity of Ideas as this Author mentions. I shall only add to it, by way of Explanation, That every Resemblance of Ideas is not that which we call Wit, unless it be such an one that gives *Delight* and *Surprize* to the Reader: These two Properties seem essential to Wit, more particularly the last of them." The reserve clause ("generally, though not always") can be held, with Addison, until the conclusion of his consideration of Locke. Before going there it is worth noting, first, that Addison's "Resemblance and Congruity of Ideas" replaces Locke's assertion that wit is an "assemblage of ideas" based on "any resemblance or congruity" the assembler can find, and, second, that Addison's emphasis on the "surprize" of wit suggests pleasure from the discovery of real resemblance in place of Locke's "beauty . . . at first sight." Both alterations are important for Addison's later propositions (par. 8) "That the Basis of all Wit is Truth" and that a beautiful thought has "its Foundation in the Nature of Things."

The essential claim of most of the rest of Addison's essay, where he appropriates Locke's dichotomy between wit and judgment into his own between two kinds of wit, is that true wit is true. The point is explicit but sometimes lost sight of because "true" wit can be taken to mean something like "genuine" or "pure" wit and because Addison also uses contrasts like "Gothic" versus "natural" (par. 9); but the starker terms are "Falsehood" and "Truth" (par. 6). The phrase probably quoted most often in summarizing Addison's position is "true Wit consists in the resemblance of Ideas, and false Wit in the Resemblance of Words" (par. 4). What he actually says is that this description covers the examples he has just cited ("according to the foregoing Instances"), among which figure prominently the familiar targets, such as shaped verses, acrostics, quibbles, and puns. The attack on puns (which false wit might call an argument ad homonym) is usually best remembered because it fits so readily the distinction between resemblances of words and resemblances of ideas. But *similarity* of ideas is not the basis of all true wit, as Addison's conclusion makes clear:

> I must not dismiss this Subject without observing, that as Mr. *Locke* in the Passage above-mentioned has discovered the most fruitful Source of Wit, so there is another of a quite contrary Nature to it, which does likewise branch it self out into several Kinds. For not only the *Resemblance* but the *Opposition* of Ideas does very often produce Wit; as I could shew in several little Points, Turns and Antitheses, that I may possibly enlarge upon in some future Speculation.

Perhaps if Addison had returned to the opposition of ideas in a later essay this passage would by now have attracted more notice. Standing almost as an afterthought, its casual tone is as disarming as the suave appearance of agreement with Locke earlier in the essay. Here Addison does much more than shift Locke's emphasis. If it is true that wit discerns differences as well as similarities, then the dichotomy between wit and judgment collapses. Having enlisted it in an argument for the truth of wit, Addison leaves Locke's distinction, so to speak, without judgment.

It may be coincidence that Addison characterized the wit of opposition as "quite contrary" to the more familiar sort Locke had described. Accident or allusion, the phrase suggests their distance, since it is the one Locke used to oppose not one kind of wit to another but the ways of difference and similitude. My brief discussion of *Spectator* 62 no doubt reveals the judgment that Addison knew exactly what he was doing. But judgment, as Locke eventually argues in some passages to which it is now time to turn, should be distinguished from knowledge.

* * *

The fourth book of Locke's *Essay*, "Of Knowledge and Opinion," begins with the proposition that because the mind's only immediate object is its own ideas, knowledge is "nothing but *the perception of the connexion and agreement, or disagreement and repugnancy of any of our Ideas*. In this alone it consists. Where this Perception is, there is Knowledge, and where it is not, there, though we may fancy, guess, or believe, yet we always come short of Knowledge" (4.1.1–2). In fact, as Locke everywhere emphasizes, we usually do come short of knowledge. Fancying, as we have seen, has nothing to do with knowledge, but we must often guess or believe in order to "know" how to live. "He that in the ordinary Affairs of Life, would admit of nothing but direct plain Demonstration, would be sure of nothing, in this World, but of perishing quickly" (4.11.10; cf. 4.14.1). Rarely in the presence of certainty, our guesses and beliefs in this "twilight" of probability are guided by judgment, the subject of a late chapter (14).

To understand Locke's account it is necessary to see what is at stake. The starting point of book 4 makes clear that knowledge—like truth, its expression in propositions—is conversant about similarities of ideas ("agreement") as well as about differences. The difference between wit and knowledge in this respect seems to be that wit *makes* similarities and knowledge *perceives* them. The question, which Addison helps indirectly to focus, is whether the same is true of judgment. Is judgment closer to knowledge or to wit?

Locke does what he can to close the gap between judgment and knowledge by associating them with each other as much as possible, and, as we have seen, the attacks on wit and eloquence in books 2 and 3 provide occasion to use judgment, truth, reason, and knowledge as near synonyms. Whatever the discriminations to be made elsewhere among the four terms, Locke seems to fuse them to compose whatever it is that is "quite contrary" to wit. Judgment ("being able nicely to distinguish") and knowledge ("perception" of agreement or disagreement) are closely associated elsewhere by Locke's tendency to speak of perceiving and distinguishing as the same thing: the mind recognizes separate ideas "at first view," for example, "by its natural power of Perception and Distinction" (4.1.4).

A broader association of judgment with knowledge by virtue of what "it" is opposed to operates in the chapter "Of the Reality of Knowledge," where Locke contrasts the knowledge of a "sober" man and a man of the "most extravagant Fancy in the world" (4.4.1). How do these two differ, Locke imagines his reader asking, if knowledge is only the internal agreement or disagreement of one's own ideas? Like the original contrast of judgment and wit, this opposition of sobriety and fancy signals a great deal of strain. Locke's answer to the question is that our knowledge is limited but consists of "two sorts of *Ideas*, that, we may be assured, agree with things," simple ideas and all complex ideas except those of substances. What he in fact argues is much narrower: simple ideas "*are not fictions* of our Fancies" because they represent things to the extent "ordained" by the "wisdom and will of our Maker," in the way we are "fitted" to perceive them; complex ideas have all the "*conformity necessary to real knowledge*" because they are "*archetypes* of the mind's own making" and were never "intended to be the Copies of anything" (4.4.3–5). When, after several paragraphs on the desirability of separating ideas from words, Locke concludes that we have "certain real knowledge" whenever "we are sure those ideas agree with the reality of things," the words come uncomfortably close to his later dismissal of enthusiasts: "They are sure because they are sure" (4.19.9). The chapter ends in a tone weirdly reminiscent of *A Tale of a Tub*:

> Of which agreement of our *ideas* with the reality of things having here given sufficient marks, I think I have shown wherein it is, that *Certainty, real Certainty*, consists. Which, whatever it was to others, was, I confess, to me heretofore, one of those *Desiderata* which I found great want of. (4.4.18)

When Locke finally comes to write of the judgment directly rather than by way of "contraries," it is still on the side of truth, but the fundamental association with knowledge no longer holds. The brief chapter (4.14) concludes with a new refinement.

> Thus the Mind has two Faculties conversant about Truth and Falsehood:
> *First, Knowledge,* whereby it certainly perceives and is undoubtedly satisfied of the Agreement or Disagreement of any *Ideas.*
> *Secondly, Judgment,* which is the putting *Ideas* together, or separating them one from another in the Mind, when their certain Agreement or Disagreement is not perceived, but *presumed.* . . . And if it so unites or separates them as in Reality Things are, it is *right Judgment.* (4.14.4; cf. 4.17.17)

In this scheme knowledge perceives but judgment puts together and separates. At least half (and if Addison is right, all) of its operations, then, seem less contrary than kindred to the "assemblage of ideas, and putting those together" previously assigned to wit. The function of the original dichotomy (2.11.2) seems in retrospect to have been to protect the "good" assemblages (complex ideas, for example) from the taint of fiction and to make a firmer claim on "things as they are" than the Lockean way of ideas can consistently justify. Having in this chapter momentarily opened the possibility that judgment may after all proceed rather like wit, Locke attempts to close it in the last sentence with the sudden introduction of "*right Judgment.*" It might fairly be objected that if we can have right and wrong judgment we can have right and wrong—or true or false—wit as well. In that case, wit and judgment are not distinct actions but different manners: one "quick," the other "careful." To Matthew Prior, at least, Locke's judgment would seem a name for slow wit.

Prior's "A Dialogue between Mr: John Lock and Seigneur de Montaigne" was not published until this century. By far most of the best of its roughly ten thousand words are given to Montaigne, whose urbanity and ranging observation are plainly more sympathetic to Prior than is Locke's earnest introspection. When Locke objects that as the "loosest of writers" Montaigne naturally undervalues "my close way of Reasoning," Montaigne replies: "All the while you wrote you were only thinking that you thought; You and Your understanding are the *Personae Dramatis*, and the whole amounts to no more than a Dialogue between John and Lock" (1971, 1:620). And the shortcomings of monodrama are as plain as the maxim that "he that does not talk with a Wiser Man than himself may happen to Dye Ignorant." "Really who ever writes in Folio should convince people that he knows something besides himself, else few would read his Book, except his very particular Friends" (623). When Locke again criticizes Montaigne's lack of method, this time enlisting Chanet, Scaliger, and

Malebranche for support, Montaigne says: "I have observed that there is Abcedarian Ignorance that precedes Knowledge, and a Doctoral Ignorance that comes after it. . . . Method! our Life is too short for it" (629–30).

Despite the breezy antipathy of these exchanges, references to arguments and examples from all four books of the *Essay* show that Prior read it with care if not respect. He is particularly attentive to Locke's suspicion of figurative language and allusions. Prior approaches allusion by having Locke boast that while Montaigne's writing is a collection of stolen goods, "I spin my Work out of my own thoughts." The claim predictably leads Montaigne to "allude" to *The Battle of the Books* and play Swift's bee to Locke's spider, with an additional shake of the metaphor: "But to come nearer to you, Mr: Lock, You like many other writers, Deceive your Self in this Point, and as much a Spider as you fancy your Self, You may often cast your Webb upon other Mens Textures." Locke answers that if he has been anticipated in some points without knowing it, "what I write is as much my own Invention as if no Man had thought the Same thing before me," while Montaigne simply copied materials from his commonplace book. To this Montaigne replies laconically: "Why the best One can do is but compose, I hope you do not pretend to Create." Finding Locke undaunted, Montaigne charges him with unwitting allusion:

> Your Ideas, as you call them . . . were so mixed and Blended, long before You began to write, in the great Variety of things that fall under their Cognizance that it was impossible for You to Distinguish what you Invented from what You Remembered. . . . When you Seem to have least regard to Orators and Poets you have recourse to both for your very turn of Style and manner of Expression. Parblew Mr. Lock, when you had writ half your Book in favor of your own Dear Understanding you quote Cicero to prove the very Existence of a God. (623–33)

In another part of this long speech, Montaigne asserts that Malebranche, like Locke, warned against misleading the judgment with figurative language but was in fact wise to ignore his own advice: "the Strength of his Argument consists in the beauty of his Figures" (633). This claim, that figurative language discovers rather than covers an author's judgment, conveys the radical difference between Prior and Locke. It emerges more resonantly in a passage that gains point when we recall that Locke's suspicion of language had led to celebrations of mathematics; on at least four occasions he had paused in particular to hope that philosophy would attain an "instrument" of "sagacity" approaching algebra (4.3.18, 20; 4.12.15; 4.17.11). In this exchange

Montaigne has just attacked Locke with two analogies, one of them taken from the *Essay*:

> *Lock*. Simile upon Simile, no Consequential Proof, right Montaigne by my Troth. Why, Sir, you catch at Similes as a Swallow does at Flies.
>
> *Montaigne*. And you make Similes while you blame them. But be that as it will, Mr. Lock, arguing by Simile is not so absurd as some of You dry Reasoners would make People believe. If your Simile be proper and good, it is at once a full proof, and a lively Illustration of Your matter, and where it does not hold the very disproportion gives You Occasion to reconsider it, and You set it in all it's lights, if it be only to find at least how unlike it is. Egad Simile is the very Algebra of Discourse. (625)

This simile (or "metasimile") falls so neatly that it may seem, as Locke would say (the actual Locke, 2.11.2), a "kind of affront to go about to examine it by the severe rules of truth and good reason." Locke's point is that the obvious inappropriateness of such an examination is itself an admission that wit is not "conformable" to the way of judgment. But whatever Prior thinks of Locke's method, he invites the reader to apply the test of truth, maintaining in fact that all similes issue such invitations. If a simile succeeds in being at once "full proof" and "lively illustration," it conveys knowledge (as Locke's agreement of ideas); if it does not, it calls judgment into action ("gives . . . occasion to reconsider") and will lead to knowledge (as Locke's disagreement of ideas). Bad similes may lower our estimate of a work; but for the reader a simile "works" whether it succeeds or fails.

Prior clearly assumes a less vulnerable reader than Locke's, one whose judgment will be quickened rather than outdistanced by wit's quickness. Exactly how much more he assumes in the passage is difficult to determine, but it seems likely that he might expect the reader who would examine the comparison of algebra and simile to be thinking of algebra as more than a shorthand notation. Considering algebra generally as the study of functions rather than fixed quantities (and the word seems to have had at least this currency), "the algebra of discourse" suggests the working-out of relationships within language. This is another way of claiming, with Addison, that wit has verity as well as brevity; in other words, it not only paints pictures but contemplates general relations. If the philosopher's desire is ultimately the Hobbesean one that words be used as the wise man's "counters" rather than as the fool's "money" (Hobbes n.d., 1.4), to seek an extralinguistic discovery procedure for moral philosophy is simply to turn one's back on the higher mathematics already at hand in the liveliest uses of language.

With different emphases but complementary doubts, Addison and

Prior both question Locke's devaluation of wit and the opposition of wit to judgment. Challenging the claim that discrimination is peculiar to judgment, Addison points politely to the collapse of the dichotomy. Prior more explicitly raises the problem of any such dichotomy (regardless of which side is "privileged") by questioning whether making similitudes and making distinctions are really separable acts of mind. This is the fundamental question at the level of common sense, and common sense sides, I believe, with Locke one moment and Prior the next: yes, we sometimes "distinguish," sometimes "assemble," and can "distinguish" between the operations; no, we cannot differentiate without comparing and vice versa. But behind this armchair antinomy the problem dividing Locke from Addison and Prior can be seen as a question with particular pertinence to our own era and criticism: does it make more sense to think of "things as they are" as represented (perhaps badly) by language or as constituted by language?

The preceding commentary suggests at several points that Locke's accounts of language in general and of figurative language in particular are efforts to reclaim indirectly an access to pre- or extralinguistic "things" that other parts of his *Essay* seal off. In suggesting now that Addison and Prior are deeply skeptical of the attempt to get past language to something firmer, I do not mean to convert them into proto-Nietzschean or proto-Derridean rhetoricians of contradiction. From the perspective of poststructuralism, both are grounded in "logocentrism." Both believe that in the beginning was the Word, the authorial will originating all subsequent meaning. Neither would know what to make of the idea that this belief should be reinscribed as "In the always-already are words." Nor would either be likely to hear more than burlesque in Beckett's version, "In the beginning was the pun." But at the same time, neither Addison nor Prior seems to share Locke's nostalgia for things and ideas untouched by words or for truths too tacit to enter the shared figures and allusions of language. If these differences are significant, then it seems we would need to speak of logocentrisms in neoclassical writing (and presumably in other literary periods) for the term to be historically useful; in the monolithic singular it is, like Locke's "wit," less descriptive of variable rhetorical practices than protective of its rhetorically constructed opposite.

Notes

1. Dryden, "A Discourse concerning Satire" (1962, 2:145). One of the best surveys of the status of "wit" (especially in relation to the opposition of wit and judgment) is the introduction by Aubrey Williams to Pope's *Essay on Criticism* (Pope 1939–69, 1:197–232).

2. See MacLean 1936, 63–66, and Bond's note on *Spectator* 62 (Addison 1965, 1:263).

3. The discussions of Locke's style that I have found most helpful are those by Colie 1966 and 1969 and Richetti 1983.

4. Turbayne 1970 discusses the implications of linguistic versus geometric and mechanistic metaphors in philosophy from Descartes onward.

Works Cited

Aarsleff, Hans. 1982. *From Locke to Saussure*. Minneapolis: University of Minnesota Press.

Addison, Joseph. 1965. *The Spectator*. Ed. Donald F. Bond. 5 vols. Oxford: Oxford University Press.

Colie, Rosalie. 1966. "John Locke and the Publication of the Private." *Philogical Quarterly* 45:24–45.

———. 1969. "The Essayist in his *Essay*." In *John Locke: Problems and Perspectives*, ed. John Yolton, 234–61. Cambridge: Cambridge University Press.

de Man, Paul, 1979. "The Epistemology of Metaphor." In *On Metaphor*, ed. Sheldon Sacks, 11–28. Chicago: University of Chicago Press.

Dryden, John. 1962. *"Of Dramatic Poesy" and Other Critical Essays*. Ed. George Watson. 2 vols. Everyman Edition.

Gay, John. 1974. *Poetry and Prose*. Ed. Vinton A. Dearing with the assistance of Charles E. Bechwith. 2 vols. Oxford: Oxford University Press.

Hobbes, Thomas. n.d. *Leviathan; or, The Matter, Forme and Power of a Commonwealth Ecclesiasticall and Civil*. Ed. Michael Oakeshott. Blackwell's Political Texts. Oxford.

Johnson, Samuel. 1984. *Samuel Johnson*. Ed. Donald Greene. New York: Oxford University Press.

Locke, John. [1975] 1979. *An Essay Concerning Human Understanding*. Ed. Peter H. Nidditch. Reprinted with corrections. Oxford: Oxford University Press.

MacLean, Kenneth. 1936. *John Locke and English Literature of the Eighteenth Century*. New Haven: Yale University Press.

Pope, Alexander. 1939–69. *The Twickenham Edition of the Poems of Alexander Pope*. Gen. ed. John Butt. 11 vols. London: Methuen; New Haven: Yale University Press.

Prior, Matthew. 1971. *The Literary Works of Matthew Prior*. Ed. H. Bunker Wright and Monroe K. Spears. 2d ed. 2 vols. Oxford: Oxford University Press.

Richetti, John. 1983. *Philosophical Writing: Locke, Berkeley, Hume*. Cambridge: Harvard University Press.

Turbayne, Colin Murray. 1970. *The Myth of Metaphor*. Rev. ed. Columbia: University of South Carolina Press.

Female Orders of Narrative
Clarissa *and* The Italian
PATRICIA MEYER SPACKS

Recent criticism has insisted on ways in which endings impose order (e.g., Kermode 1967); Nancy Miller's definition of "euphoric" and "dysphoric" plots for the heroines of eighteenth-century novels (1980) makes narrative outcomes crucial to understanding the fictional place of women. To concentrate instead, however, on the happenings preceding those outcomes generates very different forms of understanding. Counteracting its compelling images of male tyranny and female victimization, *Clarissa* delineates a woman who acts effectively by constructing and enforcing her own story, its ending in some ways less momentous than its action. Later, Ann Radcliffe's Gothic novels developed intricate plots with "euphoric" endings for beleaguered heroines quite unable to control interpretation of their stories. Competing narratives, in Radcliffe's fiction, issue not only (as in *Clarissa*) from characters with interests opposed to those of the heroine, but from the heroine herself. Unable fully to order her own narrative, the Radcliffean maiden may act courageously in less claustrophobic circumstances than Clarissa's, but finally she, too, reveals woman's socially enforced weakness.

For both Richardson and Radcliffe, Christian belief provides material for personal narrative orders—and even for some sorts of narrative disorder. In Richardson's case particularly, Christianity of course functions as far more than a narrative device (see Damrosch 1985 and Doody 1974); but the novel also brilliantly employs religious conviction as a strategy for characterization and structure as well as an ethical standard. I propose to concentrate on a single aspect of Clarissa's role in the competition of ordering narratives (see Castle 1982 and Warner 1979): her use of the Christian story for paradoxical self-assertion. In *The Italian*, on the other hand, the diminished place of religious myth, reduced from action to feeling, helps to focus attention on new ways of defining narrative, of ordering the rhetoric of fiction at the century's end. Both Richardson and Radcliffe, I shall argue, explore specifically female possibilities for adapting Christian principles of interpretation.

*   *   *

Unlike her precursor, Pamela, Clarissa neither invokes Christian authority nor relies on Christian comfort as she initially struggles for minimal autonomy against the impositions of father and brother: a fact that helps specify her individual relation to narrative. The heroine early finds herself forced into severe doctrinal selectivity. Her father claims godlike authority yet abrogates paternal responsibility, failing in attentiveness and in moral awareness. "Honor thy father and thy mother" therefore takes second place for Clarissa to a notion of "steadiness" inculcated by her religious mentor, Dr. Lewen. "*Steadiness of mind* (a quality which the ill-bred and censorious deny to any of our sex) when we are absolutely convinced of being in the right (otherwise it is not *steadiness* but *obstinacy*) is a quality which, as my good Dr. Lewen was wont to say, brings great credit to the possessor of it; at the same time that it usually, when *tried* and *known*, raises *such* above the attempts of the meanly machinating" (Richardson 1932, 1:93). Clarissa does not yet doubt her own rightness or her capacity to rise above her enemies. But her parentheses call attention to her uneasiness about the story she is in the process of constructing, a story that, in her version as in Anna Howe's, will emphasize Clarissa's virtue. Although she believes in the possiblity of getting "great credit" for her steadiness, she knows how sexual stereotypes may control interpretations of her actions. And she imagines the specific reading of her character ("not *steadiness* but *obstinacy*") that will help articulate the family conflicts generating the novel's complex narrative. Indeed, she tacitly realizes her violation of an absolute moral imperative in her failure to yield to her father, despite his wrongness. The "pride" she will later declare her besetting sin urges her on, but her awareness of interpretive ambiguity already troubles her.

Clarissa's "steadiness," she points out,

is deemed stubbornness, obstinacy, prepossession, by those who have a right to put what interpretation they please upon my conduct.

So, my dear, were we perfect (which no one *can* be), we could not be happy in this life, unless those with whom we have to deal (those more especially who have any control upon us) were governed by the same principles. But then does not the good doctor's conclusion recur—that we have nothing to do but to choose what is right; to be steady in the pursuit of it; and to leave the issue to Providence? (1:94)

Parenthood creates the right of interpretation, in Clarissa's view, but other people's views hardly matter to her. "Providence," at this point in the narrative, sanctions a simple order of events and of story: "we have nothing to do but. . . ." The young woman, more concerned about approaching perfection than about achieving happiness, appears confident of standing higher than her parents in the moral hierarchy (not being perfect, but adhering to proper principles). As she often does, she here tells a microcosmic version of her entire story: her unyielding steadiness, interpreted as obstinacy, will make her unhappy because her family lack her principles; her theological self-justification will support her in her choice; she refuses to acknowledge concern about outcomes, all acceptable because necessarily providential. Inflexible moral logic creates her orderly syntax of necessity. Possible unhappiness has a rationally comprehensible cause, suggested by *since*; a connective of causality (*So*) leads to the hypothesis of perfection that produces a necessary effect, given imperfection elsewhere; the final rhetorical question declares the inevitable conclusion. Clarissa sounds a little smug, a little blind, unaware of terrible experiential possibilities. But she also sounds *right*: the Christian premise generates its own inexorable logic.

Like the reader, Clarissa comes to know logic's insufficiencies. Her obligations to others conflict with her responsibility to God. More and more clearly, events force her to understand the painfulness of choice: choice, it sometimes seems, about whom to hurt. The individual's relation to Providence becomes murky. What if, by trying to avoid trouble between James Harlowe and Lovelace, Clarissa intercepts "the designs of Providence" (1:413)? She has earlier assumed that Providence will ratify her virtue. Gradually she lowers her sights: Enough if she can be "*justly* acquitted of wilful and premeditated faults. The will of Providence be resigned to in the rest: as *that* leads, let me patiently and unrepiningly follow! I shall not live always. May but my *closing* scene be happy!" (1:420). This depressed utterance foreshadows not only the conclusion of Clarissa's earthly career but the degree to which events focus her attention on death rather than life. Although Providence remains the figure for cosmic order, she no longer feels confident of her relation to its operations; her anxiety about her own "presumption" and her desire to "follow" contrast with her earlier certainties.

If while she remains in her father's house Clarissa's religious allusions become increasingly depressed and confused, though her faith remains strong, after she leaves home her theological references at first dwindle further. Struggling to work out her own fate, she explores the limits of self-reliance, never abandoning Christian conviction but telling her story, for a time, by means of other allusions. Lovelace lavishes on her the language of divinity ("angel," "divine") while he plots her debasement and she struggles to discern her proper course through his mazes. She describes herself as "one who ever endeavoured to shun intricate paths" (2:378), but no other paths reveal themselves. After she has eloped but before she is raped, Clarissa cannot even define the shape of her own narrative. Is she involved in a love story or a tale of seduction and betrayal? Will she or will she not, can she or can she not, choose marriage as its ending? Does she fill the role of heroine or of victim? Asking such questions, she implicitly wonders about the position and possibilities of a female self in a Christian universe.

Her mistake, Clarissa concludes, consisted in self-dependence; she considers herself a "presumptuous creature" for relying on her "own knowledge of the right path" (2:263). On the other hand, when challenged she continues to declare her self-reliance, reinterpreted as indirect dependence on God. Her hesitations about marriage, she explains to Anna Howe, come from her heart, from "Principles that *are* in my mind; that I *found* there; implanted, no doubt, by the first gracious Planter: which therefore *impel* me, as I may say, to act up to them" (2:306). Although she acknowledges in the succeeding paragraph that "The heart is very deceitful," she here declares her confidence in the divine origin of her moral convictions. Yet self is the grand misleader, Clarissa concludes, commenting on her secret vaunting of her "good inclinations"; self "is at the bottom of all we do, and of all we wish. . . . Is it not enough to make the unhappy creature look into herself, and endeavour to detect herself, who, from such a high reputation, left to proud and presumptuous self, should, by one thoughtless step, be brought to the dreadful situation I am in?" (2:379). But she will not allow herself to repine; she will rely on her divine Father.

Clarissa's mistake, not yet punished by rape, has brought her to desperate self-denial, to a vocabulary of abnegation. The story she tells is undeniably Clarissa's story, but who, now, is Clarissa? A woman whose heart impels her unerringly toward rectitude, or an "unhappy creature [i.e., created being]" helpless to find the good? A self focused on virtue, or a "proud and presumptuous self"? These fundamental interpretive questions lie at the heart of Clarissa's difficulties about her narrative: hers is not merely the familiar problem, Who am I?, but the equally fundamental one, How, and what, do I *mean*? The same question, in the third person, troubles Lovelace, who by compulsive plotting tries to resolve the problem of Clarissa. Does she possess the same meaning as his fantasies of the female nature? If he can believe in some alternative version of female meaning, he thinks he can write Clarissa's story with a happy ending. As for Clarissa herself, almost 250 pages before the rape (in the Everyman edition) she has reached an apparent nadir of selfhood. Unable to assert value in herself, she employs Christian rhetoric to deny that her story has a heroine.

This denial continues to the novel's end. More and more distinctly, Clarissa defines herself as a soul seeking salvation—a definition given urgency by the rape. After the rape, her increasingly insistent Christian interpretation of self and world serves a new narrative purpose. The violation that utterly changes Clarissa's life also redirects her rhetoric and, paradoxically, allows her most grandiose claims. Leopold Damrosch invites us to "admire the subtlety with which the struggle between self-assertion and ethical convention is embodied in the imaginations of the characters themselves" (1985, 220). More subtle still is the gradual *identification* of self-assertion and ethics that takes place in Clarissa.

Immediately after the rape, Clarissa's fragmentary utterances on paper recur obsessively to the problem of self while rejecting the language of religion. She denies her continued identity, she declares herself ignorant of her own name. Her parable of the lady with the young lion or bear or tiger concludes that "what *she* did was *out* of nature, *out* of character, at least" (3:206); succeeding fragments reiterate the self-humbling inherent in her suffering: "I was too secure in the knowledge I thought I had of my own heart" (3:207). If she no longer knows who she is, she has no doubt about Lovelace: "O Lovelace, you are Satan himself" (3:210). God appears in these meditations only as a conventional allusion to forgiveness or punishment; Clarissa can feel herself in no vital relation to her Creator.

Yet only the utterly destructive experience of rape enables her fully to assert herself. The crucial paradox dramatizes the social nullification of women by playing out the full implications of one woman's self-acceptance as *nothing*. Replacing all worldly hopes with heavenly ones, Clarissa adopts the language of religion to convey rage and outrage and to assert the only power allowed her, a power intimately allied with death.

Clarissa's new self-definition is not only unworldly but emphatically unsexual. Belford, praising her angelic nature, declares it impossible "to have the least thought of sex"—that is, of her existence as a woman—when with her (4:248). By converting herself to asexual angel, the woman conveys that life as a woman has been made impossible for her. She denies her own physicality, making herself pure spirit, concentrating her physical concerns on arrangements for a coffin to contain her body, that entity she has declared insignificant and transformed into a profound symbol. Her physicality has enabled her violation; her determined spirituality encapsulates her rage at that violation.

Clarissa's ever-more-concerted self-narration as all spirit in effect appropriates her society's professions. As many commentators have noted, the Harlowe family epitomizes capitalist society. The family aggrandizement that troubles Clarissa centers on money; the male Harlowes speak obsessively of the financial. But this society believes and declares itself Christian. Clarissa's strategy (identical in many respects with her conviction) derives force from its exploitation of the social gap between profession and practice. Lovelace himself professes Christianity, in an offhand fashion; so do the heartless Harlowes; so, even, does Mrs. Sinclair, far from atheistic, who wishes no parson at her deathbed because of her agonizing fear. Everyone believes; no one takes seriously belief's implications.

Clarissa adopts as her own the Christian story of humiliation, sacrifice, and transcendence. What her community accepts as a vague and on the whole comforting symbolic structure, Clarissa relentlessly literalizes. At the same time, she dramatizes in her own person the precise implications of what Lovelace has done to her. As she observes in her will, he has once in a manner seen her dead; she will turn metaphor into fact. He has destroyed her bodily integrity; she will discard her body. He vacillates between thinking that rape hardly matters (since its effects can be repaired by marriage) and believing that it matters enormously (i.e., it will definitively subordinate Clarissa). Clarissa demonstrates the truth of both judgments: rape doesn't matter, since it affects only her body; on the other hand, it matters so much that she must die. The young woman's increasingly powerful effect derives from her overwhelming assertion of unity between her story and her life. She acts what she professes, thus reproaching all who do not; she obsessively tells and writes the story given authority by her action and suffering, thus making her presence and its meaning inescapable. While abrogating the luxury, and the futility, of verbal reproach, she makes herself a reproach to endemic hypocrisy as well as to more active sins.

Although Clarissa recognizes the sinfulness of despair, her initial turn toward Christian narrative derives from something close to that emotion. Previous narrative possibilities have disappeared for her. She can neither tell nor enact her society's preferred fable for young women, the tale of contented compliance with male wills; nor can she play out the structure of romance; nor is the story of repentance and reconciliation available to her in her lifetime. As her "mad" fragments reveal, narrative coherence has vanished with the rape. She eludes the tragedy of incoherence (one of Lovelace's fates) and rediscovers herself by carrying self-subordination to its logical extreme, absorbing herself in a larger story.

A single instance—the important letter in which Clarissa expresses her hope of meeting Lovelace again after her return to her father's house—may suggest how powerfully the heroine appropriates the Christian story. (That this transparent allegory confuses and deludes both Lovelace and its other readers emphasizes the underlying religious alienation of the society.) Obsessively concerned with her relationship to her own literal family, Clarissa longs for parental blessing; her father's curse preys on her mind. For the date of her death on her coffin she substitutes the date on which she left her father's house. Her earlier insistence on defining the world by its origins in "one family" suggests a strategy: by metaphorical transformation she can enlarge her family of origin. She claims the Smiths and her doctor and Widow Lovick as surrogate parents, she incorporates Belford into a symbolic family structure, she makes her will an act of unification. Her most fundamental enlargement and substitution, however, insists on the equation of God and father.

"Sir,—I have good news to tell you," Clarissa writes Lovelace. "I am setting out with all diligence for my father's house. I am bid to hope that he will receive his poor penitent with a goodness peculiar to himself; for I am overjoyed with the assurance of a thorough reconciliation, through the interposition of a dear, blessed friend whom I always loved and honoured" (4:157). The allegory, based precisely on biblical promises, also stays close to immediate emotional and physical actualities: hence its ready misreadings. Reminding the reader how Clarissa's hopes have failed her, the transposition into divine terms expresses her sole remaining possibility for emotional stability.

But it also both expresses and defends against self-assertion and aggression. In its transparent Christian meaning, it subordinates all earthly concerns to the task of salvation. "I am so taken up with my preparation for this joyful and long-wished-for journey that I cannot spare one moment for any other business, having several matters of the last importance to settle first" (4:157). Preoccupied with her death and her eternal welfare, Clarissa announces her negligence of worldly matters, thus defending against any imputation of self-concern. Not her mortal *self* but her undying *soul* preoccupies her.

But "this truly divine lady," to quote Lovelace (4:157), employs her "divinity" for her own purposes. Her desperate need, she feels, justifies her use of Christian revelation as deception; the reader may recall Dr. Johnson's dictum that there is always something Clarissa prefers to the truth. Yet her allegory tells the vital truth of her anger and her will to triumph. In her postmortem elucidation to Lovelace, she reminds him of his inadequacies and of her superiority: "indeed, sir, I have long been greatly above you: for from my heart I have despised you, and all your ways, ever since I saw what manner of man you were" (4:437). She quotes biblical "threatenings" about "the wicked man," recalling the diction of her written "meditations," which often adopt the Bible's aggressive language to characterize those who have failed or denied her.

God is always on Clarissa's side, a student of mine once commented. The remark calls attention to the heroine's self-aggrandizing uses of piety. To quote the Bible to Lovelace in an effort to reform him constitutes unexceptionable Christian behavior. To add "I have long been greatly above you" reminds readers from Lovelace onward that Clarissa has by no means disappeared as a "self." On the contrary, she has discovered her self in denying it.

Clarissa claims power by stating the actualities behind Lovelace's professions and manipulations. She wishes, she says, "to awaken you out of your sensual dream" (4:437); her posthumous letter of clarification insists on what lies at the dream's heart. A "gay, cruel, fluttering, unhappy man!", Lovelace has in his "barbarous and perfidious treatment" of Clarissa hazarded his immortal soul, using "the name of gallantry or intrigue" to disguise his baseness (4:435). Clarissa deals in facts rather than names; her linguistic deception reveals fact. Her little plot has worked as well as any of Lovelace's, her trickery equals his, and she, unlike him, presumably achieves what she wants, in heaven if not on earth.

The "father's house" letter implicitly reproaches Clarissa's family as well as her violator. Penitence helps her not at all with her unforgiving earthly parent; the interposition of dear friends proves fruitless. The divine Father hypothesized in Clarissa's text will, she believes, prove *just*, as the earthly father has not. For her, the language of Christian forgiveness belongs to the realm of fact, asserting compensatory order and enforcing her superiority to her family as well as her capacity to rise above Lovelace. Her capacity to sustain simultaneous consciousness of utterly separate planes of being informs her rhetorical strategy. Thus she writes Lovelace, "You have *only* robbed me of what once were my favourite expectations. . . . You have *only* been the cause that I have been cut off in the bloom of youth. . . . I will *only* say that, in all probability, every hour I had lived with [such a man as you] might have brought with it some new trouble" (4:434; my italics). *Only* stresses Clarissa's repudiation of earthly standards: neither what Lovelace has done nor what she can say about him matters from an otherworldly viewpoint. From the point of view of readers

more committed to the life of the world (including Lovelace), *only*
emphasizes the horror of what has happened. Envious Bella has
insisted that Clarissa's brilliant letters consist *only* of rhetoric, that her
sister possesses persuasive skills independent of actual feeling or
happening. But Clarissa has earned her linguistic doubleness. Her
attention directed to heaven, she literally believes what she says.
Inasmuch as she still belongs to the world, however, her language also
supplies a rhetoric of superiority, reorganizing the family's lost order
with herself as triumphant exemplar. To achieve such triumph, she
must die. Death gives her language and her self the authority they
could not fully claim in life.

* * *

A narrative couched in the third person, *The Italian* does not
deeply penetrate its characters' consciousnesses. Ellena, its heroine,
shares with Clarissa only the compulsory beauty and virtue of eighteenth-century female protagonists, and she fills a less dramatic role
than Clarissa's in the novelistic action. She, too, however, tries to
formulate her own story; her relation to the narrative she attempts to
construct elucidates Radcliffe's compelling preoccupations.

If *Clarissa* takes advantage of the gap between ideal and actual, *The
Italian* works in the space between nightmare and actuality. With
much of the same narrative material as her predecessor, M. G. Lewis
(*The Monk*), and her successor, Charles Maturin (*Melmoth the Wan-
derer*), Radcliffe, unlike them, never literalizes the dire possibilities
she announces. Such possibilities remain constantly before the
reader, however, because they inhabit the characters' imaginations.
Ellena's uncertainties about not only what might but what *can* happen
generate an atmosphere more disturbing if less horrifying than either
Lewis or Maturin can achieve.

Although *The Italian*, set in eighteenth-century Italy, indicts the
Inquisition and the imagined excesses of certain nunneries, it delineates "good" as well as "bad" convents, and Ellena's Catholicism
imbues her virtue as Clarissa's Protestantism does hers. For Ellena,
Catholicism implies compliance, and she seems docile indeed. Or-
phaned, as she believes, she has been told of the identity and the
deaths of both parents; she wears around her neck a miniature of her
father. No mystery about family or life circumstances plagues her; her
sense of security seems palpable from the first.

Yet the narrative immediately announces its concern with questions
of interpretation. An Englishman shocked to discover that assassins
haunt churches receives a manuscript to help him understand what he
has seen; he must figure out its meaning. The manuscript opens with

the hero's first sight of the heroine: "The sweetness and fine expression of her voice attracted his attention to her figure, which had a distinguished air of delicacy and grace; but her face was concealed in her veil. So much indeed was he fascinated by her voice, that a most painful curiosity was excited as to her countenance, which he fancied must express all the sensibility of character that the modulation of her tones indicated" (Radcliffe 1981, 5). Vivaldi, trying to deduce a woman's nature from her voice, finds possibly moral qualities ("delicacy and grace") in the physical but remains curious about the further moral revelations he imagines in her face. The sequence epitomizes the novel's method. In more momentous matters as well, characters must interpret inadequate and ambiguous appearances. Their fancies prove less benign than Vivaldi's.

Predictably, Ellena's security soon vanishes. Her aunt dies, leaving her alone in the world; Vivaldi's parents bitterly oppose the idea of his marrying her. Mysterious kidnappers abduct Ellena, depositing her in a mountaintop convent, where she faces an enforced choice between nunhood and arbitrary marriage. Courageously, she rejects both, though warned of possibly horrible fates as a result. Vivaldi rescues her, but another group of kidnappers wrench her from the altar just before the couple can exchange marriage vows, taking her to a lonely spot where a would-be murderer, the monk Schedoni, appears in the middle of the night. Yet Ellena is miraculously spared; the nun who earlier befriended her turns out to be her mother; she comes from a better family than she thought, has more money, and proves an appropriate match for Vivaldi, to whom, in the final pages, she is married.

This partial summary suggests the multiplicity and unpredictability of the novel's events. Beyond the fundamental problem of survival, the heroine confronts the central difficulty of making sense of her experience. She constructs a series of mininarratives as new happenings refute each successive interpretation. Ellena's ways of "making sense" create orders of fear. She imagines herself walled up alive in a convent's dungeon, or separated forever from her beloved Vivaldi, or too weak to travel a few yards. "As they crossed the garden towards the gate, Ellena's anxiety lest Vivaldi should have been compelled to leave it, encreased so much, that she had scarcely power to proceed. 'O if my strength should fail before I reach it!' she said softly to Olivia, 'or if I should reach it too late!'" (134). Olivia points out that the gate is very close, but a few minutes later, "breathless and exhausted, she was once more compelled to stop, and once more in the agony of terror exclaimed—'O, if my strength should fail before I reach it!—O, if I should drop even while it is within my view'" (134). Such extreme anxiety repeatedly defines Ellena's condition. Although her imaginings rarely correspond to actuality, they convey truth.

Matters finally work out well for Ellena, but not as a result of her independent action. Her capacity for resistance—negative action—protects her, and she undergoes genuine terror without being overcome. But she has no power to make anything happen: only to keep things from happening, or to endure the pain of her experience. Her intense anxiety calls attention to the desperation of dependency. Feeling nightmare ever imminent, Ellena dramatizes the predicament of the powerless.

The novel's most brilliant sequence occurs when Ellena's abductors abandon her at Spalatro's lonely seaside house. She decides that the villainous-looking Spalatro wishes to murder her. After she rejects the poisoned milk he provides (one of her important refusals), he tells her she can walk on the seashore. A storm lowers; Ellena watches it and thinks "of her own forlorn and friendless situation," perhaps tracked "by the footsteps of the assassin." Her female fantasy of friendlessness, isolation, and persecution hardly exaggerates; she errs only in her understanding of the source of danger. Failing to see Spalatro, she congratulates herself on a possibility of escaping, then notes a monk walking along the shore. "'His, no doubt, are worthy musings!' said Ellena, as she observed him, with mingled hope and surprise. 'I may address myself, without fear, to one of his order. It is probably as much his wish, as it is his duty, to succour the unfortunate. Who could have hoped to find on this sequestered shore so sacred a protector!'" (220).

This unique instance of Ellena's hoping when she should fear (but still telling the wrong story) emphasizes the degree to which Radcliffe's novel, although it explains away supernatural manifestations, yet deals in the seriously disturbing. Though Ellena will not be murdered, her assumptions about the sources of security will be utterly violated. A monk, a "father," functions as symbolic parent; like a literal father, he should help the unfortunate. Ellena trusts in the parental role. But this powerful father, allied with Vivaldi's comparably powerful mother, seeks her destruction. Ellena's experience of parental betrayal exceeds even Clarissa's. Like Clarissa, she tries to deny it.

The monk passes and repasses Ellena, then asks her identity. "I am an unhappy orphan," she replies, her formulation reiterating her concern about parents (221). Schedoni becomes sufficiently explicit about his enmity to make Ellena faint, but he then forgoes his opportunity to lay her unconscious in the surf and thus eliminate her. For Radcliffe plays with the reader's fears and expectations as well as with the characters'. Far more specifically than Ellena, we know of Schedoni's dire plans and ruthless nature and expect him to take advantage of the easy chance for murder. How easy it is to make us expect the worst, how readily our fantasies cooperate! Although the reader's imaginings will probably prove less lurid than Ellena's, the fiction forces its peruser to confront his or her own vulnerability to suggestion, to the expectation of evil. It invites identification not with villainous plotters but with their victims; it places its readers in the imaginative dilemma of victimization.

Ellena's confrontation with a dangerous father continues. Imprisoned once more, left "again to solitude and terror" (224), she awakens to a loud call from Schedoni, who has just dropped the dagger with which he planned to murder her. "Be merciful, O father! be merciful!" she pleads. Schedoni reiterates, "Father!" He has seen the portrait round her neck, he demands the image's identity. "This was my father," Ellena finally responds, "pressing it to her lips" (235). The miniature, as Schedoni explains after sustaining suspense as long as possible, represents him as a young man. "Unhappy child!" he says at last, "—behold your more unhappy father!" (236). The girl inquires why Schedoni has entered her room at midnight and supplies her own explanation: "Did you come to warn me of danger?" (238). Hastily accepting this hypothesis, Schedoni departs.

The narrator, attributing Ellena's subsequent narrative interpretations to "the ingenuity of hope," calls attention to an important principle of her storymaking: "The suspicions, however, which she had formerly admitted, respecting his designs, were now impatiently rejected, for she was less anxious to discover truth, than to release herself from horrible suppositions" (242). Ellena cannot face an actuality worse than her worst imaginings. As Schedoni realizes that he, too, has made up a self-gratifying story, about Ellena's inadequacy as a mate for Vivaldi and about the need to get her out of the way, and that he has thus defeated his own best interests, Ellena tries desperately to construct a new narrative that will allow her to love her father. Clarissa can assure herself of her parents' good intentions; Ellena, if she faces the facts, can find no such comfort. Clarissa, rising to her apotheosis, forgives her parents their wrongs; Ellena, with a form of religious faith less adaptable to her psychic needs, could hardly forgive a father's attempted murder of her. More important, she could not sustain any vision of an ordered universe if that universe contained a parent who wished to kill his child. For Ellena and for the reader, Schedoni's character threatens fundamental assumptions of coherence.

Ellena's Catholicism (it strikingly resembles deism) supports emotional but not narrative coherence. Unlike Clarissa's Christianity, it implies no story. Like Clarissa's faith, it helps its possessor to transcend her experience, but it does not help her interpret it. *The Italian* distinguishes clearly between acceptable and unacceptable versions of Catholicism, embodying both in members of the clergy. The evil abbess who imprisons Ellena "with the most perfect self-applause, was violating some of the plainest obligations of humanity and justice" (120). Her counterpart, the benevolent abbess, on the other hand, possesses a religion "neither gloomy, nor bigotted; it was the sentiment of a grateful heart offering itself up to a Deity, who delights in the happiness of his creatures; and she conformed to the customs of the Roman church, without supposing a faith in all of them to be necessary to salvation" (300). In other words, good character makes good religion, since religion corresponds to "sentiment."

Ellena's devoutness, too, consists in sentiment. In the power of kidnappers, en route to an unknown destination, she responds to the mountain scene, "revived and elevated by the grandeur of the images" and reflecting, "If I am condemned to misery, surely I could endure it with more fortitude in scenes like these, than amidst the tamer landscapes of nature! . . . It is scarcely possible to yield to the pressure of misfortune while we walk, as with the Deity, amidst his most stupendous works!" (62–63). A strange instance of comparable response occurs during her captivity, when she gazes out the window at the mountains.

> Here, . . . looking, as it were, beyond the awful veil which obscures the features of the Deity, and conceals Him from the eyes of his creatures, dwelling as with a present God in the midst of his sublime works; with a mind thus elevated, how insignificant would appear to her the transactions and the sufferings of this world! How poor the boasted power of man, when the fall of a single cliff from these mountains would with ease destroy thousands of his race assembled on the plains below! How would it avail them, that they were accoutred for battle, armed with all the instruments of destruction that human invention ever fashioned? Thus man, the giant who now held her in captivity, would shrink to the diminutiveness of a fairy; and she would experience, that his utmost force was unable to enchain her soul, or compel her to fear him, while he was destitute of virtue. (90–91)

The worship of God through the mountains somehow leads to the wishful identification of virtue with power. More curious is the location of Ellena's enemy as "man"—at first apparently generic man, but more clearly masculine as the passage continues. The specific location of "man" on the battlefield, armed for destruction, suggests maleness;

and the final image of man as a giant, shrinking to a fairy, makes gender more specific. In fact a woman, the abbess, holds Ellena in captivity, and the only clearly identified enemy so far is Vivaldi's mother. Yet the battle of the sexes informs this novel as it does *Clarissa*—and as in *Clarissa*, it is a battle of opposed values.

Ellena's meditations on the mountains indicate that she proceeds not by logic but by feeling and imagination. Her religion derives from and fosters both but, unlike Clarissa's, it implies no narrative order. The sheer energy of Ellena's alogical progress from pieties about the Maker and his works to fantasies about virtue's unmanning of power declares hidden anger. On a larger scale, the unpredictable shifts of Radcliffe's complicated plot have a comparable effect. The plot pits traditionally female qualities of emotion and attachment (here embodied in Vivaldi as well as in women) against traditionally male ambition and force (exemplified by Vivaldi's mother as well as by male characters). Feeling wins. But narrative interest depends not only on feeling but on the kind of action possible only for men. Clarissa discovers narrative itself as action and as order and discovers in Christianity a sanction for the narrative to which she has triumphant recourse. Ellena finds only false and temporary narratives, declaring the disorder of experience. And her religion, based on feeling, encourages emotional incoherence—her strength and her weakness.

Radcliffe probably knew little about Catholicism: hence its vagueness in the novel and its assimilation to deism. Moreover, history tells us of the weakening of traditional religious belief through the late-eighteenth century. Even if Ellena had belonged to the Church of England, she might well have sounded less lucid than Clarissa in her commitment of faith. But the change in the narrative function of religion between Richardson and Radcliffe suggests also a more general shift in narrative, from plots whose action derives from movements of power to those incorporating sensibility, too, as a principle for generating happening. If the cost of such incorporation includes breakdowns of narrative order, Radcliffean fiction also in some respects radically challenges the hegemony of order itself.

Works Cited

Castle, Terry. 1982. *Clarissa's Ciphers: Meaning and Disruption in Richardson's Clarissa.* Ithaca: Cornell University Press.

Damrosch, Leopold. 1985. *God's Plot and Man's Stories: Studies in the Fictional Imagination from Milton to Fielding.* Chicago: University of Chicago Press.

Doody, Margaret Anne. 1974. *A Natural Passion: A Study of the Novels of Samuel Richardson.* Oxford: Oxford University Press.

Kermode, Frank. 1967. *The Sense of an Ending: Studies in the Theory of Fiction*. New York: Oxford University Press.

Miller, Nancy K. 1980. *The Heroine's Text: Readings in the French and English Novel, 1722–1782*. New York: Columbia University Press.

Radcliffe, Ann. 1981. *The Italian; or, The Confessional of the Black Penitents*. Ed. Frederick Garber. Oxford: Oxford University Press.

Richardson, Samuel. 1932. *Clarissa; or, The History of a Young Lady*. 4 vols. Everyman Edition.

Warner, William Beatty. 1979. *Reading Clarissa: The Struggles of Interpretation*. New Haven: Yale University Press.

Clocks, Calendars, and Names
The Troubles of Tristram and the Aesthetics of Uncertainty
J. PAUL HUNTER

The "oddness" of *Tristram Shandy*, once regarded as the single source of its canonical place, has long ago slipped into ordinariness, perhaps an indication of the inability of the seeming center to hold, perhaps a sign that in literary tradition the core ultimately absorbs what once were margins. But there is no disputing that Sterne's first readers— with as yet no firm expectation of the novelistic tradition but with quite rigid generic notions—felt the oddness strongly, and it is only a longer perspective on the tradition that enables us to see *Tristram* as a "characteristic" novel—central to the tradition of innovations and ultimately even definitive of the novelty the species asserts and demands.[1] Still, *Tristram Shandy* is not always easy to label or place. Its location on a proper shelf, I want to argue, has to do with the seeming oddness and unpredictability that, seen in larger perspective, "fits" precisely with a cultural situation that it identifies. Samuel Johnson's classic remark about *Tristram*'s oddness—"Nothing odd will do long. 'Tristram Shandy' did not last" (Boswell 1934, 2:449)—reflects not only conservative formal allegiances but the anxiety of Sterne's contemporaries about his cultural analysis, and it suggests the tendency of Sterne's critics, then and since, to use superficial observations about its eccentricities to evade its deeper questions about the seductive attractions of order. In this essay I want to consider the "oddity" question as a cultural issue, to try to see why Sterne's rhetorical disorder seemed so strange to Johnson and his contemporaries, to ask what the oddity ultimately has had to do with the lasting qualities of *Tristram Shandy*, and to consider how Sterne's rhetoric reflects the deep disturbances of his social moment.

The mindlessness of early responses to *Tristram Shandy*—and the trendy lionizing of Sterne himself—makes it easy to understand Johnson's suspicion and conclusion. Sterne was treated more like an exhibitionist than a writer; the spectacle of a clergyman turned jester meant instant celebrity, and the world of conversation, especially in

London, was said to have reflected the jokes and special effects of the book, creating a rage of Shandean imitations in conversation and daily conduct as well as in letters, periodicals, and books. Trendy argot, invented hobbyhorsical eccentricities, and Shandean symbols, signs, and postures were widespread, and Sterne himself devoured the personal attention, becoming an exhibitable "wonder" in London. He was the first bona fide literary "personality" to arise in the new literary marketplace, a star, a pacesetter, proof of the power of writers and booksellers to create effects across a broad range of society.[2] Sterne found almost unlimited opportunities for "gallantry"; a country dance was named the "Tristram Shandy"; and even prostitutes were said to have hawked their wares through metaphors from *Tristram Shandy*: "Sir, will you have your clock wound-up?" they are said to have offered (*Clockmaker's Outcry* [1760] 1974, 70). Few books in any age or country, and none before in England, could be said to have made such a quick and wide impression. *Tristram Shandy* certainly had its timing right; it seems to have been perfectly calculated for an audience that, whether it knew it or not, had needs and desires for which Tristram's disordered rhetoric was perfectly appropriate. Despite Johnson's evaluation and prophecy, *Tristram Shandy* did last precisely because of its ability to realize a cultural moment and project it into a text in a way that has come to be rhetorically and aesthetically satisfying.

*   *   *

Among all the innovations and strange things that Sterne has given us, no single theme, strategy, or device can be said to account for the spectacular public response to the first two volumes of *Tristram Shandy* shortly after their first publication in late 1759. But the account of Tristram's conception received, from the first, a disproportionate emphasis, and Tristram's lopsided attention to the determinism of his odd putative begetting remains the center of a whole cluster of fascinations with event, character, and philosophical assumption. In one sense Sterne seems simply to have gone eighteenth-century-novel conventions one better, moving backward one more step in time, pushing the novel past its promise to tell the "all" of a life. "I was born . . . ," the typical first-person novel begins, and, if a novel looks back (as most do) to ancestry and to earlier events that explain the hero or heroine, those matters come as later digressions or asides. Tristram's decision to trace himself ab ovo, while distinctly unepical and blissfully un-Horatian, takes to its logical extension the novelistic ideal of beginning at the beginning. If, in the novel, every hero and heroine is some kind of Adam or Eve—recreating life anew in some individual way yet reflecting the whole history of human-kind—Sterne pursues beginnings to the Idea, the Word, the Logos that creates and orders. The family clock on the stairs that, properly wound, tracks time and destiny is presented as the beginning of time for Tristram. Sterne even instantly provides (since life, to a novelist, is a warfare upon earth and a journey to destiny) a sexual battle and a putative travel account of the homunculus. Literally, of course, Sterne does not trace Tristram *ab ovo*; nothing in *Tristram Shandy* is direct, and it would be too much to expect to get a temporal tracing of Tristram, a straight narrative of the journey of sperm or an account of the taking of the egg. All is interruption and digression, and the narrative we are treated to is circumstantial, about Walter and Mrs. Shandy and habits and moments. Life, family, tradition, and authority are implicitly pitted against particulars and time. Walter, we are told, as part of his "extreme exactness," had made it a rule for many years of his life,

> ——on the first *Sunday night* of every month throughout the whole year,
> —— . . . to wind up a large house-clock which we had standing upon the
> back-stairs head, with his own hands: —— . . . [H]e had likewise gradu-
> ally brought some other little family concernments to the same period, in
> order, as he would often say to my uncle *Toby*, to get them all out of the
> way at one time, and be no more plagued and pester'd with them the rest
> of the month. (1.4.6)[3]

So it is that clocks and sex become connected in the minds of Walter and Mrs. Shandy, and thus it is that Mrs. Shandy comes to interrupt her husband at the oddest moment: *"Pray, my dear,* quoth my mother, *have you not forgot to wind up the clock?"* (1.1.2). Tristram complains that his parents did not mind what they were doing during his conception, but his narrative follows their lead and equally leaves Tristram unregarded. For Tristram as well as for Walter and Eliza-beth—and for countless readers as well—the clock suddenly becomes the center of attention, and poor proto-Tristram is left to wait. Thus, and so quickly, does time get to be central to *Tristram Shandy*. As the writing moves on, temporal relations come to take on, for Tristram, increasingly complicated functions, some of them nearly as bizarre as the positioning of the clock in the opening chapters. And as the novel proceeds, unlikely and intrusive circumstance continues to occupy the center of attention, distracting the narrator often from the pro-gress of his own life. Writing lags, life waits; time rules, clocks preside.

Time is many things in *Tristram Shandy* and makes its presence felt in many different ways. The novel reflects, in its going-and-coming way, fifty years of contemporary time, and it alludes to many centuries more, all the way back to Genesis 1. Considerations of psychological time, and of the different uses of time in literature, regularly make Sterne a central figure, and the elaborate chronology of events in *Tristram Shandy* has been laboriously worked out, proving that Sterne had thought out the full history of his mythical family quite carefully and knew, whatever he was tracing or refusing to trace at the moment, how all the events fit together.[4] There is a history behind *Tristram Shandy* that is only partly manifested in it. Time does not so much march as pulse or jump fitfully on, but we are ever aware of its power and presence: never is it far from the narrative surface of things, and the necessity of keeping our measure of it wound up is as apt to pop into the reader's mind as into Walter's or Mrs. Shandy's. Time appears to order all things.

And yet time, as symbolized by the clock in the hall and in the heads of the senior Shandys, is also a great distracter, interrupter, misleader, and sometimes a liar. If it can measure, when properly maintained, human events with accuracy and become a way not only of dating matters but of remembering them by association with other unrelated matters (as with the question of the bull in volume 9), it can also become a tyrant and a false icon, a figure for confusion and radical disorder. The clock is not, of course, time itself, but only time's indicator, one of its amanuenses of which Tristram, as a historian, is another. That such a mere recorder may have the power to interrupt time itself, to stop its flow momentarily or alter its normal course of events, is one of the novel's central propositions, and the clock early suggests that subjective notions of time not only transcend but alter reality. Whatever disruption the clock causes in the Shandy household, it becomes a symbol of what may happen rather than what must. It testifies to the power of circumstance rather than to a course of inevitability, and, even if Tristram first conceives it as a symbol of causality and a vehicle of determinacy, it reigns over the opening of the book as a guarantor that plans, hopes, and heritage may be interrupted or altered and the course of human events affected by the way they are perceived or recorded.

Tristram's authority—his ability to read, to know, and to order—is an issue from the start, not least because the book's first interruption casts doubt, for Tristram himself, on his ability either to live his life sensibly or record it faithfully. His first novelistic breath betrays disappointment in himself. Already in his first paragraph he speaks nostalgically of what a "different figure in the world" (1.1.1) he might have cut had his beginning been different. From the first, in fact, the emphasis is on what went wrong, for notwithstanding Tristram's en-

gaging forthrightness and liveliness, he sees himself, first and last, as a
failure. Most of the early volumes seek to suggest why: he begins with
the story of his conception because that is the moment that influences
most the Shandy family's sense of him and his sense of himself as a
Shandy. It is thus a moment crucial to family myth and to Tristram's
self-conception, the moment that determined his identity, if Walter's
theories are right. Sounding more like Walter than at any other time
in the whole nine volumes, Tristram explains an elaborate theory of
animal spirits that ought to have accompanied the poor solitary homunculus on its journey, and from the dispersal of these spirits
Tristram dates his doom. The clock is the culprit, or rather the
memory of the clock; Mrs. Shandy's question breaks Walter's concentration and sends the animal spirits flying in spite of Walter's
manly attempt to keep control: "*Good G—!* cried my father, making
an exclamation, but taking care to moderate his voice at the same
time,—*Did ever woman, since the creation of the world, interrupt a
man with such a silly question?*" But an even sillier one immediately
follows, and the pattern of interruption in Tristram's writing gets its
start. A dim male reader, failing to see that to "interrupt" conversation
may not be just a matter of words, interjects to ask, "Pray, what was
your father saying?" (1.1.2).

Sometimes it seems as if Tristram never forgives his mother, for it is
really her verbal acknowledgment—especially ill-timed or, as Tristram puts it, "unseasonable"—of the Shandean link between sex and
clock-winding that Tristram makes the culprit of the early chapters. It
is not the passive clock that provokes Walter's wrath or Tristram's,
though that is the novelistic object that remains—along with a
forceps, Susannah's leaky memory, a window sash, and Walter's incomplete works—to stand for frustration, failure, and bad timing. Nor
is Walter the villain in either Tristram's mind or Walter's own, although it is Walter whose bizarre mind links winding and copulating,
his desire for pleasure having long since given way and his efficient
sense of duty and ritual having settled into custom and habit. No,
Mrs. Shandy's mere acknowledgment of Walter's association, a mere
reflection of the process of her husband, draws the fire, yet one more
example of her failure to perform even the most elemental of functions
with grace and a fair sense of destiny. Tristram's portrait of her—or
rather his almost complete lack of one—seems the ultimate punishment of Mrs. Shandy, for her few and unmemorable appearances,
usually in capitulating dialogue with Walter so that we have virtually
no sense of how she could have been the woman who negotiated the
London lying-in clause or brought off an actual London trip through a
false pregnancy, provide little characterization. Tristram gives her no

credit or only negative credit, for his birth, and there is no concern expressed for her safety and health in Tristram's difficult delivery. It is no wonder, in the context of this novel, this family, and this set of male opinions, that sages can develop a theory that a mother is not really kin to her own child. It is as if Tristram, never mind Walter's theories, wanted it that way. Let me offer two wild speculations about Mrs. Shandy as a way of getting past the clock that guards the entrance to Tristram's book. The first is a mere trifle, and I am almost ashamed to mention it. It involves the phrase "to wind up the clock" that Mrs. Shandy uses. To wind the clock came to mean to Sterne's contemporaries to have sex, or, more particularly, for the male to be sexually stimulated and satisfied, as in the prostitute's offer to wind a client's clock. Did it already mean something like that to Mrs. Shandy? Was the metaphor already realized within the moment that the book memorializes? If it already existed in the moment, what did Mrs. Shandy mean? Had Walter "forgotten" to wind the clock? Did his clock remain unwound? Such a question is a little perverse, of course, rather like Judith Wilt's provocative reading of *Clarissa* (1977), but *Tristram Shandy* prompts the reader to ask perverse questions about second and third levels of meaning, especially when they involve sex or sexual organs. And the theme of impotence is rife in *Tristram Shandy*, suggestions regularly tainting the various wounded male Shandys, even including the grim-faced bull at the very end. Besides, there is something radically wrong with the clock story as it is patriarchically passed down from Walter to Toby to Tristram, and the question of winding the clock, empowering time and destiny, seems to be linked literally to propagation of life and name. The novel raises crucial questions, beyond comic dislocation, of what really happened on that fateful interrupted night and whether it is relevant to know.

The second speculation involves why Tristram is so unforgiving of Mrs. Shandy as to be virtually unable to paint her into the family portrait or discuss her rationally. This speculation will take much longer, and before I tackle it I want to digress to consider not just Tristram's betrayal by the clock but all of the Shandean wounds he is heir to.

*   *   *

The story of the conception is the first of five narrative segments that Tristram offers to explain the misfortunes of his life. Those five segments together comprise most of the action in the first five volumes, although literally hundreds of unrelated things—the vignettes of my uncle Toby, the inset pieces from other works, the verbal play and self-conscious manipulation of the structure, the interaction with

the reader—may constitute the "soul" of the novel. But the five
segments order the movement of the novel and host what suspense
there is. They represent not only Tristram's desire to explain himself
but his desire to understand, as well. Still, they appear to confirm
Tristram's low self-esteem more than actually account for his conduct
or the shape of his life. He is at his least characteristic when he offers,
in the very first chapter, the firm Walterly reasoned-out opinion about
what went wrong on the night of the clock. He is uncharacteristically
too anxious to offer finality here; he mouths Walter's platitudes with
approval, as he does not elsewhere, and here their implications
deeply involve his identity.

The four other stories represent Walterly ideas as well, and (like the
first) they ought to be thought of as etiological narratives, the family's
official explanation of Tristram's life: each tries to explain something
about how Tristram got this way. Tristram does not, however, argue
their validity or insist on their importance, as he does in retailing the
episode of the clock. Rather he narrates the approved standard version of the family myth and makes clear Walter's role as mythmaker
and fumbling patriarch. Still, in detailing the stories at all, and
especially in making so much of them, Tristram seems to admit his
human failure and to confirm his father's devastating judgment of him,
in spite of the fact that he often becomes ebullient and celebrative,
even cocky, when he thinks of his writing instead of himself. In the
shadow of Walter, Tristram is a disaster and records himself so, but
when he escapes into digressions or otherwise frees himself from the
narratives that are supposed to contain and explain himself, he is an
artist, in control himself rather than being controlled by his Shandean
destiny. That is a central paradox of the novel, and if we are to
understand Tristram's role in his own novel we must grapple with its
disordering contradictions and why they are there.

Each of the five stories involves a ritual moment in Tristram's early
life, and for each Tristram offers an official, sacramental version. The
narratives of Tristram's much-delayed birth and then overhasty naming—replicating a novel-long pattern alternating unconscionable delay and unseemly haste—much resemble the story of the conception
in their plain illustration of Walter's theories of determination, but
their tone is quite different. Gone is the distancing wit, and
throughout the account of Tristram's birth and christening a sad
undertone resists the surface humor. The birth itself puts long and
painful emphasis on the matter of the forceps, and readers do not have
to be male readers, nor do they have to subscribe to Walter's theories
or believe in the failures of Tristram, to find the account excruciating.
Tristram's loss of his nose, even at the moment of the loss, seems more

than the loss of a nose—even without Walter's theory of noses, Slawkenbergius's tale, or the family history of noseless patriarchs. From the explanation of Mrs. Shandy's marriage articles and the history of the neighborhood midwife, to the collision of Obadiah and Dr. Slop and the helpless shuffling of all the loitering males while the real labor goes on upstairs, all the preliminaries to the birth help heighten the issue of the nose. Every rhetorical delay and every digressive trick raises the ante: the ending of volumes and beginning of new ones twice before the birth actually occurs in volume 3, the insertion of a sermon read in full, the Shandean debate over midwifery, the display of the arrogant incompetence of Dr. Slop as accoucheur, the metaphoric journey by my uncle Toby to the bridge of his choice, even an epical history of the weapon before the forceps does its duty. After so much waiting and building, the importance of the nose to Tristram's future and his self-conception escalates mightily.

The family history of flat or otherwise incapacitated noses narratively explicates the anxieties of impotence that permeate Tristram's book. Are the worries Tristram's? It is hard to say. Walter seems to speak for the family in its tradition (signaled by the botched nose) of concern about posterity, and, with Bobby's demise and Tristram's lack of progeny, we know by the end of the novel that we are looking at the end of the Shandy line (Piper 1965, 25). But the anxiety about impotence is more than a question about posterity. Tristram seems to agree with Walter that his future has been compromised at birth, but the terms of the agreement remain to be worked out, sex or sonship. How Tristram's flattened nose allies him to the family's history or compromises the Shandean future is not made explicit, but his book is the history of the end of the name. Like the naming episode that perversely makes the narrator Tristram rather than who his father intended him to be, the birth seems to Walter a terminal thwarting of Shandean hopes. Tristram no more than Walter articulates his loss as sexual pleasure, not even symbolically, but his book seems written under the influence of anxiety, and the anxiety is of more than one kind.

The terrible affair of the window sash—another of Tristram's etiological narratives—seems to threaten Tristram's future more concretely: "The chambermaid," narrates Tristram, "had left no ******* *** [chamber pot] under the bed:——Cannot you contrive, master, quoth *Susannah*, lifting up the sash with one hand, as she spoke, and helping me up into the window seat with the other,—cannot you not manage, my dear, for a single time to **** *** ** *** ****** [piss out of the window]? . . . [S]lap came the sash down like lightening upon us;—Nothing is left,—cried *Susannah* . . ." (5.17.449–50). If the forceps don't get you, then the window sash will. But again Tristram regards the episode less seriously than his father does, and refuses to specify whatever worries he may have about his own generative syntax.

"'Twas nothing," Tristram insists, "—I did not lose two drops of blood by it. . . . [T]housands suffer by choice, what I did by accident" (5.17.449), and Tristram goes on to treat the episode as a circumstantial circumcision. A little later, in fact, Walter sums up all Tristram's disasters—conception, birth, christening, circumcision, and catechizing—in terms of ritual and sacrament gone awry, of order disordered. "[T]his *Tristram* of ours, I find," he tells Yorick, "comes very hardly by all his religious rites.—Never was the son of *Jew, Christian, Turk*, or *Infidel* initiated into them in so oblique and slovenly a manner" (5.28.461). The last of the etiological narratives—about Tristram's botched education because Walter cannot complete the *Tristra-paedia*—works similarly. It shows Walter's system hard at work—and failing. Again Tristram seems to accept passively Walter's theory, and he subtly alters Walter's determinism to lay the blame on experience, making Mrs. Shandy again a villain. "[T]he misfortune was," Tristram reports of the incomplete *Tristra-paedia*, "that I was all that time totally neglected and abandoned to my mother; and what was almost as bad, by the very delay, the first part of the work, upon which my father had spent the most of his pains, was rendered entirely useless,——every day a page or two became of no consequence.——" (5.16.448). The value of Walter's wisdom for Tristram's early upbringing may be questionable, but the failure of the *Tristra-paedia* is yet one more instance of reality gone wrong, messy life not living up to the orderly expectations of Walter's theories. Tristram's life is again Walter's proof, the working-out of the entropic Shandy family myth, but for Tristram himself the story is quietly and hesitantly different. He remains loyal and deferential to Walter and swears fealty to his theories and his patriarchy, while showing increasing uncertainty and narrative anxiety and placing more and more emphasis on circumstance as a radical disordering force.

All the etiological narratives heavily depend on circumstance, often on a combination of random events. For example, in the circumcision, beyond Susannah's sloth, there is the faulty window—"nothing was well hung in our family" (5.17.449), Tristram laments in a resonant moment of Shandean reflectiveness—and behind that the whole scheme of my uncle Toby's fortifications that had brought Trim to borrow the window weight to fortify the bridge. And then it was Tristram's original bridge—or rather the need for such a bridge—that had seemed to predict (in a gross version of secular typology) the sash and circumcision. So many things fall. So much is mutilated. Everything depends. Things seem to relate and go in a circle, but the ultimate direction is always downward, as Sigurd Burckhardt shows (1961), toward matter, bodies, lower selves, genitals, and for Tristram toward disorder and disaster. In *Tristram Shandy,* destiny sinks under the weight of circumstances or simply falls when counterweights are missing. Outrageous fortune has forged its slings and arrows into clocks, forceps, hinges, incomplete manuscripts, lazy and stupid servants, incompetent curates, window weights, or sashes transformed to guillotines.

Tristram is terribly anxious, perhaps unduly anxious, to detail the history of each disaster down to the slightest circumstance in order to convince us—or himself—of his damaged destiny. The anxieties of Tristram have a lot to do with Walter's theories, but it is not immediately obvious why a nontheoretical Tristram is so anxious to prove, to his own detriment, theories that seem to doom him and undermine the very foundations for writing his life and opinions. He makes himself, to justify Walter, more of a failure than he is. What is the matter with Tristram? Why does he have such low self-esteem? Why does he adopt such an excessively Walterian posture in telling about his own childhood? Why is he so anxious to please his father and affirm his failed sonship? Why is he most anxious of all to justify the conception narrative? Will Tristram rise above his conception and overcome his birth defects and aborted sacraments? Can he live his life independent of Shandean systems, clarify his opinions, and complete his novel? And what about the clock, the noses, and the Shandy bull?

*   *   *

The question of the relationship of Tristram to Walter's theories is part of a larger question about the relationship between Walter and Tristram. Issues of identity are central to *Tristram Shandy* from the start, and Tristram is the focus of most of them. "——And who are you," asks the commissary in volume 7; "Don't puzzle me; said I" (33.633). The ultimate question of identity is, however, one that Tristram never clearly articulates, although his text is full of hints about it. It involves Tristram's paternity, the ultimate question about Tristram's place in Shandy history. The rhetoric of the novel insistently raises the issue time and time again, starting with Tristram's account of his conception. There is, in the rhetorics of order that inform *Tristram Shandy* and measure its relationships, a worse alternative than being a carelessly conceived, flat-nosed, misnamed, ill-educated, wounded, and perhaps impotent end-of-the-line Shandy. Supposing Tristram is *not* a Shandy. The seeds of doubt are planted early even though Tristram is rigid and dogmatic. It is a matter of mathematics.

Tristram's initial problem is not with a clock but a calendar. He locates his conception on the first Sunday in March because of his father's whereabouts and health. The event is dated by habit and circumstance: Walter is a first-Sunday man, and Tristram eliminates dates before and after March on the basis of his father's travels and sciatica. *That* Sunday is the only possibility, and besides it is "as near nine kalendar months as any husband could in reason have expected" (1.5.8), a serious miscalculation for Tristram to be dogmatic about. A century ago a writer in *Notes and Queries* deadpanned the first scholarly contribution to this issue. "In 'Tristram Shandy,' by Sterne, there is a curious mistake. . . . [I]nstead of . . . nine, it is only eight months; and it is, in the first place, remarkable how such a mistake occurred, and, further, how it escaped the critics" (C. 1895, 29). The wonderful flat sentence about this remarkable mistake seems a little too good for *Notes and Queries* and is nearly worthy of Swift's Irish bishop who found *Gulliver's Travels* to be "full of improbable lies" (Swift 1963–65, 3:189). But what is truly remarkable about this issue is that, while often noted, it has gotten so little serious and detailed attention. No doubt many finger-tallying readers before the *Notes and Queries* correspondent noticed Tristram's miscount, and modern readers—including undergraduates—regularly chuckle over Tristram's arithmetic and Walter's insufficiencies, but analytical discussion has been astonishingly scarce. The only extended consideration of the matter is in a 1973 essay by John Hay, in which an elaborate analysis of rhetorical tropes is invoked to prove that, in the story of the Shandy bull in the last chapter, Tristram's birth is "demonstrated" to be premature (1973). There is good reason, however, not to resolve the matter so neatly. For all Tristram's professed certitude, Sterne leaves the careful reader in doubt for nine volumes and several long years.[5]

The rhetorical downfall of Tristram's certitude resides in his don't-puzzle-me dogmatism. "I am positive I was," Tristram says, speaking of the moment of his beginning on the night in question (1.4.6). He can be "so very particular," he goes on, because of the regularity of his father's habits, a memo documenting his father's travels in April, and his father's sciatica during December, January, and February. That, says Tristram, "brings the thing almost to a certainty. However, what follows in the beginning of the next chapter puts it beyond all possibility of doubt" (1.4.7). What follows that puts it "beyond all possibility of doubt" is Tristram's inaccurate count of "nine kalendar months" (1.5.8). He protests too much about the fruits of his deduction: "I am positive," he says; it is "beyond all possibility of doubt."

Tristram's repeated insistence on his certainty, while odd and amusing, might seem merely whimsical—an example of Tristram's ineptitude and not his radical uncertainty—were it not for other matters that taunt the text later on. The first five chapters are odd enough to bury or at least obscure the issue at first. Here are wonders of comic obfuscation: the ab ovo topos, the spermatozoan journey, the eccentric association of clockwork with coition, the mechanical husband who needs mnemonic devices to pursue his pleasures, the spacey wife whose sense of timing has nothing to do with either clocks or coition, the demoralized hero willing to trace himself to such a disorganized and demeaning origin. But all these facts and devices are irrelevant if Tristram did not begin on that night, and once a reader begins to question *why* Tristram is so anxious to tie himself to Walter, the text presents suspicious passage after suspicious passage.

Tristram's dogmatic adoption of Walter's animal-spirits theory in the conception—whereas he usually distances himself from Walter's systems and only reports them—is another early clue of unacknowledged anxiety. So are some of Tristram's habitual locutions. His too-frequent affirmation of Walter as "my father" may be argued to be simply a convenience, but the insistent references to "my uncle Toby" have always seemed so odd that critics consistently refer to him that way in third-person discourse, as if his initials were M. U. T. Similarly, the title-page identification of the hero by name holds a persuasive but ambiguous sway over the whole text. Misnaming may involve more than a hero's first name. Eighteenth-century novels characteristically take on as theirs the name of their hero or heroine, but the fact of the name makes no guarantee of accurate identity. Moll Flanders, for example, admits that her entire book (and life) goes under the auspices of a false identity and that her true name cannot be used "no, not tho' a general Pardon should be issued" (Defoe 1971, 7). Robinson Crusoe is really Robinson Kreutznaer; Evelina's first name and Humphry Clinker's last are both calculated to mislead us about who they will ultimately turn out to be. More to the point, though, novels like *Joseph Andrews* and *Tom Jones* go under the cover of false names precisely because the supposed circumstances of their birth and infancy turn out to have been misreported and communally misunderstood. Sending forth such novels under an assumed name is a kind of plot necessity; Fielding could not call his novels *Joseph Wilson* or *Tom Allworthy* without ruining the elaborate plot, and we continue to refer to these characters under their wrongful names even after learning their rightful identity. There are, of course, novelistic title characters before *Tristram Shandy* who are who they claim or believe themselves to be and whose title pages turn out to be accurate, but there is a significant tradition—fed not only by the old, irrepressible conventions of romance but also by the century's taste in novels for gypsies, hermits, unaccountable strangers, changelings, bastards, orphans, and unpredictable couplings—that casts a steady doubt over nominal arrangements. Far from guaranteeing Tristram's identity as a Shandy, Sterne's title-page claim merely engages the ambiguous, provocative tradition, and, together with the speciousness of Tristram's arithmetic and dogmatic certitude, projects a lingering doubt across the inflexible text. Despite the dogmatisms of oral tradition and the permanence of print texts like the one Tristram is promulgating, not even a nominal certainty is available in the fogs and mists of rumor and communal misassumptions stabilized by the sponsoring patriarchal myth.

The most tangible and frequent reminder of paternal anxiety is the Shandy coach. The coach dramatizes the family concern for posterity and integrity, for somehow it has come to bear a coat of arms that suggests illegitimacy. It had happened, we learn, when Walter's coach was repainted to include Elizabeth's arms at their marriage, but how it occurred is not clear: "[I]t had so fallen out," says Tristram, "that the coach-painter, whether by performing all his works with the left-hand. . . . or whether 'twas more from the blunder of his head than hand—or whether, lastly, it was from the sinister turn, which every thing relating to our family was apt to take—It so fell out, however, to our reproach, that instead of the *bend dexter*, which since *Harry* the Eighth's reign was honestly our due——a *bend sinister*, by some of these fatalities, had been drawn quite across the field of the *Shandy*-arms" (4.25.372–73). The matter comes up in the novel just as Walter is trying to undo the misnaming of Tristram. "It would have made my story much better," Tristram says, "to have begun with telling you" about the altered coat of arms (372). Better in what way is not specified, but had Tristram "begun" that way, the coach would have supplanted the clock as the presiding symbol of Tristram's begetting. But once mentioned, the sinister arms on the coach come to haunt the novel. Walter, we are told, had hoped to have the matter mended long ago, but the coach never does get repainted. Walter spends a lot of time trying unsuccessfully to reverse things, but here he is provoked by more than his inability to set matters right. "'Tis scarce credible," Tristram reports, "that the mind of so wise a man as my father was, could be so much incommoded with so small a matter. The word coach—let it be whose it would—or coach-man, or coach-horse, or coach-hire, could never be named in the family, but he constantly complained of carrying this vile mark of Illegitimacy upon the door of his own; he never once was able to step into the coach, or out of it, without turning around to take a view of the arms, and making a vow at the same time, that it was the last time he would ever set his foot in it again, till the *bend-sinister* was taken out—but like the affair of the hinge, it was one of the many things which the *Destinies* had set down in their books—ever to be grumbled at (and in wiser families than ours)—but never to be mended" (373).

"Ever to be grumbled at . . . but never to be mended." The phrase stands for Walter's view of life and seems to describe everything he feels responsible for, including Tristram. Certainly it represents, in Tristram's novel, more than a paint job and suggests that, however easy revision may seem, things do not undo themselves and are not by others undone. Tristram records such matters and allows their implications to ramify without seeming himself to consider what they may mean. Never does he add up the signs, and when he shows anxieties about his identity, his father, and the Shandy family generally, he refuses to focus them. Often it is hard to tell whether the concerns Tristram records about illegitimacy involve his own fears about identity, reflect Walter's doubts, or suggest family insecurity more generally. Sometimes Tristram goes out of his way to be evasive, and sometimes Walter seems to show paternal anxiety but, because he is so negative about Tristram's sonship more generally, one can never be sure. In any case, the anxiety is one with the checkered past and dim future of the Shandys: there are suggestions that the whole long line of flat-nosed Shandys was for years barely able to keep the name going—perhaps only with a little help from their friends—and Tristram at the time his book ends has, at the age of forty-nine, no heir, no prospects, and perhaps no live possibility of extending the name.

Other hints of Tristram's illegitimacy are scattered throughout the text as well. During the long wait for Tristram's birth, for example, Toby inevitably begins a discourse on fortification, and Walter says what is on his mind: "I would not, brother *Toby* . . . have my head so full of curtins and hornworks.—That, I dare say, you would not, quoth Dr. *Slop*, interrupting him, and laughing most immoderately at his pun" (2.12.128). Similarly, in the incident involving the coach's sinister coat of arms, we learn, almost incidentally, that it was the damp of the coach lining on a previous trip that had brought on the disabling sciatica at the probable time of Tristram's conception (4.25.374). And the final chapter of the final volume, although it does articulate the issue of prematurity, as Hay argues, also implies that the Shandy bull's inabilities replicate human incapacities in the family.

All the hints are essentially of the same kind: they suggest illegitimacy or doubts about paternity without allowing us to say definitively that Tristram recognizes, or consciously plants, them. Often the hints seem to come through in spite of his attempt to censure them, as with the long-delayed account of the coat-of-arms that Tristram admits he should have given at the start. Sometimes it seems as if the family story is known by everyone but Tristram and that his role of scribe and interpreter is doomed to failure by his own reluctance and by intransigence on the part of the other Shandys, who wish the myth to stay murky. Tristram puzzles over his identity some, associates himself with Walter's sense of interrupted destiny as often as he can, and flees into dogmatism in his rhetoric, starting with the very first sentence of his life and opinions. He raises our suspicions without quite raising into articulation his own doubts and concerns. *Arma virumque*, he sings, fitfully. But whose arms? And what man? Walter's arms, certainly, whatever they may signify; Toby's arms, too, in a different but always present sense. And despite his sexual embarrassment and doubts about himself as a carrier-on of the Shandy tradition, story, and name, Tristram is clearly the man on whom attention (and anxiety) center. But what other arms might have had a part in his story, Tristram is reluctant to say.

*　*　*

Who begat Tristram Shandy? There are few plausible candidates. The world around Shandy Hall is not a large one: "a small circle . . . of four *English* miles diameter," according to Tristram's definition of "world" (1.7.10)—that is, a clocklike circle just over twelve miles in circumference.[6] It contains few paternal possibilities. We hear nothing of Elizabeth Shandy's friends. Like Bridget Allworthy, she could have had early adventures the narrator has not disclosed, but we know her only as an echo to Walter Shandy; Tristram apparently wants it that way. It is hard to imagine Elizabeth Shandy in the adulterous arms of someone else, but it is hard to imagine her sexually at all, and the anecdote of the clock does not help. To think her an adventurer is not much more of a task than imagining her scheming for London, or living in London, or living at all. The number of Lady Macbeth's children may be irrelevant, but Elizabeth Shandy's unrecounted life takes on a certain relevancy because it is so pointedly, perhaps even passionately, ignored.

An alternate list of candidates for paternity within practical reach of

Shandy Hall is thin: my uncle Toby, Yorick, Dr. Slop, Trim, Obadiah, and Jonathan—a motley lineup. It would be neat for the novel—and wonderfully climactic for my essay, as well as our Western patriarchal sense of order—if I could here produce a lost chapter or a new volume in which a strolling player, a king of the gypsies, or a Mr. Wilson slips into the picture and resolves the issue. But unfortunately the novel refuses to offer even fanciful candidates who, like the Man of the Hill in *Tom Jones,* become a rhetorical possibility. Only the unnamed commissary at Lyons, who puzzles Tristram with his question about identity, may raise, for just an instant, the suggestion of disguised fatherhood in Tristram's mind or ours. The text offers nothing more.

Of the real possibilities, Trim is the only one with a known (or strongly suspected) capacity to copulate, and he is the only man around (at least metaphorically) for all of Tristram's other sacramental episodes. (I count him as causally present in the matter of the sash.) His symbolic role is as somebody else's man, and the similarity of his name to Tristram's might seem to be faintly suggestive to the Sternean suspicious. But probably not. His sexual concentration is a little hard for him to maintain even in the matter of Bridget, and the text offers no persuasive connections.

Obadiah and Jonathan are so shadowy as to be hardly worth speaking of. Among the rest, it is worth asking what role they took in Tristram's other sacramental disasters, for if Sterne were operating analogically or cryptogrammatically in the matter of Tristram's paternity, the question of presence at ritual moments in his life might be a clue. Dr. Slop is, of course, there for the birth and naming, and he is called in quickly after the circumcision; but symbolically he is everywhere *less* an agent than he should be, rather than more. In the two cases where we might expect a primary role for him, the birth and circumcision, he is called in only to clean up the mess, and in the matter of the naming and the *Tristra-paedia* he takes no significant part. He is ever a second, and none of his actions suggest vicariousness. The only faintly suggestive thing about him involves Mrs. Shandy's wish not to have Dr. Slop as her obstetrician; my uncle Toby believes it is due to her modesty, a reluctance "to let a man come so near her ****" (2.6.116).

Yorick is curiously absent at all the crucial sacramental moments, but his surrogacy is several places an issue. His curate is a key figure in the naming, and in the birth the midwife is elaborately proved to be his vicarious presence. In the matter of Tristram's education and catechizing, we strangely hear nothing of Yorick at all; Yorick's only role is as a listener to the parts of the *Tristra-paedia* that Walter, in a singular display of impotency, decides too late to read—to adults. And there is nothing of Yorick, ceremonial or otherwise, in the circumcision. Tristram, for all his fondness for Yorick, never lets him get physically close to the central action, and Yorick is curiously distant, too, from the novel's sexual ambiguities, an odd exclusion. He is almost too removed. I shall return to Yorick.

The sentimental favorite has to be my uncle Toby. An unpublished master's thesis purporting to prove that my uncle Toby is Tristram's father may be instructive, even though its evidence is not persuasive, for it illustrates what more sophisticated readers and critics may be reluctant to admit, a human preference for the influence of my uncle Toby (Brenner 1964). Despite Walter's intellectual pretensions and his desire to turn life into a rational and orderly system, Walter remains unattractive, especially to academics and intellectuals, perhaps because he is a parody of what we sometimes fear we may become, while Toby, simple and silly as he often is, appeals to our nonjudgmental side. The two brothers are each half-men as Sterne portrays them, but my uncle Toby is the better half. Walter seldom evokes much sympathy even in his disappointments and defeats, although at moments— such as the poignant time when, after failing to name Tristram aright, he is reduced to tears, despair, and total silence and stasis—he seems quite human and a little pathetic. But Tristram gets little from Walter except neglect and the details of his failure. He does not inherit Walter's intellectual curiosity or passion for systems, although he tries to imitate the former and in his book parodies the latter. Tristram's inability to complete things and his tendency to digress may owe something to Walter, but nature and nurture are in competition here, and Walter's main influence seems to be in making Tristram feel inadequate—fatherly intimidation, not inheritance or genes.

On the other hand, Tristram has not only learned from my uncle Toby—he describes what he learns from Toby's sentimental release of the fly as his most important lesson in philanthropy (2.12.131)—but he also shares emotions and human sympathies. The question, in fact, posed by the fly anecdote is ultimately whether Tristram "learned" compassion or whether he merely discovered a sympathy already deeply embedded in himself. The one issue in which Tristram's humanity fails when my uncle Toby's does not is in regard to Tristram's mother. Toby is the only one in the novel to take her seriously (though he sometimes seems nervous around her) while Tristram, for whatever reason—suspicion or anxiety, general misogyny, or particular distrust—can scarcely bear to mention her. It would be satisfying, perhaps even liberating, to think that Toby begat Tristram.

And there are some few suggestions that it might have been so. He is present physically or symbolically at all Tristram's sacramental

moments. He is there but shadowy at the birth, naming, and catechizing; the stolen weight for his fortification makes him a party to the
circumcision, and for the conception story he is the only source and
authority. I have already mentioned Tristram's too-insistent claim of
the uncle/nephew relationship, and my uncle Toby's repeated insistence on his total lack of knowledge of women may also be read as
protesting too much: he claims he doesn't know the right from the
wrong end of a woman (2.7.117–18). His modesty derives, we are
told, from a wound in the groin caused by a blow from a stone that fell
from "a horn-work" (1.21.75); because of it he cannot bear to hear of
Aunt Dinah's sexual commerce with the coachman, the source (says
Tristram) of all his differences with Walter over the years. Nothing in
the text forces us to read his horn-work wound allegorically, but
metaphors, once introduced, tend to linger and infect tenor as well as
vehicle.

The history of Toby's wound *proves* nothing, but it leers, textually.
And there are suggestive, even suspicious, pieces of dialogue as well.
One involves the discussion of Tristram's begetting while the as-
sembled males await Tristram's birth:

> Brother *Shandy*, [said] my uncle *Toby*, looking wistfully in his face . . .
> you do increase my pleasure very much, in begetting children for the
> *Shandy* family at your time of life.——But, by that, Sir, quoth Dr. *Slop*,
> Mr. *Shandy* increases his own.——Not a jot, quoth my father.
>
> My brother does it, quoth my uncle *Toby*, out of *principle*.—In a family-
> way, I suppose, quoth Dr. *Slop*.—Pshaw!—said my father, — 'tis not worth
> talking of. (2.12–13.133–34)

Another conversation, only a little later, involves surrogate begetting.
Dr. Slop and Walter are discussing family governance and which
rights a husband and father might be willing to forego: "I know not,
quoth my father . . . what we have left to give up, in lieu of who shall
bring our children into the world,—unless that,—of who shall beget
them.——One would almost give up any thing, replied Dr. *Slop*.——
I beg your pardon, —answered my uncle *Toby*" (2.18.169). A third
instance, troublesome especially in its ending, involves yet another
conversation between Walter and my uncle Toby about begetting.

> . . . believe me, dear *Toby*, says Walter, the accidents which unavoidably
> way-lay [children] . . . in the article of our begetting 'em . . . are well
> worth considering . . . [and] little need is there to expose them to unnec-
> essary [dangers] in their passage to it.——Are these dangers, quoth my
> uncle *Toby*, laying his hand upon my father's knee, and looking up
> seriously in his face for an answer,——are these dangers greater now

o'days, brother, than in times past? Brother *Toby*, answered my father, if a child was but fairly begot, and born alive, and healthy, and the mother did well after it,——our forefathers never looked further.——My uncle *Toby* instantly withdrew his hand from off my father's knee. (3.6.192–93)

He then begins to whistle *Lillibullero*.

All these passages may be regarded as proof of my uncle Toby's squeamishness or bashfulness or both; they do not prove his fatherhood, although an interesting rhetorical case could be made, using arguments similar to John Hay's, that he is sometimes Walter's other half—for feeling and pleasure—and sometimes his surrogate, so that my uncle Toby is the implied father. But for all his verbal teasing and insistence on close, implicative reading, I do not think Sterne builds plots that way. He plays with symbols and surrogacy, syllogisms and tropes, but he uses them to extend suggestivity, not to build a narrative logic. One other suggestive passage works rather differently, by analogy; it doesn't logically involve my uncle Toby at all, but it hovers over him in the text. It is part of the Rabelaisian history of family noses and involves a discussion three generations old about inadequacy: Tristram's great-grandmother insists on an especially large jointure "'Because,' quoth my great grandmother, 'You have little or no nose, Sir'——S'death! cried my great grandfather, clapping his hand upon his nose,—'tis not so small as that comes to;—'tis a full inch longer than my father's. . . . You must mean your uncle's, replied my great grandmother" (3.32.259). But who can say whether analogy applies to future generations?

The case for Yorick is rather different, for it involves absence rather than presence. Important as he is to the novel, Yorick is a shadowy figure in the plot, and he is seldom around. "And where's Mr. *Yorick?*" Walter asks when he is needed for the christening. "Never where he should be, said *Susannah* . . ." (4.14.343). His elusiveness contributes to the sense of furtiveness in his character and underscores his curious interaction with the Shandy household. The relationship is an intimate one, and Tristram pays him high tribute, but he kills him off quickly, midway through volume 1, before he himself is even born, in a gesture that seems consonant with Yorick's shadowy presence in the narrative.

We know little about Yorick's personal life, but he is a fellow of infinite jest, like the clergyman he reflects, and his idea of a good joke might just be to beget a Tristram Shandy. No doubt Yorick has the opportunity, and if we are to regard him as standing for Sterne, he evidently had the weapon. And the product resembles Yorick enough in his sense of humor and general quirkiness to be a plausible son.

The textual evidence is taunting but scant. Yorick and Walter have three different conversations about the relationship between begetting and the behavior of the child, all of them suggestive. For example, when Yorick reports on the tribunal consulted about Tristram's renaming, he first reports on its sophistry, then makes a strange statement, possibly a slip. "[N]o mortal, Sir," Yorick tells my uncle Toby about Tristram's existence, "has any concern with it—for Mrs. *Shandy* the mother is nothing at all akin to him—and as the mother's is the surest side—Mr. *Shandy*, in course, is still less than nothing—In short, he is not as much akin to him, Sir, as I am——That may well be, said my father, shaking his head" (4.30.393). But we cannot father the deed on Yorick with any certainty. Yorick would make a lovely grandfather to the text, but he can be linked to it only circumstantially. There is no smoking gun.

Tristram may have probable cause to think himself someone other than Walter's son. Certainly the disturbances in the text plant suspicions and indicate that there is something beyond placidity in Tristram's dogmatic etiology. Others in the family and community, including Walter, may have considered it, and the oral traditions of the families, like their physical symbol, the coach, enshrine innuendoes. But the text leaves the whole matter dramatically in doubt: Tristram might have simply arrived early (though Dr. Slop's quip about hair on the head in the last chapter makes it doubtful), or Walter could conceivably have braved his sciatica or varied his ritual (though Walter is Walter). But perhaps Mrs. Shandy for once in her life did something adventurous, with Yorick, or my uncle Toby, or Trim, or a mysterious stranger, perhaps a fugitive from some other story who wanders, Woody Allen–like or (rather) like a Fielding gypsy, into this one.[7] The text seems to hold a secret but refuses to deliver.

* * *

Why does Sterne go to so much trouble to raise doubts about Tristram's identity and paternity and then leave the issues unresolved? Two reasons, I think, one textual and contextual, the other personal and philosophical. The first makes a firm point about narrative, mimesis, and cultural psychology; the second raises questions about the factitiousness of fiction and, typical of Sterne, half undercuts his premises, suppositions, and postures in the novel. But finally the two points are one.

First, the textual reason. The portrayal of Tristram as writer, historian, and would-be novelist seems central to *Tristram Shandy*, and making him a central mystery, in part to himself, seems one of the novel's major strategies, the character equivalent of the digressions in plot. For however important other characters may be, Tristram is the focus; it is his book, about his life, and the attention is on his attempt to explain himself, account for the eccentricities of his life and art, and unravel the question of his identity, although in Sterne's odd order of things he cannot succeed. Alas, poor Tristram: we don't know him too well. And neither does he know himself, although he tries, within his inhibitions. Sterne leaves us with a lot of ironies and little resolution: the central uncertainty involves the question of how to read all the assembled data about the history of a family—for he adds that scope to the novelistic repertory, not settling for the history of a hero or heroine. But the history may turn out to be—because of one crucial event, the very first in the novel—bogus. Here is the end of the Shandys, as bloodline and as name, and the line break could have occurred a generation before the name ended, unknown perhaps even to the family historian, who, unknown to himself, was an imposter. As in Swift so in Sterne: plenteous circumstantial details do not necessarily add up to accurate history (see Zimmerman 1987 and Stoval 1984).

But in making Tristram so doubtful a historian of himself, Sterne also makes him referential and culturally resonant. The uncertainty of identity fits a pattern in eighteenth-century English novels that seems to reflect a deep cultural anxiety at that historical stage in the patriarchal society. Blame it on economic change, urbanization, or social insecurity, or consider it an implication of a widened reading public, of growingly uncertain distinctions in a society where money seemed to be challenging land as a basis for family identity and continuity, or of male anxieties about competition from females in the marketplace, especially the literary marketplace and particularly the novelistic one. For whatever cultural reason, novels about that society evidently touch a vital nerve in describing anxieties of identity. At least the ones that caught and retained large numbers of readers regularly, somewhat repetitiously, try. Foundlings abound, bastards proliferate, families degenerate but hold tight to their claims, identity crises are everywhere. With ideas of consciousness and individuality being redefined, family structures under attack, and son-following-father professional expectations breaking down, novelists had plenty of material, and their representations involved, more often than not, an individual uncertain of how to deal with the world because of anxieties about identity and place. Fathers feel their authority slipping away and try to add to the ancestral land; mothers feel their influence lessen and try to knot the strings that bind; sons seek fortunes elsewhere, daughters drift and flee. Only marriage or death seem to bring about the recovery of the old values and reestablish family ties in the novels that became most popular in the mid-eighteenth century, and Sterne differs from his fellow novelists primarily in refusing to resolve the anxiety while other novelists rescind the ambiguity and have their protagonists discover, or recover, an identity that secures a heritage and promises posterity or eternal life. The *Tom Jones* solution may seem a romantic throwback, but is in reality contemporary fright and anxious avoidance. Some of Sterne's female contemporaries, incidentally, pose the identity issue differently. Burney, for example, gives us an Evelina who knows who she is, but is not sure the world will acknowledge her true identity or her right to it; through almost all of her novel she faces the prospect of having to live as someone else because her father will not acknowledge her. Even when women know their identity they often (in novels by men or women) cannot assert it. Men, as created by male novelists, habitually doubt their identity. Women acknowledge the patriarch but are not sure it helps you get on with your life; men seem to be losing confidence that they have power over the line, and often they are unsure whether they are *in* it. Is it the rise to articulation of middle-class values and anxieties in a culture dominated by aristocratic sexual anarchy? increasing nervousness about the independence of women? or just that most of the most-read novelists were men past middle age with wives who made them nervous about their present and past? The oddness of the issue of individual identity in the eighteenth-century novel generally is that it pops out so readily, unfettered by the conventions of traditional modes designed to house universalist assumptions. The great cultural insecurity in the English mid-eighteenth century seems to have involved not the death of God or retirement of providence, nor the shifts of wealth and the rise of colonial insurgencies, nor yet the loss of the sense of land and the decay of communal life. Rather, insecurity seems to derive from a pervasive male sense that men were holding their place only nominally and that women were beginning to control energy, vitality, and ultimately identity. In reflecting such anxiety as other novelists do but allowing its resolution to be even more open, scary, and (for Tristram at least) largely unperceived, Sterne makes his gesture at writing the epic of his time. In a lot of ways it represents the cultural change so precisely as to embody just that epical sense, and it is no wonder that its odd accounts of paternity and anxious sense of patriarchy gained a ready reception.

But there is another side to the issue, the specifically Sternean personal side. In my analysis of character, identity, and anxieties of paternity, I have been pretending that Tristram is a real person and that the novel *Tristram Shandy* is self-existent, independent, with its characters living out their lives entirely in its made-up world. But that, of course, is not exactly the case, not even in the classic formalist sense. *Tristram Shandy* has an author who sometimes refuses—relentlessly refuses—to be separate from his creation. He keeps the novel going for eight years, adding more and more volumes, at first promising to continue forever, so that life (Sterne's life, as well as Tristram's) keeps impinging on the text's ability to go on and bring itself to closure. Tristram may fail to move his narrative forward because he is borne back ceaselessly into the past, but Sterne is present as complicator as well, sending volumes forth in spurts and then, in part at least, living his novel out in public. *Tristram Shandy* is, at once, a fictional world apart and a refusal to be one. Sometimes it is not so much reflective or representational as interchangeable and confusing.

When I say that there is a personal reason for Tristram's anxieties about paternity, I do not mean that Sterne worried about his own paternity or his own lack of a male heir, although he might have done both. Rather I mean than Sterne in part refused the convention of factitiousness in the novel, exposed the novel's close ties to autobiography, and clung to a confusion between the mimetic world of the novel and the world referred to in it. In the months that followed the publication of *Tristram Shandy*, Laurence Sterne became Yorick, symbolically and then really, in publishing his sermons under that name, and he became Tristram, too. As Alan Howes has said, "Yorick, Tristram Shandy and Laurence Sterne became hopelessly entangled in the public mind" (1974, 5). And perhaps in Sterne's mind as well. Certainly, the three are all mixed up in the novel, and no account of bloodlines will precisely suggest who is father to whom. Each is a creation of another, Tristram and Yorick of Sterne (in his London phase), just as surely as vice versa. Such a befuddlement of identities, and of confusion between the world of fiction and the world of fact makes, however Sterne happened upon it, an important aesthetic and philosophical statement, about the relation of life and art, a statement that refuses to draw the line, a decision to live and write along the margin, somewhere between genes and imagination. Sterne is the father of Tristram and of Yorick, and in a metaphorical sense, perhaps, Yorick helps create Tristram, half in his own image; but fatherhood transcends bedrooms and the pages of books, and neither clocks nor calendars prove the issue or delimit the author's begetting. Genealogies deteriorate on the margin, and one cannot say to whom fatherhood really belongs. It is and is not a metaphor. Sterne's novel makes a philosophical statement about relationship and creation in the new species even as it leaves Tristram in limbo and readers in doubt. The ultimate joke in *Tristram Shandy* is that no matter how real it all seems, no matter how accurately it reflects a real culture with real anxieties about individualism, identity, and family lineage, it does not exist, curious reader, except in your mind and mine and Sterne's, who jointly agree to suppose a world twelve miles in circumference. Ultimately, there is no interruption in Tristram's conception and no paternity to be assigned because there is no copulation, no Shandy Hall, and no clock. But there are things and processes that all those figures stand for—life, place, and time—and they are the stuff of life suspended *between* fiction and fact.

Tristram Shandy is a vast many things. Intellectually and emotionally it leaves few ideas unexamined and leaves no tone un-Sterned. Odd in its own way, it is also ordinary, so ordinary that it refuses to honor artificial distinctions about privileged texts, to sort out distinctions between fiction and fact, or to give a definitive answer to questions that fictions readily settle but in ordinary life may stay unanswered. And it has lasted not so much because it puts things in a universal way, as because it reflects, crucially and brilliantly, the oddness of things in a temporal, changing world that is the age of both Johnson and Sterne, neither of whom was very comfortable with issues of paternity or family posterity, though the two chose to deal with those matters in very different ways. The odd and unsettled particularity of *Tristram Shandy* justly represents general nature, too, in a world of clocks, calendars, and uncertain names.

What is certain, even in the confusing and disordered world of *Tristram Shandy*, in which philosophers try to explain away the obvious, is that Tristram is his mother's son. In spite of her problematic status in Tristram's text, the text itself as he gives it to us is an important inheritance from her, for even in her absence (*especially* in her absence) she is finally the figure of the novel's subversive creative imagination that begets without regard to linear or patrilinear order. In the internal logic of *Tristram Shandy* it is right for Tristram to hate and fear her even as he celebrates his embodiment in her spirit of uncertainty and disorder. The Shandy family myth tries desperately to hold the male line. It is a mark of the times and of Sterne's generic insight into the times that the line will not hold nor the narrative order contain.

Notes

1. Victor Shklovsky may have been the first to discuss (in 1921) *Tristram Shandy* as a characteristic novel; Shklovsky called it "the most typical novel of world literature" (*The Theory of Prose*, as quoted in Alter 1975, 30). Occasional assertions of the oddness or antinovelistic strategies of *Tristram* still surface from time to time, but Alter pretty well speaks for contempo-

rary received opinion in finding Sterne at the center of the tradition of self-consciousness and therefore at the center of the tradition of the modern novel.

2. For the contexts of Sterne's place, see Braudy 1986.

3. All references to *Tristram Shandy* are to book, chapter, and page number in the Florida edition (1978–84).

4. See Byrd 1985, 125–26, Piper 1965, 42–65, and especially Baird 1936. For larger scale treatments of Sterne's ideas about time and narrative, see Mayoux 1971 and Mendilow 1952. Curiously, two more recent considerations of time and narrative pointedly avoid discussion of Sterne. Ricoeur 1984 mentions Sterne once, Tobin 1978 not at all.

5. Howard Anderson's Norton Critical Edition seems to have been the first to footnote the eight-month issue (Sterne 1980). The Florida edition notes that "There are . . . a good many hints of Tristram's illegitimacy throughout the work" (3:52).

6. The center of this circle is the midwife, surrogate for Yorick. The "world" ruled over by the emperor of Lilliput is just this size: "five thousand Blustrugs, (about twelve Miles in Circumference)" (Swift 1965, 1.3.42).

7. The habit of characters moving from one eighteenth-century novel into another is an interesting and largely unexplored phenomenon. Fielding's expropriation of Richardson's creations into *Shamela* and then *Joseph Andrews* is the famous parodic instance, but "minor" novels quite often take over characters from well-known novels (as well as from "life") as a way of establishing their own world.

8. I refer to Swift's critique of Defoe in *Gulliver's Travels*, a matter I have discussed in detail in a forthcoming essay (Hunter forthcoming).

Works Cited

Alter, Robert. 1975. *Partial Magic: The Novel as Self-Conscious Genre*. Berkeley and Los Angeles: University of California Press.

Baird, Theodore. 1936. "The Time-Scheme of *Tristram Shandy* and a Source." *PMLA* 51:803–20.

Boswell, James. 1934. *The Life of Samuel Johnson LL.D*. Ed. George Birbeck Hill. Rev. L. F. Powell. 6 vols. Oxford: Clarendon.

Braudy, Leo. 1986. *The Frenzy of Renown: Fame and its History*. New York: Oxford University Press.

Brenner, Sandra. 1964. "An Ancilla to *Tristram Shandy*." M.A. Thesis, Emory University.

Burckhardt, Sigurd. 1961. "Tristram Shandy's Law of Gravity." *ELH* 28:70–88.

Burney, Frances. 1968. *Evelina; or, The History of a Young Lady's Entrance into the World*. Ed. Edward A. Bloom. London: Oxford University Press.

Byrd, Max. 1985. *Tristram Shandy*. London: Allen and Unwin.

C., H. R. P. "A Mistake in *Tristram Shandy*." *Notes and Queries* 8th ser., 7 (12 January 1895):28–29.

The Clockmakers Outcry against the Author of the Life and Opinions of Tristram Shandy. [1760] 1974. Reprinted in *Sterne: The Critical Heritage*, ed. Alan B. Howes, 67–71. London: Routledge and Kegan Paul.

Defoe, Daniel. 1971. *The Fortunes and Misfortunes of the Famous Moll Flanders*. Ed. G. A. Starr. London: Oxford University Press.

Hay, John A. 1973. "Rhetoric and Historiography: Tristram Shandy's First Nine Kalendar Months." In *Studies in the Eighteenth Century*, ed. R. F. Brissenden, 73–91. Toronto: University of Toronto Press.

Howes, Alan B., ed. 1974. *Sterne: The Critical Heritage*. London: Routledge and Kegan Paul.

Hunter, J. Paul. Forthcoming. "*Gulliver's Travels* and the Novelistic Tradition." In *The Genres of Gulliver's Travels*, ed. Frederick N. Smith. Newark: University of Delaware Press.

Mayoux, Jean-Jacques. 1971. "Variations on the Time-sense in *Tristram Shandy*." In *The Winged Skull*, ed. Arthur H. Cash and Joan M. Stedmond, 3–18. Kent, Ohio: Kent State University Press.

Mendilow, A. A. 1952. *Time and the Novel*. London: P. Nevill.

Piper, William Bowman. 1965. *Laurence Sterne*. New York: Twayne.

Ricoeur, Paul. 1984. *Time and Narrative*. Chicago: University of Chicago Press.

Sterne, Laurence. 1980. *The Life and Opinions of Tristram Shandy, Gentleman*. Ed. Howard Anderson. A Norton Critical Edition. New York: Norton.

———. 1978–84. *The Life and Opinions of Tristram Shandy, Gentleman*. Vols. 1 & 2 (text), ed. Melvyn New and Joan New (1978). Vol. 3 (notes), ed. Melvyn New, Richard A. Davies, and W. G. Day (1984). Gainesville: University Presses of Florida.

Stoval, Bruce. 1984. "*Tristram Shandy* and the Art of Gossip." In *Laurence Sterne: Riddles and Mysteries*, ed. Valerie Grosvenor Myer, 115–25. Totowa, N.J.: Barnes and Noble.

Swift, Jonathan. 1963–65. *The Correspondence of Jonathan Swift*. Ed. Harold Williams. 5 vols. Oxford: Clarendon Press.

———. 1965. *Gulliver's Travels*. Ed. Herbert Davis. Oxford: Blackwell.

Tobin, Patricia Drechsel. 1978. *Time and the Novel: The Genealogical Imperative*. Princeton: Princeton University Press.

Wilt, Judith. 1977. "He Could Go No Farther: A Modest Proposal about Lovelace and Clarissa." *PMLA* 92:19–32.

Zimmerman, Everett. 1987. "*Tristram Shandy* and Narrative Representation." *Eighteenth Century: Theory and Interpretation* 28:127–47.

Contributors

J. DOUGLAS CANFIELD is Professor of English and Director of the Graduate Program in Comparative Literature and Literary Theory at the University of Arizona. His latest book is *Word as Bond in English Literature from the Middle Ages to the Restoration* (1989).

MICHAEL J. CONLON is Associate Professor of English at the State University of New York, Binghamton. He has written articles on Dryden, Swift, and eighteenth-century parody and is currently at work on a study of Swift and contradiction.

JACKSON I. COPE is Leo S. Bing Professor Emeritus at the University of Southern California. His latest book is *Robert Coover's Fictions* (1986).

JOHN IRWIN FISCHER is Professor of English at Louisiana State University. He has recently coedited *Contemporary Studies in Swift and His Contexts* (1989).

J. PAUL HUNTER is Professor of English at the University of Chicago. His latest book is *Before Novels* (1989).

MAYNARD MACK is Sterling Professor of English Emeritus at Yale University. His latest book is *Alexander Pope: A Life* (1985).

CLIFFORD EARL RAMSEY is Professor of English at the University of Arkansas at Little Rock. He has written on eighteenth-century topics, Shakespeare, Virginia Woolf, and Faulkner, and is presently engaged in a study of Pope's debt to Montaigne.

JOHN SITTER is Samuel Candler Dobbs Professor of English at Emory University. His latest book is *Literary Loneliness in Mid-Eighteenth-Century England* (1982).

PATRICIA MEYER SPACKS is Professor of English at the University of Virginia. Her Latest book is *Gossip* (1986).

JAMES THOMPSON is Associate Professor of English at the University of North Carolina, Chapel Hill. His latest book is *Between Self and World: The Novels of Jane Austen* (1988).

ROSE A. ZIMBARDO is Professor of English at the State University of New York, Stony Brook. Her latest book is *A Mirror to Nature: Transformations in Drama and Aesthetics 1660–1732* (1986).